LONDON MADE US

ALSO BY ROBERT ELMS

Non-fiction
The Way We Wore: A Life in Threads
Spain: A Portrait

Fiction
In Search of the Crack

LONDON MADE US

A MEMOIR OF A SHAPE-SHIFTING CITY

ROBERT ELMS

CANONGATE

First published in Great Britain, the USA and Canada in 2019
by Canongate Books Ltd, 14 High Street, Edinburgh EH1 1TE

Distributed in the USA by Publishers Group West
and Canada by Publishers Group Canada

canongate.co.uk

1

British Library Cataloguing-in-Publication Data
A catalogue record for this book is available on
request from the British Library

ISBN 978 1 78689 211 9

Typeset in Goudy Old Style by Palimpsest Book Production Ltd,
Falkirk, Stirlingshire

Printed and bound in Great Britain by Clays Ltd, Elcograf S.p.A.

To Alice, Alfie and Maude, Londoners all.

CONTENTS

Introduction   1

1. Becoming Londoners   13
    The Avernus Returns   49

2. The Knowledge   54
    On Fridays We Ride   84

3. Up West   87
    Do You Fancy a Schvitz?   115
    Lord of Lord's   118

4. Dinner Time   121
    Every Day I Take Coffee with the Portuguesers   146

5. Kicking Off   149
    There Are Dead People All Over the Place   176
    Down By the River   181

6. At Night   185
    Jesus's Blood   218
    Who's the Best Dressed Man in London?   221

7. Leaving Home   225
    The Brigadistas   256

8. Finding Home   260

Postscript   289
List of Photographs   297
Acknowledgements   299

Introduction

'This is no longer my London.'

These were the words of an old lady, born by the River Thames, almost eighty-five years before she was about to expire by the Euston Road. Propped up in a hospital bed, she was eager to reminisce, but increasingly short of the energy to do so. When she had a burst of will, however, and a lungful of bottled breath, she took to talking about the city where she had lived all her long and eventful life; she knew it wasn't there.

'This is no longer my London,' she said with a wave of her veiny hand and a resigned but somewhat slighted melancholy. She was mourning the passing of her home town as she awaited her own demise.

That lament for a lost metropolis wasn't exactly my mother's final utterance. Her last words were spoken so softly through an oxygen mask as to be inaudible, but they probably involved love. And while she hadn't fallen out of love with her city, which she once knew so well after years as a clippie on its crimson double-deckers, she no longer felt part of it, didn't understand it. The town she had so rarely left had left her; disappeared or transmogrified so as to be unrecognisable, and she was disorientated by the changes. Her mind was still sharp, but her mental map was way out of date.

This became obvious when I was trying to mine the last nuggets of her memory. I have always been fascinated by the old tales of the tumultuous corner of West London the Elmses had called home for generations. We were Westies, and there had been members of my father's family bowling along Ladbroke Grove and Portobello Road, working its markets and angling its alleyways, from the very start of its story back in the mid-nineteenth century. But long before my mother's imminent departure, not one was left, not a single cousin or aunt flogging their wares or raising their kids, not a trace of our blood flowing amid those once crumbling stucco terraces.

Instead we had all been re-housed and resettled, scattered in a cleansing diaspora of gentrification. In our absence those once condemned houses had been tarted up and filled up with well-scrubbed, floppy-haired families in pastel cashmere sweaters to match their pretty pink and lilac abodes. The neighbourhood had been transformed more dramatically than any other in all London. But my mum hadn't seen that movie. Shaking her frail almost translucently silver head she said with all the vehemence she could muster, 'Notting Hill is a slum.'

She no longer knew London because the London she knew no longer existed. It was well aware of her though.

On the morning of the day in 2011 that Eileen Elizabeth Elms, née Biffen, breathed her last in University College Hospital, I went to take some air outside the hospital. I was seeking respite from the emotionally suffocating ward on the seventh floor, where my mother was slowly slipping over the eternal precipice. The screeching junction of Tottenham Court Road and the Euston Road, with the underpass sucking in traffic, is one of the most noisy and noisome in the entire metropolis. It is not exactly the best spot for a breather and a moment of quiet contemplation. So I moved a few yards south and found myself pacing philosophically between Spearmint Rhino and PC World.

I was wiping tears from my face and musing on the inevitability of passing and the raw sadness of imminent loss, outside a lap dancing emporia. I then remembered that this had previously been a dodgy 'Cockney Cabaret', where thespians in flat caps and braces with Dick Van Dyke accents did the Lambeth Walk for Japanese tourists scoffing soggy fish and chips, and even managed a half smile.

At this point a black cab rolled by, slowing to a halt at the lights. The driver shouted out of the window, 'How's your mum?' Surprised but not shocked, I didn't want to holler 'She's dying' over the throb of the traffic, so placed my hands together by my head in what I hoped was the internationally recognised symbol for sleeping. Forced by the lights to move on, the concerned cabbie left me to my solemn, sodden ruminations. Or so I thought.

For a couple of minutes later the same handsome old Hackney carriage was back. He must have whipped round the fiendish one-way system and then barged through the morass to pull over by the kerb in front of me.

'Do you mean she's resting, Robert?' he said. Now I didn't know this taxi driver from Adam, but guessed he must be a listener to my daily BBC London radio show. I had spoken on air so many times about my mum, shared her stories; and she would occasionally call up and take part in the show, so the listeners felt like they knew her.

They also knew she was ill and my absence from the airwaves had alerted them to her worsening condition. He looked really concerned about an old woman he'd never met. I wiped my eyes and spoke to him.

'To be honest mate she's dying, won't make it through the day.'

At that point a large stubby hand reached out from the drivers' window and held mine in a truly touching embrace, warm and kind.

'London is thinking of her,' he said before rolling gently away into the workaday madness. Blimey, that didn't half make me think about London.

The black cab and its knowledge-encrusted driver – themselves an endangered urban species in this age of satnavs and Ubers – are such a totemic symbol of my city, mobile golems arising from the rat runs: it was the most fitting and touching way for this metropolis of millions of souls to deliver succour to one of their own. My mum would have loved that.

She loved a black cab, always said riding in one made her feel posh. I returned to her impending deathbed and told her what had happened. I hope she heard. Later that day, surrounded by those who loved her, she left London. But as her presence faded with the procedures and bureaucracies of death, so the idea that her London had itself passed on, that in essence your city dies with you, really began to haunt me.

*

Eileen Elizabeth Elms, her middle name recognition that she was precisely two weeks younger than the Queen – two baby girls born into entirely different worlds, just two miles apart – was every inch of her five-foot, two-inch frame the Londoner. Yet she no longer knew this place, because the city she had grown up in, courted my father in, raised her sons, mourned her husbands, buried her friends, kept an eye on her neighbours, cradled her grandchildren and great-grandchildren in, was indeed no longer there. It had, by stages and increments, street by street, shrunk and vanished just as she did.

Some of her city had been knocked down, slum cleared, town planned or redeveloped away. But for a girl who had survived both the Blitz and the building of a motorway right above her house, who could cope with Jerry-bombed streets and jerry-built estates, that wasn't really what threw her. It was more that the patterns she had spent a lifetime absorbing and memorising, the detailed sociospatial 'knowledge' all Londoners accrue after years in this place, had twisted, shifted, moved and mutated to such a degree that it was a totally different picture.

This constantly restless city is happy to shed its skin of brick and stone for steel and glass, to unsentimentally jettison the unprofitable, to abandon the unfashionable, to discard the undesirable. London is a giant kaleidoscope, which is forever turning. Take your eye off it for more than a moment and you're lost.

And yet. Well, and yet the past is also remarkably resilient in this living palimpsest. A few months after my mum's funeral, I had arranged to meet my wife at the Tate. Not the Modern one, which deep down I still think of as a distant, disused power station in a largely abandoned bit of town where rave parties are occasionally held, but the old, neoclassical, slightly stuffy British one on the north side of the river at Millbank.

I jumped into a sherbet and for once was early, so got out intending to walk the last bit. I wasn't too sure of my bearings, but was enjoying a meander in the vague direction of the Thames in an area I don't really know. After a few minutes, hopefully heading towards my rendez-vous, I thought I ought to check exactly where I was, so I looked for a sign. The nearest one said Tachbrook Street SW1, and I was standing outside number 64. That rang a bell.

The most bittersweet task of the whole post-death rigmarole is going through personal papers. Old ladies can accrue a bizarre collection of cuttings and mementos, school reports and insurance documents, poems, recipes, drawings, Green Shield Stamps, swimming certificates, scrap books and rent books, and she had all of those. Her birth certificate was in there among the paper detritus of a life. A yellowing, folded form with the faded yet absolute authority of a pre-digital age. I remembered that the stated place of birth of this baby girl, born roughly equidistant in time between the world wars, was 64 Tachbrook Street SW1. I had, by absolute serendipity, stopped precisely at the point where my mum had started. A sign indeed.

I had never knowingly been here before, and I don't suppose she had been back since her family – which at that point consisted of her mum, dad and two older brothers – upped sticks in the early 1930s. They headed to a council house on a vast new estate near then-suburban Shepherd's Bush, when she was but a small girl of four or five. I knew little about her short time in Pimlico (she actually always referred to it as Westminster), except that the five of them lived in two rooms, one of which had been the venue of her first breath and almost her last.

A month premature, painfully underweight, suffering from chronic jaundice, little Eileen had been administered the last rites in that one room where her brothers also lay, as they expected her to add to the infant mortality statistics. But obviously she pulled through and lived to see two further girls and another brother join the brood.

Her vague recollections of life in Westminster were of what she called a 'tenement'. A crowded, crumbling block, stained black by smoke and soot, chock full of poor families spilling over on to rumbustious streets where her snotty-nosed, scabby-kneed siblings ran amok. Outside toilet, shared cooking facilities on the landing, insanitary, undesirable. But I was looking at an elegant late Georgian terrace, manicured to within an inch of perfection, swag curtains adorning its vast sash windows, luxury cars lining its otherwise tranquil kerbsides.

I was obviously looking a little too intently, because a smartly attired man suddenly opened the Farrow and Ball-coated front door, with its proud brass knocker, and asked me nervously what I wanted. I explained that I wasn't casing the joint, but that my mum was born here in this very house many Londons ago. This gentleman kindly asked if I wanted to come in and have a look round, but I declined, knowing that this place would bear no resemblance to her life. These elegant walls held no traces; the pieces were all still there but the kaleidoscope had turned so many times. Besides, I had to meet my wife at the old prison on Millbank.

And it wasn't just here in her first home that my mother's home town had vanished. Hers was a resolutely working-class city; flat-capped and overalled in the week, suited and booted on Sundays, talking from the side of its mouth and smoking from the back of its hand. It was a hard-working city with factories, breweries, distilleries and power stations lining the river, sulphurous and stained, battered, bombed, scarred and dark, foggy and damp. But life in her smoggy, dank and dimly lit London was brightened by dance halls, tea rooms, picture palaces, hair salons, public baths, launderettes, football terraces, street markets and unruly pubs.

The London she lived in and loved was a vast, grimy, largely Victorian sprawl. Made intimate by the proximity of family and friends, and the continuity of life in run-down streets and squares, where kids frolicked and women nattered, and people who spoke the same language, with largely the same accent, knew each other's business and told them so. The old adage about London being a collection of villages was still largely true and many people stuck to their village for generations. *Passport to Pimlico* and all that.

Of course, even in my mum's prime time, just after the Second World War and before this city started to swing, there were other Londons. The parallel world of the privileged and the posh was only ever a few streets away, where stately prams were wheeled through Hyde Park by uniformed nannies and clipped voices commanded staff to complete their tasks. Her mother: my deferential, softly spoken grandma, had been in service. She was a parlour maid, a few hundred yards from Tachbrook Street in a grand house in Belgravia when she met the man who would become my grandad and fell awkwardly pregnant. They married quickly.

Over in the City was another city still, where bowler hats and pinstripes were the order of the day and the middling sort took trains to suburbs in Surrey and suchlike. Soho was bohemia, Clerkenwell was Little Italy, Kilburn was a displaced Irish county, the East End was Yiddish and – by the time the *Windrush* had arrived – Notting Hill, where she met and eventually married my father, was home to a pioneer band of Caribbean families adding a tropical swagger to the crumbling streets.

My mother herself was part Jewish, my father's family partly Romany street trader stock; this was always a metropolis drawn from a wide gene pool. But its predominant culture was definitely white bread. Pie and mash, pale ale, pease pudding and a packet of Woodbines. Quick witted, good at getting a couple of bob, savvy as a saveloy, staunch, eager for laughter and dancing, tribal and territorial but also communal and convivial.

She loved that London: the walks through Kensington Gardens arm in arm with my lefty father, talking politics. The jokes with her bus driver lost in a pea-souper somewhere down Clapham way. The market pitches and costers with their saucy patter, the charabanc rides to the coast paid for in instalments at the rumbustious local. The jive at the plush Palais de Dance in Hammersmith, the trips up West (actually east of where she lived, but some London conventions defy logic), pictures at Leicester Square with tea and cake in a Lyons' Corner House complete with nippies.

Hers was a town of sing songs, knees ups, even occasional punch-ups. But like all Londons, as she lived it, so it was dying out; its inevitable extinction a function of perpetual urban evolution.

Which is why I decided to write this book. When the tears of my mother's passing dried, and her ashes joined my dad's long-gone cadaver in a pretty West London graveyard near the languorous river, I became a fifty-one-year-old orphan boy adrift in the city. If I manage to live as long as my mum, I am already roughly two-thirds of the way through my journey. That means that two-thirds of my London, the town I have made my life from and by and in, the city I have loved with an intensity that has occasionally baffled even me, has already been and gone.

London changes: that is a given and a constant. As a Londoner, you know you are a tiny part of a perpetually morphing organism. You also know that the details of every life lived on these streets, including your own, passes. Yet we hope that the essence of this great city, our collective character, manages somehow to survive the maelstrom of innovation; that we are part of an eternity even as our era disappears.

My mother's London was already vanishing by the time mine was forming. I came of age in a broken 1970s city where factories, docks and workshops were evacuated and eviscerated, rotting hulks of a former economy. The blackened, exhausted terraces of once poor but stable neighbourhoods were condemned and demolished, replaced by soaring concrete towers, and entire social orders were dismantled. That resolutely blue-collar, grey-streaked, yellow-lit London of post-war certainties was crumbling away, and the ragged inner city of my youth was close to derelict and all but abandoned.

Between 1945 and 1985, inner London lost almost half its population. The one-time teeming streets from Paddington to Hackney, Brixton to Bermondsey were dismantled and decanted of working-class families in a mass suburban displacement. This 'slum clearance' programme meant I grew up not in Notting Hill but half-a-dozen miles away on the Watling: a huge, distant, 'overspill' estate in Burnt Oak at the far end of the Northern line.

Another remarkable fact is that almost half of all Londoners lived in what we then called council estates, which were genuinely affordable and even desirable. My family swapped an albeit tumbledown Georgian terrace with an outside toilet and a leaking roof in W10 for a two-up, two-down council house in Burnt Oak. And were pleased to do so. After all, their Notting Hill was a slum.

But by the time I was unleashed, it was a fabulous if occasionally dangerous playground. Bombsites that we called 'debris' competed with the street-long craters created by town planners who vied to outdo the Luftwaffe in their destructive power. Vast swathes were swathed in a rickety armour of graffiti-covered corrugated iron, occasionally colonised for deathly adventure playgrounds staffed by idealistic but anarchic middle-class hippies.

Much of the old inner city, which by the 1970s was a literal shorthand for decay, deprivation and danger, had been left to ruin and rot, like a mouth with half the teeth broken or missing. Think *Steptoe and Son* with amphetamines.

As I grew into the explorative mania of teenage life, fuelled at first by Red Rovers, pocket money and collected Corona bottles, later by all kinds of part-time jobs, so my horizons expanded and my personal mental map developed. Each area could be encapsulated by a shorthand that estate agents would shy well away from. Our ancestral Notting Hill homeland meant blues parties, squat republics, reggae shops and drug runs. King's Cross was toothless hookers and junkies, warehouse raves and squalid squats. Camden Town was second-hand record shops, Irish pubs full of dossers and cheap digs. Tower Bridge was deserted wharves, artists' lofts and arty parties. Hoxton, if you even knew it existed, was villains, National Front supporters and acres of nothing. You could fire a shotgun down Curtain Road in the middle of the day back in 1979 and nobody would even notice, let alone get hit. I know a man who did just that.

And it wasn't just what geographers call 'the Zone of Transition', that ring of one-time low-rent, often immigrant, working-class neighbourhoods circling the centre that had fallen down on their uppers. The epicentre of our collective universe: Soho, dear Soho, the heart of London's supposedly glamorous West End, the dark but mesmerising soul of our city, was shabby and shady, swerved by all but the furtive and the brazen. The notorious redoubt south of Oxford Street, which is now so swish and buzzing, was a seemingly forlorn place of frayed shadows, peopled almost exclusively by wide boys in grubby bookshops, dirty men in dirty macs, the occasional old-school queen and a few sweaty old boozers in sweaty old boozers. Unless, that is, you knew which door to knock on, which stairwell to descend, which name to drop in our thrillingly un-square mile. Then it was big fun.

In my youth the post-industrial wasteland of this 'sick man' city was ripe with piratical possibilities. Every empty warehouse was a party, every abandoned block a free home. Fancy living in Clerkenwell or Bankside? Just climb up and clamber in, but watch out for the speed freaks or the glue sniffers upstairs. There was also a splendid stock of tawdry, tacky discos, often run by men in camel coats, just ripe for a spot of one-night-stand entrepreneurship to turn them into the coolest clubs for the hippest kiddies. The Blitz, the Wag; the nights we had. Inner London was ours to do with as we pleased, an anarchic wonderland of endless possibilities. It was punk. It was great.

Of course, that has all changed. I've seen this city flip inside out in my lifetime. The once-crumbling centre has been transformed into the most desirable real estate on Earth. London has become an international success story, regularly and perhaps rightly deemed the greatest city in the world. Its population has soared back up to pre-war levels as its popularity has increased.

But these are different people in different places; smarter, richer, blander Londoners in a nicer, wealthier, blander London. Zone One in particular has been gentrified and sanitised, maxed out with luxury flats, swanky shops and posh restaurants. Like a colouring book where every page has been filled in, leaving little room for creativity or spontaneity.

It seems unbelievable now, but until I took her to one on Charlotte Street in about 1985 my mother had never, ever been to a restaurant. There weren't that many back then, certainly not for people like her. From a culinary desert to a gourmet destination, we have witnessed a remarkable risotto-drenched 'Risorgimento' of this busted, has-been old town. As a result, even areas like Peckham and Dalston, Harlesden and Brixton are now considered hip and 'desirable', where not so long ago they came complete with dire health warnings and ferocious front lines. From murder mile to estate agent's wet dream in what seems like a matter of months.

Yet simultaneously, the outer, leafy suburbs, once the aim and ambition of so many, the place my parents fled to from their W10 slum, are all too often neglected and derided, desultory and threadbare. Look at where murders take place now and it is out on the sullen, unloved edge, our very own harshly polyglot périphérique, where the poor and the careworn gather. Would any sane family choose Burnt Oak over Notting Hill today?

In many respects, what we have witnessed is a wonderful urban renewal: incredible new architecture, bridges, galleries, Gherkins and Shards; amazing transformations of those post-industrial ruins, and a Klondike-like land grab, which has burnished and rebranded so many run-down neighbourhoods from docklands, along the South Bank, to Shoreditch and Bethnal Green. My city has become truly cosmopolitan, sophisticated, arty and al fresco: continental in its ways and bourgeois in a way I could never have imagined. Shiny, modern, affluent, a picture of pale wood and gleaming glass, but perhaps just a little dull in comparison to the tumultuous, tumbledown town I grew up in.

All change is a double-edged sword: it gives and it takes away. So much of that scruffy, gritty, edgy London of my youth – a place simultaneously wrecked yet redolent with possibilities – has vanished that I now reside simultaneously in two cities at once. I live and work, ride and walk, play and parent, eat and drink, occasionally even think in this twenty-first century success story, a tastefully lit, gracefully designed global metropolis. But as I move through this thoroughly modern Babylon, I can never truly escape the ghosts of my grotty but beloved old London.

I regularly find myself seeing things that are not there any more. I float through a cityscape of apparitions, remembering and re-experiencing the so many stories, adventures, misadventures, lies and romances contained in the walls or even the shadows and shells of the former walls of my town. That city, my city, is still here, all around and deep inside me.

This is a book about that lost and vanishing London, while I can still recall what it smelled like. It is a compendium of stories that may never have happened and a guide to things that no longer exist. It is my mother's town and my town in me; our town in all of us. It is a memoir of a shape-shifting city.

CHAPTER ONE

Becoming Londoners

In the end there is nowhere to go but where you began, so I shall begin there. This is a journal of journeys, urban excursions, which take place both now and then, in times plural and space singular: one city, many cities, my city.

This is a book about being here and being part of this monster, this all-pervading, all-providing, all-devouring behemoth of a birthright. I am a Londoner, which means I am but a fragment. I cannot hope to tell the story of the whole, nor even begin to grasp the whole story.

There are so many different cities, and I have moved between them, yet I was born squarely into just one of them. The London of the Elmses – a working-class family making their lives from and on the streets – was sure, solid, yet without foundation. There were no known origins: we were just here and from here, which determined who we were, how we spoke, dressed, danced. There was no arrival story, no founding mythology, no doubt. The Elmses: a London mob.

I, though, have always sought stories. I need to know and tell the tale, and so have settled on the saga of Little Freddie as my personal Romulus. Because, in this and that London, I have walked the same space, along the same streets as little Freddie Elms so many times. In fact, I have retraced a few of Fred's steps practically every other Saturday for half a century, sometimes on Tuesday evenings too. 'Come on URRRs.'

On my repeated, repeated, obsessive, compulsive journeys to football, I occasionally fancy I see Freddie along the way, flogging a Granny Smith off a barrow or treating himself to a beer. I haven't known him for very long, but he has always been there in me, pacing the Uxbridge Road.

For I, too, am a Freddie – Robert Frederick Elms, son of Albert Elms – and I've got a big brother called Reggie, which matters in a way that will soon become clear. For all the available evidence I have been able to uncover suggests that Fred was the first of our London lineage.

I did a little distinctly amateur research into the Elms family tree, only to discover that it's all a bit bonsai. There are Elmses all around Ladbroke Grove from the end of the nineteenth century onwards: Horace and Emily, Clarence and Mary, James and Alice; namesakes all over the gaff, cousins, aunties, uncles-aplenty. But as I go back a generation or two, we seem to stop at little Fred, his mum Jane and his sister – or more probably his half-sister – Eliza.

Frederick Elms was born in 1862, Eliza a couple of years later. Both of them delivered in the Uxbridge Union Workhouse, both of them noted as 'father unknown', their young mother signing her name on the forms with only a cross. A destitute illiterate giving birth to the illegitimate, and I love her pretty bones. I have picked her as my great-great-great grandma and her two poor little Victorian bastards, sired by God knows who, delivered into gaunt penury in a punishing red-brick institution in a distant Middlesex village where I once saw the Sex Pistols, as my favourite forebears.

Having chosen Freddie as my abiding ancestor, I have invented a story of his arrival. I do not know that he tramped from the workhouse up the Uxbridge Road to Shepherd's Bush as a fourteen-year-old boy and decided to go no further, but it seems like a likely scenario. I imagine him as a likely lad, a coster, like so many of his offspring, setting out his stall where he stopped and setting up home just up the road in Notting Hill.

Once ensconced in the neighbourhood, he began begetting. There was an Albert, who in turn begat a Reggie, who in turn begat an Albert, who in turn begat both Reggie and me. (He begat my brother Barry too; God knows where that name came from.)

So Elmses came from Uxbridge – a place I once went to. Linked directly to London by its umbilical, eponymous road, it is now an outer suburb with a university named after Isambard Kingdom Brunel, where on 16 December 1977, the Sex Pistols – Cook and Jones, prime Shepherd's Bush street urchins – played their last ever London gig. Sid looking like a smack-scarred god with his top off, Lydon with a hankie on his head.

I got there by hitching a lift from outside a boozer on Bush Green while wearing bondage trousers. One ride all the way along the Uxbridge Road with my legs tied together, from a photographer for *Sounds* magazine.

That was the one and only time I have ever made that epic schlep way out west. I did it almost exactly one hundred years after Freddie presumably did precisely the same trip in the opposite direction. Turfed out of his grim institution, as he would have been at the age of fourteen – Lord knows what happened to poor Jane and Eliza – he made the fateful trek into town, perhaps sporting a battered stove-pipe hat, and never went back. He might, I guess, have hitched a ride on a coach, but more likely he footed for thirteen miles in hobnails until his sore feet would go no further. That is how we became Londoners.

Later on, the various Fredericks and Reginalds and Alberts that followed can be picked up in the census forms on Lancaster Road, Charles Street (now Queensdale Place), Cornwall Crescent and Latimer Road. Never migrating more than a few hundred yards in nearly a hundred years, around Notting Hill, or more accurately Notting Dale.

The Dale is the disreputable W10 neighbour down the claggy slope towards the Bush, always the poor bit, always the forgotten bit. Poor Freddie had found a home here and founded a West London dynasty, a QPR family. Hence my repeated visits to their decaying Fray Bentos tin-style stadium just off the Uxbridge Road, to be deeply disappointed by men in hoops. Hence why I see so many ghosts along the way.

Actually, a little further digging on my behalf has suggested that Freddie's forebears probably originated in a village in Wiltshire known as Lacock, where almost every Elms has his or her roots; leaving the hungry land for London's purportedly gold-strewn streets and winding up in a workhouse. This serves to bolster my belief that people settle in the side of the city from which they arrive. If you came up from Kent you'll be doomed to remain 'sarf' of the river, while men of Essex populate the East End, and vice versa. We came from the West Country.

That's why, for example, the Irish were in Camden Town; straight off the boat train to Euston, and as far as you can walk before you put down your suitcase and take a drink and a room. The Scots went round the corner from King's Cross to the Caledonian Road, and the Welsh set up dairies and chapels near Paddington. It's also why Ugandan Asians who landed at Heathrow in the 1970s got only as far as Southall.

It all goes to show that all that cockney bollocks about Bow Bells is just that: Londoners are Londoners; choose these streets and they will shape you. I don't think a single member of my family had ever been east of Aldgate, but we were Gord Blimey to the apple core.

Then came the Westway.

'Luxury' and 'apartment' is currently the most reviled combination of words in the London lexicon. A plague of Bubonic virulence, its high-rise glass and steel pustules promising glamorous metropolitan living but in fact delivering little more than safety deposit boxes with balconies for the globally avaricious.

The current land grab, what some know as the Great London Flat Race, has driven out those who cannot afford millionaire price tags. Ordinary families exiled, banished to the edges, unwanted in the heart of this bright and shiny (or maybe shite and briny) twenty-first century Babylon. It is social cleansing, no doubt, threatening the cheek-by-jowl, rich-by-poor pattern of London life, which has existed since the hovels of Houndsditch were close to the mansions of Mansion House. But it certainly isn't the first time London has witnessed a centrifugal spasm of social exclusion, expulsion and expansion. It happened to the Elmses.

There may have been a touch of Victorian melodrama at play when Notting Dale was described as 'the Avernus of Kensington' – an avernus being the gateway to hell in the lurid parlance of nineteenth-century social reformers – but there's no doubt that the Dale was a strong contender for worst slum in town. Also known as North Kensington, Charles Dickens himself called it 'a plague spot, scarcely equalled for its insalubrity by any other in London'.

Adjacent to, but a million miles from, the grand and gracious houses of Holland Park, this clay-bound enclave of potteries and piggeries was said to have the highest death rate in the entire capital. It was a venal swamp of acute poverty, chronic overcrowding and ubiquitous drunkenness, peopled originally by the product of a bout of forced social cleansing.

Many of the residents of Notting Dale had previously been turfed out of the notorious gin-soaked Rookery of St Giles. That's the one-time leper colony, plague pit and gallows breeding ground hard by Centre Point, which will feature large later in this book. The rookery was razed to the ground and New Oxford Street driven through it in a civic slum clearance scheme of the late 1840s, designed specifically to clean up the West End. So the unclean packed up their meagre belongings and headed further west to North Kensington.

The expat denizens of Hogarth's Gin Alley were joined in the then distant Dale by London's largest gypsy community. You can still see remnants of that traveller gathering in the cluster of spick and span caravans and abandoned fridges that make up the gypsy encampment under the northern end of the stained concrete confluence of the Westway. And traveller blood flows through the Elmses' veins.

Between the Romany settlers and the Rookery survivors, they created a rollicking redoubt of totters and tearaways, costermongers and scrap dealers, horse traders and numbers runners, washerwomen and brothel keepers, which wasn't entirely unrecognisable by the time my own dad, Albert mark two, was born there in 1924. He arrived in a house at 345 Latimer Road, which has long since gorn.

Latimer Road was once twice the length it is now, running almost all the way to Shepherd's Bush and was as close to a high street as lowly Notting Dale ever got. It was here, a couple of years after my father's first appearance, that one of my favourite tales from that era also emerged.

I have made it a life-long mission to collect arcane London stories, the history in the margins, and the case of the missing monkey jazz band of Latimer Road is a pretty good one. It centres on the activities of one Thomas Murphy, a travelling showman of Irish origin who made his final fortune from building and running dog tracks in the 1930s, and whose eternal mausoleum lies over in Southeast London amid the remains of his long gone Charlton stadium. But it is no surprise that he was originally based in W10.

The area, with its strong gypsy connections and its myriad stables for all the local totters (*Steptoe and Son*'s Oil Drum Lane and their horse Hercules were actually in the Dale), always attracted fairground and circus folk. I can still recall peering through the fence of a local yard where the carnies stored their gaudy equipment well into the '70s.

There had even been a short-lived racecourse, the Notting Hill Hippodrome, the footprint of which can still be seen on maps and the memory of which is kept alive by a short street called Hippodrome Place. It failed because of the quagmire nature of the soil, which meant the going was always heavy, and so were some of the local characters. The well-heeled followers of the sport of kings didn't much like mixing with the local vagabonds, slum-dog residents of what was then known as Cut Throat Lane.

Anyway, before Mr Murphy invested in racing dogs, he had a thing about monkeys, specifically monkeys who could play jazz. Jazz bands were the big craze of the Roaring '20s, so obviously Thomas Murphy put together a troupe of thirteen simian swingers to entertain the happy flappers. I have to say at this point that I have no idea if there was some kind of awful racist joke going on here, nor do I have a clue exactly what sort of racket these animals actually made, but I do know that when they escaped from Murphy's yard on Latimer Road in November 1926, it became a major national news story.

It seems that the syncopated apes were released inadvertently when a gang of hardened chicken rustlers raided the gaff, thinking it was a full of potential Sunday lunches, only to discover that their foul crime had actually let the monkeys out of the bag. Mayhem ensued, with the freedom-intoxicated primates storming a corn chandlers round the corner on Bramley Road and scoffing twenty-eight pounds of biscuits before a team of eight coppers, armed with whistles and handcuffs, managed to round some of them up.

But a few evaded capture for days and held the nation enthralled. Two of them settled under the arches at Latimer Road station and would not be enticed out, while Bimbo the drummer boarded a train bound for Ealing. The intrepid band leader Franko made it as far as

Rugby in the Midlands, where the fugitive jazzer was finally captured in a local pub, the Saracen's Head. The report in the *Guardian* read, 'The captured monkey travelled to Rugby by train and was seen to jump out of the window of a first class carriage. He then walked sedately towards the barrier, and treating the ticket collector with scorn, cleared the barrier with a flying leap.'

Nowhere in the papers does it ever question quite why a bloke in Latimer Road had a troupe of Dixieland monkeys, nor can I ascertain if they ever performed again after their great escape. But I do cherish the idea that my infant father, perhaps even sitting outside his house in his pram, as was the way in those days, might have actually witnessed this splendid brouhaha.

Quite where on Latimer Road this occurred I have no idea. Because that area has been so remorselessly bashed about it's hard to pinpoint exactly where anything was. I learned a little more when my own son Alfie started playing football for QPR's Centre of Excellence as a half-decent, ten-year-old centre half in the early 2000s.

Every Thursday evening for years I had to take Alf for training on the plastic pitch, the one you see way down on your left as you swoosh past, high above on the eastbound elevated carriageway of the A40 approaching Paddington. It looks like you need a parachute to get there, but actually it's in the atmospheric warren of rain-streaked concrete under-crofts behind Ladbroke Grove, which utilises the space beneath the flyover.

Watching schoolboys trap and pass, trap and pass, trap and pass, for week after week, gets deeply dull, so I would often wander off searching for memories. I scoured the scrambled and disjointed ways, exploring the dead ends and blind alleys made by the imposition of a vast concrete barrier across these old streets, trying to picture what was there when we were, before the Westway was.

Today there's a splendid if ramshackle array of bizarre endeavours beneath the roaring road, including tennis courts, fives courts, horse paddocks, skateboard runs, guerrilla gardens, graffiti walls, shooting galleries, art galleries, dance studios, crack dens, breakers yards, rubble

. . . loads of rubble. It is an above-ground yet still subterranean other-world, where time has somehow stood still since this leviathan on stilts crashed into the landscape. I was searching amid all this for family traces, some sense of the life lived here before the cataclysm, but never quite finding them.

Then one weekend I told my mum, Alfie's doting Grandma, that her boy was playing for Rangers, the team her beloved husband had loved so dearly. Her accent had one of those old London quirks which rendered an A as an E.

'Where does Elfie train?' she asked, pleased but not particularly surprised that Alf/Elf should have been chosen to wear the holy hoops, as if somehow this was his birthright. I told her it was on the astroturf pitch off Barlby Road, a space she would once have known so well.

'Show me on a map,' she said, so I did. 'That is almost exactly the spot where the house your Dad was born in used to be.'

And it is no longer there, because of the Westway.

If luxury and apartment are the current pox upon London life, then back in the 1960s it was 'town' and 'planning'. London has tradition-ally been resistant to *Grand projets*, the overarching schemes that have shaped other more malleable cities. Paris is essentially the product of Haussmann's monomania; Manhattan a carefully considered grid. But when the Great Fire razed the City of London, Sir Christopher Wren's proposal to rebuild the whole lot on a rational, ordered masterplan, with wide boulevards and symmetrical squares, was thankfully stymied by the fact that Londoners wouldn't wait for high-minded architects and bureaucrats, so they began re-constructing their houses, shops and taverns along the twisting, claustrophobic medieval street pattern that survives to this day.

This city has a mind of its own, organic and anarchic, at its best when it grows from the gutter up. But in the futuristic, car-crazy '60s town planning was all the rage, and the part of town that has every reason to rage against the planners was poor old W10. For the neigh-bourhood Frederick Elms chose as his own was pretty much obliterated by men with bow ties and sharp pencils. They decided that it would have a motorway or two driven through it, high-rise council estates placed upon it and its close-knit inhabitants hounded out in a petty diaspora to Perivale, Northolt, Greenford and other far-flung 'overspill' estates way out west on the Central line.

From W2 to W12, Bayswater to the Bush, a swathe of charismatic inner West London was devastated, divided like some little Berlin by this flyover, which showed no mercy as it took out whole communities all around it: town planners made the Luftwaffe look benign. Paddington, once the most densely populated place in Britain, never really recovered, Ladbroke Grove was split into two and Notting Dale essentially disappeared.

My mum and dad – who had met while jitterbugging at the Hammersmith Palais, courted while the bombs fell during the Blitz, running across Westminster bridge holding hands to avoid a doodlebug, who had survived an offer of accommodation from John Christie at nearby 10 Rillington Place, shouted down Blackshirts at Speakers' Corner, navigated double-deckers in pea-soupers and witnessed the notorious Notting Hill race riots at the end of their road – opted for a two-up, two-down council house on the Watling Estate in Burnt Oak. They chose to live at the end of the Edgware Road, on the outer reaches of the Northern line, where nothing ever happens. And truth be told, they were happy to go, because don't forget: 'Notting Hill is a slum.'

It is important to acknowledge that poverty is never nice and rarely romantic. Notting Hill/Dale was certainly not an avernus by the time my mum and dad were living there. The worst areas of nineteenth-century deprivation and overcrowding, especially around the notorious Bangor Street section, had already been cleared and cleansed, replaced by a pleasant little park and blocks of early social housing named after Charles Dickens' son Henry, a local councillor and social reformer. But well into the 1950s, '60s and '70s, this was still a run-down and deeply deprived part of London.

The housing stock was made up largely of threadbare and careworn three- or four-storey, early Victorian terraced houses, which had been degraded and divided and divided. They squeezed in more and more rent payers, most of whom lived with outside toilets, shared cooking facilities, leaking roofs and windows, rotten floorboards and damp in all directions.

This was one of the few parts of London where the signs did not always read 'NO Irish, NO Blacks, NO Dogs', so consequently there were lots of all of those. Add in a large Spanish community, in exile after the Civil War, and a smattering of Italians, Africans, Cypriots and Maltese, all attracted by the cheap rents and crammed into those tiny rooms, and you have arguably the first example of true multiculturalism anywhere in Britain.

But it was the influx of fantastically well-dressed West Indians in the wake of the *Windrush* which would define Notting Hill for generations. These newcomers, with their tilted trilbies and languid gaits, gave the area a natty sway and a swagger. Caribbean music coming

from every basement blues and open window; exotic herbs hanging in the air; exotic fruit and veg – okra, breadfruit and plantain, which the costers dubbed 'queer gear' – appearing on the barrows.

In West London, it was largely Trinidadians and small islanders – St Lucians, Antiguans, Guyanans – who settled in those blistered and blackened terraces. The new Jamaican arrivals tended to congregate over the river in Brixton. That's why Carnival, a Trinidadian tradition, but never a Jamaican one, found its natural home in Notting Hill. And long before Carny started in 1962, there were blues, steel bands and calypso ringing in the air.

But it wasn't only West Indian life. Shebeens, spielers, showbands, rock'n'roll and dog crap were all part of the everyday as the cultures entangled, even if they didn't always get along. Add to that mix the effluent peddled by one Peter Rachman, whose name became a synonym for evil slum landlords everywhere. His dubious career started in an office in Shepherd's Bush and his malign practices served to further diminish the reputation of the wider Notting Hill area. (His enforcer was one Michael X, who will also pop up again later in this book.)

The neighbourhood was blighted by bad housing and even worse landlords, and among the litany of slogans which adorned those grimy walls was a graffito on a wall in Notting Hill for years, which read 'Not Lords of the Land but Scum of the Earth'. There were others saying 'KBW' – 'Keep Britain White'.

There were undoubted tensions, particularly between young West Indian lads and indigenous local youths, the latter perhaps enraged and envious of the sexual success of the former. This famously flared up in 1958, in what have become known as the Notting Hill race riots. More accurately, they took place in Notting Dale. Local Teddy Boys, including brothel-creeper-clad relatives of mine (I take no pride in the prejudice), egged on by Mosley's fascists, fought it out with some of the local West Indians (augmented I'm told by Jamaican reinforcements from down south) over three nationally shaming nights of violence.

Overcrowding and poverty, as well as the all-too-prevalent racism of the time, were undoubtedly major factors and W10 was certainly in need of some severe TLC. But did it really need knocking down? Town planners back in the '60s were of the absolutist, year zero persuasion. Call in the bulldozers, drive through the motorway.

The idea that the car should take precedence in the urban pecking order is now deeply unfashionable, but in the '60s, the prevailing paradigm suggested that the future belonged to the automobile. The centre of the city, town planners decided, was no place for decent, modern, middle-class people to abide. Heavily influenced by American suburban ideals, the idea took hold that inner London would primarily be a place to work; a high-rise downtown where you would drive in to your swanky office on a network of lovely new motorways from your outlying home in leafy Acacia Avenue. The poor sods that did stay in the centre would be decanted into tower blocks between the *autostrade*.

It has always struck me as somehow a bit sneaky that nice bourgeois academics and architects convinced working-class people that the houses they lived in were unfit for human habitation, then moved into them like a shot once the oiks were cleared out. The streets that survived the wrecking ball in W10 and W11 are now among the most valuable on earth. A four-storey gaff in Portland Road, where my cousin once lived, is roughly six million quid a pop, quite a sum for a slum. But I am prepared to accept that actually the motives of most of the slum clearance schemes were honourable.

The Utopian urges and socialist motives behind the big brutalist blocks like the large Lancaster West Estate and Erno Goldfinger's handsome Trellick Tower, which replaced the notorious but glorious Southam Street area in Kensal Town, just north of Notting Dale, were admirable. People originally loved having indoor toilets, fitted kitchens and central heating. But smashing apart a community to build a road in the sky is perhaps less benign. Doing it twice is surely close to criminal.

To paraphrase Oscar Wilde: 'To lose one house to a motorway scheme may be regarded as a misfortune; to lose a second is bleeding ridiculous.' But that is precisely what happened to the Elmses. The Latimer Road abode was subsumed beneath a football pitch beneath a flyover, but by then my dad's mob had already moved a little further west-southwest, back towards Shepherd's Bush, where Freddie first arrived from Uxbridge. They settled in a short, rather pleasant no-through road called Norland Gardens. At least it was pleasant until some brainbox dreamed up the London Motorway Box.

The nominal head of the Norland Gardens house was my dad's dad Reg, always known as Grandad Weenie because of his tiny stature, but it was really run by Aunt Glad, my father's eldest sister and a phenomenal character, despite also being a shade less than five feet in height. (The diminutive stature of that generation of the old Elms clan is what makes me assume Freddie was also little.) Glad and her husband ran a fruit and veg business in Norland market, played honky-tonk piano in the local boozers, cleaned local schools and smoked thousands of fags a day.

Aunt Glad became my de facto grandma after my dad's actual mum, a fiery, red-haired Romany lass, prone to rolling up her sleeves to fight her corner, died just as I was being born. Glad was the absolute epitome of the caustic, caring, all-encompassing working-class woman, quick of wit, sharp of tongue, full of love. When I think of Notting Dale, I think of Aunt Glad, the embodiment of a largely lost world.

Her place in Norland Gardens was the house my dad called 'home', even though he lived in exile with his half-Yiddisher wife and three sons, half-a-dozen miles and two bus rides away on the Watling Estate. My mum's family 'home', the abode of the Biffens, was on the White City estate, just the other side of the Westway, and even closer to QPR. So every Saturday, without fail, and for much of the school holidays, we would make the pilgrimage from Burnt Oak back to the ancestral homelands to see both sets of families. These weekend trips back 'home' were a feature of estate life for most Burnt Oak families, who maintained their ties to their old inner London communities in Islington, King's Cross, Paddington and Notting Hill. Everybody had a 'home' to go to in town.

My abiding memory of those Saturdays is of waiting for countless eternities for a Number 52 at Cricklewood bus garage in the freezing cold, snuggling beneath my mum's coat for warmth. We didn't have a car to drive up that modern flyover, which had wreaked such destruction, so we were doomed to wait for buses that never came. But despite the cold and the wait, it was worth it. For somehow I knew, even then I knew, that we had been banished from what I thought of as *real* London, *proper* London, *our* London.

This was now the soon-to-be-swinging '60s, yet there was not even a hint of modernity in the vocabulary of those dark, brown and still essentially Edwardian West London interiors we visited every weekend. A litany of splendidly archaic words such as: Anaglypta, antimacassar, scullery, scuttle, doily, spittoon, bolster, meat safe, tin bath, outside privy, front parlour, linoleum, Lincrusta, candlewick, winceyette, eiderdown, counterpane, chamber pot, Izal, Omo and carbolic.

Being at both of those deeply old-fashioned West London homes also involved arcane rituals. Tanners were pressed into palms upon arrival; bacon sarnies proffered, always doused in malt vinegar; milk bottles kept in buckets of cold water were produced to drink. The best bit was running age-inappropriate errands; placing a bet for Grandad Weenie at the bookies and fetching beer from the offie counter in the General Smuts pub for Grandad Biffen.

My mum's mum's little house was part of the sprawling White City site, which had originally been constructed in 1908 for a huge Franco-British Exhibition and the first London Olympics. It was the gleaming vision of one Imre Kiralfy, an Austro-Hungarian burlesque impresario, huckster and conjurer. Kiralfy was a protégé of P.T. Barnum, and he decreed a vast white marble-clad Xanadu (hence the name 'the Great White City'), stretching from Shepherd's Bush roundabout virtually all the way to Wormwood Scrubs. The showgrounds (as it was still known to older locals) was later used for a series of Empire exhibitions and trade fairs and boasted scenic railways, ferris wheels, vast pavilions, lakes, waterfalls and exotic themed 'villages' displaying the wonders of the rose-hued world, all in gleaming white.

In its day, the Great White City attracted hundreds of thousands of chaps in boaters, and ladies in fancy bonnets; one of the wonders of the age. But each exhibition and fair was a little less successful than the last, and it slowly dwindled to desolation. Its grand proscenium arch entrance could still be seen by Shepherd's Bush bus garage, rotting gracefully away, leading only to a collection of breakers' yards, dodgy car dealers, dubious lockups and shabby light-industrial units. It was finally demolished in 2005 to make way for the gargantuan twenty-first century pleasure dome called the Westfield shopping centre. I think that's called progress.

The royal box at the White City Stadium, the largest stadium in the world when it was constructed for the 1908 Olympics, was exactly 26 miles, 385 yards from Windsor Castle, where the marathon running race started, which is why all marathons are now that precise distance. (There is, at time of writing, still a line in the pavement, in between Tesco Express and Starbucks, next to a nondescript 1980s BBC building, marking precisely where the finish line was).

Later, the White City Stadium became the home of British grey-hound racing, a car-coat and flat-cap mecca, a cathedral of broken dreams and torn betting slips, which was within jogging distance of QPR's much humbler, but longer lasting ground at Loftus Road. This was evidenced by the fact that Stanley Bowles, the shaman of Shepherd's Bush, the greatest footballer ever to grace the hoops, a carefree maverick and an inveterate gambler, could occasionally be seen running from White City to Loftus Road, with a mac over his kit and a biro behind his ear just moments before kick-off.

The White City housing estate itself was built on the site of the decaying showgrounds in the 1930s and became a bastion of tough, working-class QPR stalwarts. Always an estate with a reputation, it was once filled with my cousins, uncles and aunts, shouting to each other over the balconies of the curvilinear five-storey blocks, peopled by a mix of old London, Irish and Caribbean families. But when that generation of White City-ites moved out, there was a stark, dark, decline.

Allowed to run down, its walkways strewn with rubbish, old cars festering in the drives, it became regarded as a sink estate, neglected and notorious for crime, crack dens and 'problem' families. I always felt perfectly safe walking through the flats to football and stopping for a pint, felt most of its inhabitants were decent people living in tough conditions. But I had to smile recently when strolling past a fancy hoarding just over the road from the estate. It was wrapped around one of the plethora of swanky new luxury developments going up in the area, and it boasted in big letters 'WHITE CITY LIVING'.

My mum's mob, the Biffens, started their bout of White City living when the estate was first built. They moved to one of the slightly 'superior' houses on the fringes of the estate from their two rooms in Pimlico in 1930–31. Perhaps they chose there because my nan and grandad had gone to Kiralfy's Great White City while courting. The last Biffen present was my Aunt Joyce, my mum's youngest sister, who had a photo of Doctor Kildare on her bedroom wall and always called me her 'little gammon rasher'. She died alone in the house in 1998. So for nearly seven decades there were Biffens at 9 Bentworth Road.

The most exciting thing about that little house as a kid was its proximity to QPR, but also to Wormwood Scrubs prison, which was directly behind it on Du Cane Road. A grim Gothic institution, there was a bell which would be rung whenever a prisoner escaped, warning the locals to shut their back door, as they may come prowling through your garden in a Magwitch fashion. I've convinced myself I was there the day the bell rang for the Cambridge Soviet spy George Blake, who went over the wall en route to Moscow in 1966.

I could also have heard a rather special piano being played. Ivor Novello spent a couple of months in the Scrubs during the war for forging petrol coupons. He clearly had special privileges as he was allowed to bring in his baby grand so that he could compose a few bars behind bars, which he then donated to the prison chapel where it still sits today. Such stories made my nan's little house seem a little more glamorous, but other than that it was a fairly anonymous two-up two-down council house. Or so I thought.

It was only years later, when I was doing some research into the history of Kiralfy's original White City, just as the last vestiges of it were about to be subsumed by the brute leviathan of the Westfield shopping centre, that I discovered something fascinating about that house. I saw a map indicating that Bentworth Road had once been on the site of the Grand Indian Pavilion, the jewel in the colonial Expo crown. This boasted turbaned Maharajas, uniformed sepoys, fakirs with snakes and a family of elephants that had camped exactly where Nan's back garden was. I wish I had been able to tell that to the Bengali family who moved in a few doors away.

Apart from the rare thrill of the prison bell, the greatest excitement of time spent at Nan's was the considerably more commonplace pleasure of being sent to collect Grandad, Isaac Silas Biffen, from the General Smuts. This boozer, named after a Boer, is now an Egyptian restaurant, shisha bar and even a little impromptu Masjid for the many Muslim inhabitants of White City. But it was once a truly rollicking local. Its denizens divided between the Irish and the West Indian, both of them dressed in suits, many in ties, both drinking the Guinness, one lot watching the racing, the other lot playing raucous dominoes, everybody smoking copiously, swearing furiously; 'Bludclot' and 'pogue mahone'. This place was rich.

I would be dispatched there at tea time to get Grandad Biffen – a solitary, grumpy, hard-drinking, usually tight-fisted man who would have to be prised out of the saloon bar of the Smuts. Despite being a famed tightwad he would occasionally bribe me half a crown if I let him have another beer and maybe a chaser before heading home. That allowed me, aged maybe eight or nine, to revel in the wanton, lubricated air of the place, rank and rowdy, thick and male. To this day I like pubs like that far too much. I like the very smell of them. Sadly there aren't too many pubs like the smelly Smuts left anywhere in London.

And I really liked going to Aunt Glad's too. The house in Norland Gardens felt tumultuous, teeming, but even then it seemed to me like an endangered species of an abode. It was actually an early Victorian terrace, four storeys including a basement, steps up from street level, an 'area' below, each floor full of family. The place was always busy with cousins and aunts, and a man known as Charlie Percy who was some sort of in-law who liked rum. There were kids everywhere, parties aplenty, a piano for Glad, a front parlour used only for wakes, and a telly in the kitchen, where Weenie sat in a collarless shirt watching the racing in fuzzy black and white. There was a backyard, which itself backed on to a totters' yard where they kept the horses.

There was also an air of cash money affluence, a typical cockney pride in always having a few bob in your pocket, 'fruit in the bowl and no one's even ill'. Grandad Weenie had been a street angler, a man who knew how to make a shilling. Aunt Glad's husband was a market trader and shouter of wares, and compared to the parsimonious smallness of my mum's mum's council house a mile away in Bentworth Road, it felt like money and song and life flowed in Norland Gardens. Us kids, especially myself and my second cousin Lee-Ann, Glad's granddaughter, ran a kind of sweet riot. The line between the house and the street was blurred, permeable, in and out, games that started in the yard often ended in the Bush. My favourite memory of Aunt Glad's house is of escaping it to run wild on the debris with the local herberts.

The whole family went to both houses most weekends when I was a small boy, and then we didn't. The family wasn't whole any more. My father, Albert James Elms, Freddie's distant heir, was a soft, hard-left, building-site trade unionist, and a tender, loving husband and father of three. Intensely proud of the contribution he made to his city as a skilled steel erector, reconstructing his bombed-out town, perched atop tall scaffolding. He would reel off a list of the jobs he'd worked on from hospitals to gas holders, council estates to the Festival of Britain. He was part of the crew that constructed the Festival Hall on the South Bank and with other local comrades helped drive Mosley's fascists from their base in Kensington Park Road. My dad was steeped deep in the London he helped to build.

Albert Elms went to work on a building site in Park Royal one rainy day and never returned. He was forty-one, and my mum was thirty-nine; I was about to be seven. Perhaps it's a good thing he never got to see his city rebuilt again by Mammon & Co, callously reshaped by the market and those who do its bidding. But it is tragic that he never got to see his three sons become men.

He was taken away by a sudden, unheralded heart attack, and I have missed him every single day since. The cause of death of my father in 1966 was given on the certificate I found among my mum's effects as 'aortic stenosis of rheumatic origin', which is now described as a condition 'rare outside the developing world'. His death left my mum bereft and me bewildered: why would such a good man go?

We would still go west most weekends. My mum now on her own with three sons, working two or three jobs, but still making that tortuous cross-town schlepp to keep the fraying family ties together.

It also meant that during school holidays, when mum had to work in Woolworths, or cleaning the houses of snobby pilots based at RAF Hendon, I would have extended sojourns with the ancients. Alternatively I went to stay with my cousin Ian, my mum's sister's boy, another West London QPR fanatic who had somehow ended up exiled in a pre-fab in Fish Island, Hackney Wick, where we regularly tried to storm Percy Dalton's peanut factory.

There are few advantages to losing your father at an early age, but I undoubtedly had to develop a certain self-reliance. Left alone for long periods I got good at solo wandering, intimate explorations of my nascent Londons. And over in our old town, around Aunt Glad's house, as I ventured out into those knocked about, beaten-up streets, increasingly resembling some kind of little Stalingrad, I was witnessing a vanishing world, a doomed way of life, but also a new one emerging. There's always fun to be had amid the ruins.

As I write, a development, hilariously but perhaps predictably dubbed Notting Dale Village, has sprung up exactly where I once cavorted with the local roustabouts in Sta-Prest and Ben Shermans. Big high street fashion companies like Monsoon, Accessorize and Cath Kidston have made their head offices in garish, overdesigned new corporate buildings where the totters' yards and horse-feed shops once stood, beardy types and flouncy fashionistas soaking up the urban vibes. But then this was always a hotbed of street fashion, home of the first Teds, the nattiest rude boys and the most ardent mods, and one of the incubators of the biggest street-style eruption of them all.

Punk was a product of two great cities on the brink of bankruptcy: New York when it was skint, dangerous, collapsing, full of loft spaces to spare; London when it was equally boracic, broken, clad in corrugated iron and overflowing with squats. Both cities when they were down on their luck, randomly violent, decaying and derided, were at their most creative. They were cheap. In New York, the epicentre of punk was the Bowery and the Lower East Side, in London it was indisputably a West Side story based on the King's Road, Chelsea, the Bush and the Grove.

Punk was initially a form of sartorial sedition, a daring new trouser tribe, and the King's Road, currently the most drearily bourgeois thoroughfare in all London, was where the action was. This was home to the cutting-edge clothes shops; Malcolm and Vivienne at World's End, Don Letts with Acme Attractions in Antiquarious, Boy and Johnson's, a radical teen catwalk of clashing street styles parading, preening and posing every Saturday. But the bands and the beat came from the Bush and its environs.

The two groups who instigated the London punk tsunami, the Sex Pistols and The Clash, were both based in this crumbling enclave. As we've already noted two of the Sex Pistols were Shepherd's Bush ragamuffins, and a third original member, Glen Matlock, was from nearby Maida Vale and is still a QPR regular. The Clash all had their roots in these streets. Mick Jones, another Loftus Road season ticket holder, whom I often see fretting at matches, lived as a teenager in his grandmother's high-rise council block overlooking the Westway. Paul Simenon grew up in a bohemian but skint household on Ladbroke Grove, while Joe Strummer, the middle-class outsider, made the squats and ramshackle short-life housing of W9 and 10 his spiritual stomping ground from when he first rocked up in London in the early '70s, until well after he could afford not to.

Strummer's first band, the 101'ers, were named after a squat at 101 Walterton Road, near Elgin Avenue and he floated around the free houses of the area for years. There was also a squat in Davis Road, East Acton, which should surely have a plaque with a safety pin. This place in 1976 was home to Mick Jones, Paul Simenon, Viv Albertine from the Slits, Sid Vicious and Keith Levene from Public Image. But the most remarkable squat of them all, literally yards from the Elms household on Norland Gardens, is among the most extraordinary tales this neighbourhood has to tell, a parable of the way London has transformed itself in my lifetime. It is the remarkable saga of the People's Republic of Frestonia.

It is difficult now to even imagine, but in my adult lifetime, property in inner London was worth so little that you would have trouble giving it away. Notting Hill, now London's stockbroker belt (actually it's more of a hedgie ghetto), was once the absolute nexus of free housing. At its height in the late '70s it is estimated that over 30,000 people in London were living in squats of one kind or another. There were Rastafarian squats, gay squats, feminist squats, squats concealing the Angry Brigade, luxury squats in Nash terraces and squalid squats in rat-infested hell holes. But most were just unloved old houses filled with young people, particularly students, artists and musicians. And by far the largest concentration were in that wedge of West London from the Dale to the Vale.

There was even an anarchist estate agent on the Westbourne Park Road called the Ruff Tuff Cream Puff Agency. Run by playwright Heathcote Williams, this centre of sedition helped over 3,000 would-be squatters identify potential properties, dished out legal advice and doled out crowbars to secure entry to empty premises, all in the W10, W11 nexus.

I myself resided in a few 'temporary' properties in the early '80s in North London, moving from house to house and finally settling in a disused fire station in South Tottenham with Sade Adu and half her band. Boy George, Marilyn and many of the fabulous devotees of the Blitz club lived in a vast, theatrically decaying Georgian mansion in Warren Street W1 that no one even claimed ownership of. How much is that house worth today?

Most commonly the squats of the '70s were humble council housing stock, owned by the local authority, who had rows, blocks and indeed whole streets of old housing in need of modernisation and deemed unfit to let out to families, but which they did not have the money to do up. Or else the sad shells of houses were awaiting demolition, because of some madcap scheme; sitting empty, often for years, rotting away. So people just moved in. This is exactly what happened in Freston Road, which was actually the continuation of Latimer Road after it was cut in half by the Westway. But what happened next is unique.

As the '60s morphed into the '70s, I watched those old streets of decent Victorian dwellings, mainly three-storey workers' houses, being dismantled from the vantage point of my house-proud aunt's front steps. Because she actually owned the property, it was safe for the time being. I saw local families we'd known for years decanted into the newly constructed Stalinist stalagmites or exiled to the edges. I watched as the houses were emptied, and then often deliberately 'vandalised' by the council, who would knock out windows and smash roofs, in an attempt to dissuade squatters from moving in, but it never worked.

As soon as the corrugated iron went up, the hippies clambered in, patched up the holes, linked up the electricity, called up their mates. Aunt Glad thought they were all long-haired, soap-swerving layabouts, and she wasn't the only one. Local youths were resolutely of the cropped-haired, tonic strides, skinhead and ska variety, and the only hairy, heavy middle-class types anyone knew worked at the nearby adventure playground, building deathly rope swings, smoking roll ups and fermenting revolution.

Scores of these lank peace-and-love warriors colonised the crumbling, abandoned old terraces all around the manor and introduced patchouli and essence of Afghan coat to the area's aromas. Those locals who had moved to the high rises, in this case the twenty-two-storey blocks of the Edward Woods Estate, literally looked down on the bedraggled arrivistes as they moved into their old houses. There was a certain tension – or perhaps mutual misunderstanding – between the old and the new, the smart oiks and the scruffy toffs. Who knew that this was actually the first sign of the gentrification to come? Hippies as harbingers of hedge-fund managers.

The biggest hippy colony of them all was set up in a sizeable tranche of land bounded by Freston Road, St Ann's Road and Bramley Road. This was a roughly triangular, roughly two-acre site spanning W10 and W11, which housed up to 150 piratical freeloaders, including a fair number of families with ragged-arsed kids. It also featured a communal garden, an art gallery, an occasional hotel and the People's Hall, a handsome red brick Victorian civic centre. This was about to become the National Theatre of Frestonia.

I can't say that I followed this story at the time, or had any idea what was going on behind the corrugated iron curtain on Freston Road. My gaze, and indeed my family, were elsewhere, but I have certainly got to know it since, especially when I was asked to write and present a Radio 4 show called 'From Belgravia to Frestonia'. This told the history of squatting, just as it was about to be effectively abolished by a change in the law, outlawing the entry to residential property. I was lucky enough to interview a couple of old Frestonians, and what a splendidly mischievous tale they have to tell.

For after a few years of a more-or-less disorderly but stable existence as a distinct, if occasionally shambolic cooperative community, the GLC decided that it wanted the land around Freston Road back. They intended to knock the whole lot down (knock it down was the GLC's default position on just about everything) and at some point in the distant future sell it off for office and light-industrial development, making lots of rubble, making the inhabitants homeless and effectively wiping out one of the last surviving stretches of old residential Notting Dale.

The first response was for 120 of the squatters to officially change their surnames to Bramley (after Bramley Road), in the hope that if they claimed they were all one family, they would have to be re-housed collectively. The council was having none of it and issued official eviction orders, and had the bulldozers at the ready. So one of the long-term residents, Nicholas Albery, former Haight Ashbury pioneer and anarchist activist, suggested that they go one stage further, and make a UDI (Unilateral Declaration of Independence). At a public meeting in the People's Hall, 94 per cent of the 200 people present voted in favour, and on 31 October 1977 they declared Frestonia independent from the United Kingdom.

Given their libertarian leanings, there was no prime minister or president, but diminutive actor David Rappaport-Bramley became the foreign minister and Heathcote Williams-Bramley was ambassador to

Great Britain. A two-year-old child named Francesco Bogina-Bramley was appointed minister for education. The nascent micro-state's coat of arms bore the legend 'Nos Somos Una Familia'. And the whole Bramley family celebrated Frestonia's independence by showing a pirate copy of *Passport to Pimlico* on a makeshift screen in the newly named National Theatre. Is that life imitating art?

There were precedents for this tongue-in-cheek, but also genuinely idealistic and potentially pragmatic, move. Christiania, a far larger hippy commune on an old army base in Copenhagen, had declared itself a Freetown in 1971 and has managed to live a semi-autonomous existence ever since, although these days it's as much a tourist attraction as an alternative society. Much closer to home, but on the other side of London, the Isle of Dogs had beaten Christiania to it by almost a year.

In 1970, the island, actually a loop of land in a massive meander in the Thames that we all now know from the *EastEnders* opening credits, was a forgotten world. A solidly working-class but terminally declining community that was largely made up of dockers and their families and cut off from the rest of London by its unique geography, the Isle of Dogs was always a place apart, accessible only by a couple of rickety bridges and ill-served in terms of infrastructure, transportation, schools, etc.

So a couple of the militant local lightermen and stevedores, heading what they called the Citizens Committee, set up a 'government' in a council flat at 27 Skeggs House. They then set about closing the bridges and issuing entry visas for 'foreign' journalists who wished to visit the island to cover the story. No less luminary a broadcaster than Walter Cronkite reported on the independent cockney island for CBS; many of the British papers put it on the front cover and two of the ringleaders, Ted Johns and John Westfallen, actually ended up meeting the then Prime Minister Harold Wilson at 10 Downing Street. Eventually, the development they were promised at that meeting led to what we now know as the soaring steel and glass towers of Canary Wharf, which I'm not sure is exactly what the left-wing dockers were after. Sometimes you have to be very careful what you wish for.

What the Frestonians wanted half-a-dozen years later was ultimately for the area to be saved for housing rather than offices or warehouses, and for the community to be allowed to stick together. They also wanted to have as much fun as possible along the way and set about accomplishing both with a gusto and brio that still shines brightly. At the same time that they seceded from the United Kingdom, the Free Independent Republic of Frestonia applied to join the EEC as well as the United Nations and indeed wrote an impressively legal-sounding letter to the UN on official headed notepaper, urging them to send a team of blue beret-wearing peace keepers to this fledgling state to protect them from the invading GLC. The tanks never actually arrived.

Border guards were posted around the corrugated perimeter, stamping the visas of any visitors. Frestonians were issued with their own passports and actually travelled internationally on them. They printed postage stamps which worked to send letters even further abroad than the UK, issued an occasional national newspaper called the *Tribal Messenger*, and kept up a constant barrage of inventive, knowing, publicity wheezes which kept Frestonia (a name inspired in part by the Marx Brothers' Freedonia in *Duck Soup*) in the headlines and kept the bailiffs at bay. The separatists received support from some unlikely sources, including Geoffrey Howe, then shadow chancellor of the exchequer, who said, 'As one who had childhood enthusiasm for Napoleon of Notting Hill I can hardly fail to be moved by your aspirations.' Even Horace Cutler, the Tory head of the Greater London Council, their avowed foe, seemed to enjoy jousting with them.

All the publicity stunts and a fair degree of public sympathy meant that Frestonia survived into the new decade, but by then the nature of some of the residents had changed. The republic was always divided between the Utopian inner-circle, many of them middle- and even upper-class idealists who chose the squatting lifestyle and those who, because of poverty or drink and drug problems, had little option. And in the later years of Frestonia, the latter became more prominent and some of the squats became more chaotic and squalid. Life was never easy in decaying old buildings with rudimentary facilities, often no heating or hot water, always no security, but some of the reports of what it was like to actually live in the Republic in the '80s are blood-curdlingly tough. *Withnail and I* with no windows and bricks by your bed to lob at drug-crazed interlopers. Anarchy in the O.K. Corral.

This darker, harsher phase of the republic was also a reflection of the great cultural shift from hippy to punk, from peace and love to hate and war, idealism to nihilism, dope to speed and smack. The young anarcho-punks who moved into Frestonia turned one of the largest buildings in the country into the ominously named, and riotously hedonistic, Apocalypse Hotel. They enjoyed smashing things up so much, it was said that in the Apocalypse even the walls were provisional. That didn't stop The Clash, who all lived a stone's throw away, from having their photo taken outside, and the art group Mutoid Waste from staying and performing their earliest shows there. The Clash, always good at combining solidarity and publicity, eager to show their men-of-the-people street cred, rehearsed and recorded their *Combat Rock* album in the People's Hall. But by now the end of the nation was nigh. The end wasn't all bad.

At some point, the older, more moderate members of Frestonia, weary of the rigours of their chosen lifestyle, morphed into the Bramleys Housing Co-operative Ltd. They joined forces with the much more conventional and established Notting Hill Housing Trust, and as a result of a public enquiry managed to get a section of the one-time independent state preserved for social housing. The original properties, except the listed People's Hall, were all demolished and some of the residents scattered. The more militant anarchists, angry at dealing with 'the man', left for other more radical squats and communes. But a block of forty small, neat, almost twee yellow brick houses, fronting on to St Ann's Road, aptly arrayed around a communal garden, are still there to this day; still a cooperative, still a close-knit community, still home to original Frestonians and their children and even grandchildren.

But none of my family is anywhere to be seen. From Freddie's arrival in the 1870s to the last Elms leaving the Dale was almost exactly 100

years. I guess that's not bad going for an urban dynasty, but I feel bad
when I think that we are no longer part of the fabric of that neighbourhood, which was so much a part of us. I feel also that the manor
is diminished, not just by our absence but by the departure of so many
of the souls whose stories are woven into those streets; good, fast,
London families gone.

I have actually felt this for most of my life, that somehow growing
up out in the Burnt Oak boondocks made me just a little less. (I think
Paul Weller, a man of a similar age, attitude and attire, whom I admire
enormously, and whose London family were exiled even further, to
Woking, carries a similar burden.) I became jealous of kids whose
families had held out, in awe of lads who came out of Holborn or
Pimlico, played run-outs among the mummies of the British Museum
or had their first snog at the Tate by Rodin's *The Kiss*.

I almost worshipped a girl in my teenage years primarily because
she had spent all her life in the flat she was born in above a bookshop
on the Charing Cross Road. To this day I feel slightly awed in the
company of people who were born in the belly of the beast, heirs to
Blake, Sheppard and Gwyn. From about the age of fourteen, I was
desperate to move back towards the centre of town, the oh-so-magnetic
pole. But exile also made me more: more ambitious, more agitated,
perhaps perversely, more passionately London.

This cockney 'saudade' is a common malaise. I hear it from surprisingly wistful cab drivers currently residing in Hornchurch, lamenting
their days growing up in the Cali or the Cross, get it from Brixtonites
who did well out of a house on Railton Road, but wonder now whether
their life in Surrey is quite so superior. Some of this is simply the
normal nostalgia of ageing souls turned sentimental, yearning as much
for lost youth as place, but there is something deeper; a communal
sense that we have all been reduced.

I feel it most at football, at Rangers on a Saturday, when people
trudge back in to haunt the haunts and share the stories. They revel
in the tight urban togetherness of a game, crowding into those narrow
streets, shoulder to shoulder in the pubs. I still give a knowing nod at

the match to tasty faces from the Grove, even though most are now statin-scoffing dads or even grandads living in Northolt. And I'm sure that yearning is echoed at West Ham, Arsenal, Spurs, Millwall, all clubs whose supporters have been pushed or pulled out of their heartlands; all places where exiled old Londoners make pilgrimages to re-affirm their tribal ties. Many of those thousands and thousands of people shell out fortunes, not just for a ticket to the football, but a season ticket to their old manor.

The Elms family ties to the ancestral Notting Dale homeland were finally severed by the London Motorway Box. The London Box was part of a truly maniacal 1960s scheme to drive a series of four elevated, orbital motorways slicing through the city, to create four roughly concentric ring roads, joined together by a network of radial links. A monstrous concrete spider's web strung over London.

The innermost motorway, Ringway 1, was conceived as a large rectangle, (hence the box) made up of four connected 'cross routes' east, west, north and south. Its construction would have taken out large chunks of Wandsworth, Brixton, Battersea, Clapham, Chelsea, Shepherd's Bush, Kilburn, Primrose Hill, Belsize Park, Hampstead, Camden Town, Islington, Hackney, Plaistow, Greenwich, Woolwich. Pretty much most of what we now know as 'Zone Two' was to have a hideous six-lane road on stilts pushed right through the middle of it. Over one million Londoners would have been living within 200 yards of a motorway. Then they would begin Ringways 2, 3 and 4, until the whole town was covered in a network of highways to nowhere. The outermost of those circuitous thoroughfares, Ringway 4, is essentially what we now know as the M25, the world's biggest car park, which has become London's de facto perimeter. They were actually going to do this.

The box wasn't the GLC's only wantonly berserk scheme to smash apart the historic fabric of old London town. Perhaps the craziest of them all was a plan to completely redevelop Covent Garden. Knock down 70 per cent of the historic buildings from Cambridge Circus to the Strand, convert the piazza into a vast conference centre, and replace the rest with high-rise offices, hotels and multistorey car parks, and force pedestrians on to walkways in the sky while the traffic roared through a series of new highways below. They came within an inch of eradicating one of London's most charismatic quarters, and – as late as 1975 – they were still trying to force this insanity through despite the concerted opposition of just about everybody.

Local residents, one of the last surviving old-school central London communities; Fleet Street printers, West End scene shifters, publicans, bumarees, cab drivers and of course market traders, formed the Covent Garden Community Association to combat this disastrous scheme. Architecture students and conservationists, displaying a growing realisation that the past is too rich, too woven into the future to be bulldozed away, joined them. The fruit and flower market itself, one of the most viscerally vivid experiences in all London, a ripe, pungent favela of flowers and salads, spilling over those ancient cobbled arcades, ringing with coarse canting cries dating back to the seventeenth century, was sadly doomed. Ultimately, it headed over the water for Nine Elms and sanitised sanity in 1974.

Of the homes in the area, 82 per cent – almost exclusively those of working-class Londoners – were going to be flattened as part of this maniacal scheme. But these tight-knit families, some of whom could trace their WC2 roots back to the Hundreds of Drury, when this was the most roguish area in all Romeville, refused to just let their neighbourhood disappear beneath the vainglorious dreams of town planners.

They put up a mighty fight: clever, witty, resourceful, staunch. Thankfully they got support from political leaders of almost every hue as the tide turned against such wanton destruction. Anthony Crosland, Labour's shadow environment minister, made a speech where he said, 'I believe with passion that it is now time to call a halt. It is time to stop this piecemeal hacking away at our city. It is time to say to the GLC . . . "Gentlemen, we've had enough. We, the people of London, now propose to decide for ourselves what sort of city we want to live in."'

Plenty, of course, no longer wished to live in the city at all. Glad to get out at a time when the place was being pulled apart; its population and its reputation in what appeared to be terminal decline. Nobody in the mid-'70s called London the greatest city on Earth, and indeed it could seem a bit like a failed Soviet state on a particularly grey day. Backward-looking, old-fashioned, early closing, tired and tatty, big chunks of it under threat of demolition . . . throw in perpetual strikes, three-day weeks, shortages, rationing and power cuts and London felt less like the capital of a great nation, and more like the bridge of a sinking ship.

My favourite anecdote from this era is straight out of an Ealing comedy. During a baker's strike in 1977, loaves were rationed, they had guards outside bread shops and a baker's van carrying a load of precious split tins and wholemeal baps was hijacked by masked men on Commercial Road in E1. That's how desperate things had become, a banana republic with a bread shortage.

But as is so often the case, when things are at their lowest is just when they are starting to look up. London's revival was heralded by punk's liberating cultural paroxysms; educated, socially mobile pioneers (don't yet call them yuppies) moving into decaying old inner-city neighbourhoods; artists, musicians and entrepreneurs taking advantage of cheap rents. Combine those with new waves of international migration, a growing realisation that the fabric of this historic city is worth saving and organised residents fighting for both the past and the future. All of these would coalesce to start nudging London's pendulum back in a positive direction. But that all came too late for Aunt Glad and Norland Gardens.

That house, which for me represented my links to my father, and via him to a particular type of London life right back to Freddie, was in my memory at least the last home standing, with a veritable battle zone of rubble and ruination all around it. The campaign to save Covent Garden was ultimately successful, and there was a similar outcry about the outrageous plan to turn London into a motorway service station. But nothing could save Norland Gardens.

Banners made from bedsheets were hung from houses and flats; women in curlers did a lot of shouting, but all to no avail. The West

Cross Route, the first part of this brave new world on wheels running from Battersea to Harlesden, was underway. The London Box was opening and so the Elms's residence was compulsorily purchased, and the last of Freddie's offspring were bought out and pushed out. The wrecking ball came in, and I watched, holding my beloved Auntie's veiny hand, as ancient Anaglypta floated in the air.

'Our' house was sacrificed for the grandiosely titled M41: talk about living in the fast lane. Aunt Glad and her family moved to a posher but more sedate home out Chiswick way. We still went to see them as often as possible, but it was never the same. She had never been more than a few hundred yards from a street market and before long they gave up the ghost, gave up on the city completely and settled for a life beside the seaside. As Lee-Ann said to me recently, 'I felt bereft, bereaved.' Their London was over.

The complaints and concerns of the Gord Blimey families of Notting Dale came to nought. Back then, even areas like Islington, Clapham, Battersea and Greenwich were still largely populated by the easily ignored, glottal-stopping proletariat. But over in Chelsea, Belsize Park and Hampstead it was a different accent, a different matter. The GLC tried to buy off the protests of the metropolitan elite with tunnels under NW2 and diversions round the King's Road. But the well-funded, well-organised, well-spoken, articulate and persistent campaign waged by the residents of the sort of inner-city areas that were never a short-hand for crime and dereliction, combined with astronomically escalating costs, finally paid off. The whole lunatic Ringway scheme was eventually abandoned. Except for one bit.

A hundred years of Freddie's lineage, a century of Elmses in the Dale, were sacrificed for 0.75 miles of tarmac, which basically went from one of our old houses to another; from Shepherd's Bush round-about to Latimer Road. It was, I believe, the shortest stretch of motorway in the world, until it was ignominiously demoted to the status of an A road in 2000. If you look closely at the point where the now named A3220 meets the Westway, the roundabout just before the football pitch where Alfie played and my dad grew up, you can see a short spur of road going nowhere. It is literally just a few feet long, heading towards Harlesden, ending abruptly; a connection never made. That's all that remains of the GLC's grandest, maddest vision for London.

And what remains of that part of my London and my part in that London? Well truth be told, it still has an air and I still hold a torch. I heard Mayfair described recently as a place for people who can't afford Notting Hill, and the joke wasn't entirely funny. Gentrification is a double-edged sword: it bringeth and it taketh away. The jet-powered gentrification that roared through W11 from roughly the late '80s onwards has brought untold wealth, elegance, good food, nice flowers and some fuck-off enormous basements with home cinemas and swimming pools.

Notting Hill now feels like a fog or maybe even a thick snowfall of affluence has settled over the streets, making them muffled, muted, calm. It is international, aspirational, like a living Patek Philippe advert. It must be an excellent place to live if you want, and you can afford, to live like that. It feels cosseted, like a boutique hotel of a neighbourhood, and I can enjoy a plush hotel as much as the next man. But I don't really enjoy what the neighbourhood has become.

On its fringes and in its crevices, however, there are still the estates and the social housing, and the occasional tatty house that has escaped the curse of the developers. People still sit on steps and drink tea. There is the odd hooped shirt on a snotty kid, or a dread's tam bobbing in the distance, a local builders' merchants, a local substance merchant, a makeshift mosque, a Baptist congregation. That shabby Spanish restaurant where you can get a late drink, that Moroccan gaff the guys go to, the social club under the flyover, the pointers to its former life still lived. And what gentrification has taken away was not all good in the first place. Ask Kelso Cochrane. Ask my mum.

But I do miss the booming bass of Dub Vendor and People's Sounds, the loping step of Rastamen waiting for the black star liner on Portobello Road when the two sevens clashed. Soon come. I long to see the 'QPR NOTTING HILL' flag flying over a run-down terrace, and a totter feeding his horse outside a pub. In my mind I still hear Jimmy Pursey from Sham 69 shouting for peace, as all hell crashed around him during a biblical riot in Acklam Hall; out-of-town racist skinheads, scattered by the fury of righteous local kiddies, black and white unite and fight.

Singing of riots, there was Joe and The Clash in the KPH with the old Irish, the SPG amassing round the corner; Geoff Travis selling me a sweet deep Al Green tune when I'd gone into Rough Trade to buy some punk. Rangers colours flying from bus stops and sweet shops all the way to Wembley in '82. This is our cave. Norman Jay spinning *Good Times*; the Mangrove, the Colville. The beautiful black-and-white images of beautiful black-and-white boys entangled in Roger Mayne's epochal lens. Love those boys, mourn those streets. Grandad Weenie standing proud on the cobbles, a kettle in his waistcoat pocket, his dad's hand-cart behind him. Oysters in the Cow. Kenny Mars Bars on his barrow. Trinny corner. Boxers from Dale Boys running early morning, hoods up, hands held high. Freddie always somewhere in the distance.

Cross over Ladbroke Grove and you cross one of London's unmarked but unmissable boundaries, a fault line in the capital's tectonic plate that you feel in the air leading down into the Dale. Still a different land. Here in forgotten North Kensington there is less affluence, less elegance, less almost everything. But it is more like ours, more like London. The Dale still feels like it is recovering from the blows, concussed, perhaps, by all the bashing, suffering from collective amnesia, like it has forgotten its own stories. Yet it also feels like a community determined to hold on, to retain its rightful place in so regal a borough.

There is (hopefully) still a pub called the Pig and Whistle, a pug ugly, flat-roofed boozer hard by the station, which is just a little like the Smuts, where you can get goat curry, a pint for four quid, a tip for the 4.15 at Uttoxeter Races and a pair of trainers if you know who to ask. But you'd better not ask. As I search for musical monkeys in the land of Frestonia, I know I never really came from here and I shall not return. You can never go home again.

The Avernus Returns

I had to look up that word again to check that it really was as chillingly apt as I thought. Avernus, from a volcanic crater in Italy, which was seen as the entrance to Hades, a perilous, sulphurous gateway to the flaming under-world, where no sane soul would venture and no birds flew. 'The Avernus of Kensington' was a commonplace description for the rancid Victorian slums of Notting Dale, where the life expectancy was the shortest in all London, and the fiery conflagration of the afterlife of the damned was ever present. It is a word that sadly has come back to haunt us.

It was on 14 June 2017 that the murderous flames of hell returned to North Kensington. Reminding us that in this ever-changing city, some things are doomed to remain the same. Grenfell Tower is/was (currently stuck in the terrible limbo between tenses) part of the Lancaster West Estate, a 1970s concrete enclave in the ward of Notting Dale. A bold, brutalist slum clear-ance scheme a few hundred yards from the old Elms house on Latimer Road, just up from hopeful, hopeless Frestonia.

The nation watched that night in horror. We all felt the pain, and maybe the guilt, of Grenfell; the flames shamed us all as we saw the tower turn to ashen crematoria, those sacrificed souls sealed and seared inside. It scorched me.

Much of the breast beating afterwards was about the disparity and prox-imity of rich and poor, but it was always thus in those streets. London is built on cheek by jowl, each learning and borrowing and stealing from the other. That social juxtaposition is London's grist and gift; it gives the poor hope, and the culture makes us all richer. The real threat is that the not rich, or the ordinary, everyday Londoners, will be expunged altogether from a borough like Kensington and Chelsea. Proximity works when respect is shown by both sides. The real burning shame of Grenfell is the attitude of the wealthy overseers to their less financially affluent neighbours.

Many of the more well-to-do locals were magnificent: Cerys Matthews, Marcus Mumford, Lily Allen, Damon Albarn and the legion of not-so-famous local people who instantly tried to help, and continue to do so, because they understood and cherished the weft and weave of the social fabric. It is that very mix that makes an area like North Kensington attractive to many people, but not to everybody. There are those who complain about the carnival, look down on their neighbours. Some wealthy people don't like to know that they share a city with those less affluent than themselves. Gated communities, anybody? Is 'exclusive' the ugliest word in the English language?

Grenfell and all the other council blocks were only perceived as poor and problematic by those in the multimillion-pound homes who were embarrassed by their shabby shadows; those who wanted to hide the shame of ordinariness in inflammable plastic. Grenfell housed a rich, diverse, coherent if complex community; a decent place to live, full of decent people, and I'm sure a few dodgy ones. It was a haven and a home for refugees and architects, barrow boys and schoolgirls, old ladies and young babies, which was allowed to become a death trap precisely because the masters of the borough did not want their like there, among the gleaming stucco and bountiful boutiques.

The past waves of social cleansing in W10, including the one that drove every remaining Elms from the area, were at least carried out in the name of social improvement and advancement. They were designed, rightly or wrongly, to help the poor: 'homes fit for heroes', 'slum clearance', modern flats and motorways. That area is full of the efforts of the well-meaning well to do, from the Rugby Club and Harrow Club, (started by Rugby and Harrow Schools) to the Dickens Estate (founded by Dickens's son) to Holland Park School (supported by Tony Benn).

Now, though, naked greed is the only motive for moving the poor away, shifting them out, knocking them down. The market dictates that those who cannot afford the prices cannot live on the land – and too many of those who do live there now, in the big houses and the posh apartments, prefer it that way. They want to reside in a financially homogenous ghetto where they don't have to gaze upon the poor and their grimy little flats.

Until we acknowledge that London is at its best when we all live side by *side and make efforts to ensure it stays that way, Grenfell will rightly damn us all. I spoke to many people in the direct aftermath of the tragedy (or was it an atrocity?), but one conversation stopped me in my tracks. It was with a local girl – not a Grenfell resident, but she lived in one of the adjacent blocks – and she said that for days after the fire, no birds flew anywhere near the charred remains of the tower. An avernus indeed.*

CHAPTER TWO

The Knowledge

Cab drivers spend three or four years scuttling round town on mopeds with maps on the front, in an intense course in memorising the streets and the tourist attractions, the patterns and the pot holes of the entire town. Apparently they develop superhuman hippocampi as a result of carrying the A *to* Z and more around in their noggins. They become seers: they can literally see a run in their heads.

Anyone who spends any time in this sprawling, baffling city will begin to develop an acute mental map of their own; unique, detailed, ingenious, full of short cuts and mnemonics, marginal gains and shrewd observations, a cerebral encrustation of accrued urban wisdoms. We all do the Knowledge.

But even the most learned Londoner's perception of their town will inevitably be full of huge gaps, blind spots and lacunas. We all live in our own individual, limited Londons, because this metropolis is essentially unknowable. It is uncontainable, spreading out in all dimensions and directions, up, down, out, back, across rivers and eras, through tunnels and through time. London will definitely exhaust you, but you can never exhaust London.

I am certainly not tired of life in the Johnsonian sense. I adore this dirty, cultured, clever place as much as I have ever done; it is my restless city of circuses. I still get that boyish buzz, dodging through Cambridge Circus's congealed jam to enter Soho's tarnished lure. Still thank a God I don't believe in when I spy St Paul's dwarfed but blessed old dome from the rise of Ludgate Circus. Still say my respects to the addicted and the rented who once paraded by Piccadilly's tourist-cursed circus. Still long for St Giles's battered Circus to entertain me again. I love London's many pasts, and many of its presents, but I am acutely aware that I am hardly up to the minute in my cognitive diagram. This city of perpetual motion moves on.

Inevitably there comes a point in your London life when you tip over from acquiring the Knowledge to losing it; a form of mental downsizing. You can no longer keep up. I know that Notting Hill nowadays is not considered a slum, but I am out of the loop on which doors to knock on in Soho at 3 a.m., or even if there are any. Is it Dalston or Clapton? Who lives in Harlesden? Why is Peckham, and what is the point of craft beers?

There was a time I was truly on top of this town. I would have taken you down a ladder into a dripping basement, deep in the City, armed only with a bottle of Chablis and a couple of paper cups, and we could have feasted on live oysters from the shell, standing among briny tanks full of sea creatures, to celebrate a good day with the bulls or the bears. Or else, we could have bought some vinyl from a portly elderly lady in Dean Street who would have sat knitting, while giving us the low down on the latest twelve-inch import funk masterpieces in a room below a brothel. Soho was a cinch.

We could have squeezed into that tiny lift above the crumbling Golden Girl club, where the desiccated 'hostesses' sat on display in the grubby Meard Street window, to see the secret Matisse masterpiece in the forgotten rooftop bar. I would certainly have pointed out the fancy cheese sign in Farringdon (it actually read 'Crowson & Sons Ltd: The Fancy Cheese People'), which was in fact a front for secret spies going about their spooky business. But I can't. They're all long gone: time and change has robbed me of some of my best party pieces.

As someone who prided himself on being in the know, who thought it was important to be on first-name terms with every doorman in town, and whose sole ambition was to be a face about town, it is a blow to the self-esteem to have to admit that some of your favourite places are no longer places. (Londoners are even proud of what we do not know, boasting about having no idea of what goes on over the water, whichever side of the divide we are from.)

Sure I can still point you to a decent tailor (take a bow, George), locate the best shawarma on the Edgware Road, get a schmeiss from a naked boxer in Bayswater and avoid traffic on the Hampstead Road by zipping round the back of the old petrol station. But that particular cut-through is about to vanish because of HS2. I need to plug my personal satnav into a computer to update it. And therein lies the problem.

As always, London mirrors life, and true knowledge – the kind of ingrained, split-second mastery which can only be earned by spending years on a moped or a lifetime on the Old Kent Road – is increasingly redundant. Why do you need to really know anything if you can look it up on your phone? There are no secrets, and concomitantly, no experts anymore, just computers.

This city, which once rewarded diligence and intimacy, valued privacy, kept its true treasures out of sight – up an alley, down the steps, back a yard – is now an open book; or more aptly an app. Take the queue at the twenty-four-hour Beigel Bake on Brick Lane, a polyglot snake of cameraphone-wielding tourists and sweetly excitable newbies. Once the kind of place you had to know about to know about, it is mobbed, spilling out on to the pavement. Which is great for the owners, and the beigels are still the best. But the only edge you can get from being a Londoner, rather than a visitor, is from loudly pronouncing them properly as you shout your order for a dozen plain and a salt beef with mustard and pickle. Let bagels be beigels.

Of course, we still scoff at tourists standing on the wrong side of the escalators, chastising them for their gaucheness. I have even been known to stand at the bar in the French House, hoping for someone to order a pint. But apart from petty point scoring there is a genuine worry about losing the collective, accumulated nous of the town. Particularly in Central London, which is increasingly a place for other people.

I had a conversation with an immaculately presented, luxuriously attired, voluminously wedged property developer, who was actively 'developing' the West End. He said to me, without a hint of dismay or even irony, 'Robert, you must understand Soho is not for Londoners anymore, it's for the world.' I felt a bit like King Canute. *Stop the bloody waves: I live here; I'm from here.*

I watched just this hollowing out process happen to Manhattan, a city I have known and loved and lived in, going right back to the late '70s. For me, the greatest pleasure of New York was New Yorkers. The swooping checker cab drivers with that strangulated nasal sneer, taking no shit, taking you anywhere. The fourth-generation Irish in a bar in Hell's Kitchen singing 'The Rose of Tralee' and describing a Dublin he's never seen. The Italian–American in a shiny suit in a 'social club' on Mott Street, playing Frank and only Frank on the jukebox. The drag queen in the Meatpacking District, talking just like Johnny Friendly in a frock. The cute waitress in the Jewish deli, who could trace her family directly to that cold-water, walk-up tenement on Delancey. The old Ukrainian guy eating dumplings in Vaselka, the Nuyorican hustler on roller-skates on Avenue A. New York incarnate.

They were the sharp, hard edge of their diamond-cut city, and I have watched them leave, disappear; a deracinated population leading to a less specific, much less charismatic Manhattan. And don't tell me that it has shifted, I don't want to go to New York and hang out in Brooklyn: I want Damon Runyon on Broadway.

And I want a London alive with people who know London. The Knowledge used to be a neighbourhood. It was where you lived, and as your knowledge expanded, so did your city. It was also what you shared; your friends were people who had developed similar cities, whose Londons overlapped with your own. As you ventured beyond youthful constraints, left your estate, took in new areas, crossed zones and boundaries, met bods from different barrios, dated girls or boys from exotic postcodes, so you started to piece the place together. All the while expanding your urban horizons and developing your metro-politan hippocampus.

I am sure my relentless desire to try to make sense of the city, an irresistible urge to venture forth and explore, was a function of finding myself stranded with my West London family way out on the very edge of the known world. Exiled as we were in the simmering periphery, I knew I had to get out of Burnt Oak and get back into town. Thankfully we had the Tube – though for years we barely used it . . .

When the very first escalator was installed on the London Tube network at Earl's Court station in 1911, this remarkable new technology was demonstrated by a one-legged man known as Bumper Harris, who travelled up and down the moving stairway all day to prove that it was safe. The theory was that if a monoped could manage to stay upright, then people with twice as many legs would surely find it a doddle. My mum needed more than a stable one-legged ex-army officer to convince her to go down there.

I thought, when I was young, that my mum's dogged (and to me, perverse) preference for the buses over the much quicker and more efficient Underground system was the result of some sort of exaggerated sense of loyalty to her old regiment. She had started as a conductress or clippie on the buses, actually on the network of trolleybuses, electric vehicles controlled by overhead cables, as a fourteen-year-old girl fresh out of school in 1940. Imagine now putting a fourteen-year-old kid to work on the buses during the Blitz.

It was actually a form of conscription, war work for young women, and she had to choose between the Women's Land Army and the trolleybuses, which was no choice at all. The closest my mum had ever been to the country was walking across Wormwood Scrubs: she had a major dislike for mud and would no more volunteer to wear wellies than she would a tin hat. But she looked just dandy in her clippie's uniform; she loved being on the buses. She hated going down into the Underground.

My mum definitely minded the gap; she also minded the escalators, she minded the whoosh of stale air as a Tube train approached and the dreaded doors that opened and closed of their own accord. She was convinced that disaster lay around every bend and twist in the tunnel. While my dad was still alive she could occasionally be convinced to get on a Tube for a family outing up West, providing everybody held hands at all times, but once she was alone, with no man to hold her hand, it was all too much for her.

I think, looking back, that she had some kind of claustrophobia, but it was only after she was gone that I figured it might also go back to her wartime experiences. Going down into the Underground meant the bombs were falling above, and I remember her saying how much she hated those airless, sleepless nights crowded on to a platform, not knowing if your house was going to still be there when you emerged blinking into the daylight. It's not a wonder she didn't want to go down there.

Just possibly she also thought, deep down, that the buses were more for people like us. The Tube, with its leafy, suburban Metro-land overtones was always the more middle-class mode of transport, ferrying chaps and their secretaries from Amersham to the City (the Metropolitan line originally had Pullman dining cars on the Tube for well-heeled commuters to take kippers on their morning commute), while the humble bus was the working man's conveyance. It was also

cheaper, and when she was a single parent with three boys, every penny counted.

Anyway, for whatever reason, we seemed to spend an inordinate amount of time on buses and even more time waiting for them – and waiting for them and waiting for them. Anybody who tells you things were better back in the old days obviously never stood in the sleet and rain for hours desperately hoping to see a Number 7 coming towards them on the distant horizon. Buses back then didn't have timetables; they had rumours, and the old stories about them hunting in packs were entirely true: you never seemed to see a single double-decker. But I learned to love them anyway.

Everybody loves the old Routemasters, with their rounded genial face and their suicidal open platforms. To this day my son still talks about the time we leaped off a moving Number 31 on Shepherd's Bush roundabout when he was but a small boy and we were late for footie. He just caught the very last of the Routemasters, but when you lived with those sumptuous machines for years of your youth, you can recount numerous tales of falling off, leaping on, bunking on, throwing up, chatting up, playing up, getting thrown off and generally larking about on a bus.

They were our playgrounds. Rush up the stairs, front seat to the right above the driver if you were alone, at the back in a gang and let the fun commence. It was an unwritten rule back then that smokers, snoggers, schoolkids and all round roustabouts went upstairs, leaving families, serious men and little old ladies with bags on wheels down below.

The view from the top deck of a bus is the best in town: you can see over walls, into gardens, into lives. You are privy. Everybody who spends any time in London adopts a bus of their own; a route which you know intimately, which carries you and your memories – and mine is the Number 52. I haven't taken a 52 in years, but it is still my bus, because it is the vehicle for so many of my stories. Originally running all the way from Borehamwood to Victoria via Mill Hill, Burnt Oak,

Willesden and Ladbroke Grove, it is a ridiculously long route, which like so many has now been severely truncated. This was the bus that took us back to the ancestors every weekend for decades. The 52 took me to football, to the open-air swimming baths in the summer with a rolled up towel and a Bovril and a Wagon Wheel afterwards; it took me into town for expeditions, took me to my first real girlfriend's house and took us both on long tonsil-exploring rides together on the back seat.

In July 1976, the Number 52 took me all the way to Victoria, wearing pink peg trousers and plastic sandals, to see the Crusaders play one of the most majestic gigs I have ever witnessed, which made me a committed jazz fan to this very day. A few weeks later it took me to Carnival to witness the infamous riot The Clash sang about, the streets of my ancestral homeland aflame, while I morphed into a spiky biker-jacketed punk. And a few years back, when my mum passed away, I went back to the Watling Estate to clean out our little council house for the very last time. I closed the door of the house, walked the routes of my memories, held her hand in mine, stood at the old stop and rode my bus for a few stops, just to remind myself. I don't know if I have ever sobbed so much on a 52 before.

Almost everything occurred on a bus, particularly when I got a Red Rover. This legendary day pass was a big thing back in the late 1960s and early '70s, and I'm fairly certain I was ten, certainly still at junior school, so it was probably 1969 when I went on my first ever Red Rover adventure. It was the first of many. I also seem to recall the small, stamped yellow cardboard pass cost three shillings: fifteen pence. Even then that was a small price to pay for the entire city. It worked like this: three or four of you, armed with your Red Rovers, would meet at the stop outside the station on Watling Avenue in the morning; everyone would have sandwiches in a plastic bag, and the words of your mum ringing in your ears, 'Make sure you're home in time for tea.'

This pass allowed you to get on and off any London bus free of charge, for one day, so that's what we did. Once we were beyond the boundaries of Burnt Oak we had no plan, no route, no timetables, just a desire to range freely, escape, explore. I remember running amok among the dinosaurs at the National History Museum and going warily transpontine to the Imperial War Museum in Lambeth with its tanks and cannons. I recall breathlessly scaling the Monument's 311 steps, and running, shouting and hollering over every bridge in town.

Our Red Rovers meant that boys from humble Burnt Oak played on Oxford Street, played in Hyde Park, played once with the busby-sporting soldiers on Horse Guards Parade. But just as often, we would find ourselves in Harrow or Alperton, Preston Park or Park Royal, getting lost, going nowhere, leaping off at a moment's notice, running for another bus to God knows where. It didn't matter as long as we were home in time for tea. We were doing the Knowledge.

There are many great London bus stories. The most dramatic occurred on the penultimate day of 1952, when a preposterously iconic combination of events combined to create a scene, which if it occurred in a clichéd London movie would be laughed off screen. One Albert Gunter, a good name for a bus driver, was taking the Number 78 (a classic RT double-decker and forerunner of the Routemaster) north over Tower Bridge. He was heading in the direction of Shoreditch, when the two sides of the famous bridge began to part and the bascule on which his bus sat rose into the air, and a void opened up before him, the river way below.

Staying splendidly calm, Albert put his foot down and literally jumped his twelve-tonne chariot across the great divide: a double-decker flying through the air. He landed safely on the other side, with all his passengers intact, although his conductor did suffer a broken leg. Albert was awarded £10 and a day off for his amazing sangfroid. Today he'd have his own YouTube channel, and quite possibly a crack at being the next James Bond.

But my absolute favourite tale of London's world-famous crimson omnibuses is the one I know as: 'Take this bus to Cuba.' This really is a piece of lost geopolitical history, which involves some of the biggest

global figures of the time, intrigue, espionage, ping-pong balls and a
fleet of red buses bound for the red island. The context of this story
is the Cold War at its most febrile, when nuclear armageddon had
come perilously close, because of the macho posturing of the Cuban
missile crisis and the trade embargo imposed on the Caribbean commun-
ists by the United States.

It is now late 1963, and the head of the Cuban Department of
Industrialisation, one Ernesto Guevara, wants a new fleet of buses for
Havana. So he decides to place an order for the most iconic and
splendidly red buses in the world, i.e. the London bus. At the time,
these are made by Leyland, then a private company based in the
Midlands. At first Che fancies double-deckers, but someone points out
they won't make it under the low-lying streetlamps of old Havana, so
instead he places an order for 400 single-storey red Leyland Olympic
buses. But this, of course, is contrary to the newly imposed American
trade embargo. So pressure is placed on the company not to fulfil the
order. But they stubbornly insist that they will not be ordered about
by bloody Yanks, and go about building the buses for that nice Mr
Guevara.

The Americans are furious, so JFK – for it is he – tries to stop the
damn buses being delivered by threatening any shipping or airfreight
companies with blacklisting if they carry this cargo. This delays them
for months, but eventually an East German freighter, the MV
Magdeburg, arrives in the Port of London to take the first consignment
to Havana. It is now 27 October 1964. JFK is dead; Lyndon B. is in
office, and it's a foggy day in London town, where a small crowd of
Jack Dash's communist dockworkers have gathered on the Dagenham
quayside to wave off the first shipment of forty-two buses, with clenched
fist salutes and fraternal greetings for their Cuban comrades.

The rusty old DDR hulk sails slowly up the Thames Estuary with a
journey of 4,500 miles ahead of it, and gets as far as Broadness Point
near Tilbury in Essex. Coming in the opposite direction out of the
murk a Japanese vessel, the *Yamashiro Maru*, bound for the Royal Docks,
suddenly appears. The two craft collide in a crash, which disturbed

families watching black-and-white television sets miles away. The *Magdeburg* was ripped open and tipped over, lying on its side in the Thames with its precious cargo of buses drowning in the water.

The collision was a big story at the time, making the front of the papers and even Pathé newsreels, but I first heard of it from listeners on my radio show decades later. One of the callers had been a young boy living in the estuary at the time, who recalled seeing thousands of lightweight plastic balls bobbing about on the water round the wreck. This seemed totally far-fetched, but it was apparently true; a technique for attempting to restore buoyancy to the craft, by pumping in air-filled orbs.

The ship was eventually righted weeks later, but the buses were a write off, ruined by salt and water, destined never to get to Cuba. I had an image of people waiting patiently at bus stops in Havana for a fleet of London buses that never came, and knew exactly how they felt. I also wondered whether the frustration is what prompted Che to give up his government position and go off to Bolivia for some proper revolutionary action.

I presumed this was the end of this brief yet brilliant story. But a few weeks later, another listener called to say he had been so intrigued by the tale that he did a little further digging. He had uncovered a small piece in the *Washington Post* in 1975 written by two reputable reporters, Jack Anderson and Les Whitten, which claimed that the *Magdeburg* and its cargo of sanctions-busting buses had been sunk by the Japanese craft under orders of the CIA with the covert assistance of MI5.

The classic, red double-decker Routemaster bus has to be a firm favourite for the ultimate symbol of London. But the roundel, that red circle with blue bar, which announces and adorns Tube stations, would run it a close second. No other city is as defined by its transport system; no other city has such an elegant heritage of everyday design.

Frank Pick is the hero of this story: managing director of the Underground in the early part of the twentieth century, he commissioned Harry Beck's perfect map of the Underground and Edward Johnston's wonderful font; he brought in architects like the great Charles Holden, whose modernist masterpieces gave so much gravitas to humble places like Arnos Grove and Hangar Lane.

The magnificent Mr Pick encouraged artists of the calibre of Graham Sutherland, Paul Nash and even Man Ray to design posters; he oversaw the fabrics used on seats, the fittings used for lights, the card used for tickets. He ensured that the process of this great metropolis going about its business was not only as efficient as possible, but as beautiful. Beautiful mass transportation: what a staggeringly splendid idea. What a man.

Mr Frank Pick was perhaps the single most civilising influence on the history of this city, and I was overjoyed when an elegant, elegiac memorial was recently unveiled to him at Piccadilly Circus station. Designed by contemporary artists Langlands & Bell it takes the form of the roundel with his name in it and used his own wondrous words to describe his mission:

BEAUTY UTILITY GOODNESS TRUTH IMMORTALITY RIGHTEOUSNESS WISDOM

He said that about Underground trains.

It is fair to say we owe Mr Pick a great deal. For me, his commissioning Harry Beck's sublime topological rendering of the city was his masterstroke. That veritable 'Mondrian meets the Mona Lisa' of maps played a massive part in my life. I can still close my eyes and see it, the colour coding, the stark simplicity of the connections, the staggeringly clever way it makes sense of the unknowable, by excluding all geography, all topography, all distance, all reality. London isn't really like that; it isn't ordered and neat and knowable, but it is when you're down there in Beck's beautiful, rational Underground.

Except they've gone and changed it, defiled it with additions, the bloody 'ginger line' indeed. They have also thereby robbed us of one of our most pleasingly arcane facts. It used to be true that there was only one stop on the Tube map that did not contain any of the letters of the word Mackerel. That was St John's Wood, but now that Hoxton has been added that is no longer true. See what I mean about change.

I mastered Beck's original purist masterpiece – based on the simplicity of electrical circuit diagrams – early on and can still recite the entire Northern line, both branches, north to south. Still get a certain pleasure in going down the escalator at Camden Town without a care in the world, while hordes of tourists are having nervous breakdowns at the most complex intersection on the entire system. I love the look on their faces as they try to work out whether they want platform 1 northbound Edgware, or platform 2 southbound via Bank, or platform 3 southbound via Charing Cross, or platform 4 northbound via High Barnet or Mill Hill East? If you grow up in Burnt Oak, you just know this stuff. If you grew up in Burnt Oak, you know how to get away.

Burnt Oak only exists because of the Northern line, which was extended beyond its handsome Leslie Green Hampstead terminus in 1924, creating new suburbs all the way to High Barnet. Still the longest continual subway tunnel in the world, it has been dubbed 'the misery line', because its complexity and length meant there were often delays, but to me it was pure joy. It was London in a jet-black line. Our station, one of those suburban vernacular cottagey stops with a parade of shops wrapped around it, actually used officially to be called Burnt Oak (Watling), because Burnt Oak is basically the Watling Estate, named after the Roman Watling Street. And Roman Watling Street is the Imperial antecedent of the Edgware Road, running all the way to Marble Arch. It's actually only nine miles from the Arch to the Oak, but the Watling Estate feels a long way from triumphal.

A vast London County Council project begun in 1927 (the LCC was the predecessor to the GLC, who specialised in building things rather than knocking them down), the Watling Estate was part of the 'Homes Fit for Heroes' campaign. After the First World War, there was a drive to provide decent accommodation for the families of men returning from the hell of the trenches. Get them out of the inner-city slums and into decent housing in leafy suburbs. Over 4,000 individual homes in the low-rise, low-density, garden-city movement style were built, on what had been open land between the more established, much more bourgeois 'villages' of Hendon, Edgware and Mill Hill. And therein lay the problem.

Despite the specific intention of filling the Watling Estate with the 'deserving poor', the kind of hard-working, working class with decent jobs and tidy families, it immediately raised the snobbish hackles of its near neighbours. They wanted a golf course rather than a council estate built on the fields. As soon as the first families arrived, many of them rehoused from a vast slum-clearance scheme in King's Cross and the Caledonian Road, It was immediately dubbed 'Little Moscow' by the Right-thinking residents of the privately owned homes all around it.

One local Tory councillor described it as 'the raw red tentacles of that housing octopus, the London County Council'. There were even calls for a Trump-type barrier to be built all the way round the estate, 'the Watling Wall', to keep the proles in their place. They never got their wall, but we always knew where we stood in the pecking order.

Our family mythology has it that when my mum and dad first visited the Watling to see if they would take up the offer of a home, my dad said that they would only live there if he could find a pub within five minutes' walk of the station. Not because he was a drinking man, but a sociable one, and to his Notting Hill head a pub meant a community. By pure chance they turned right out of Burnt Oak station, up the slope towards the Edgware Road and four minutes later there was the Bald Faced Stag, an old coaching inn that pre-dated the estate, so they took the house. If they had turned left he could have walked all the way to Mill Hill Broadway without seeing a boozer, and we would have lived somewhere else. Because the 'improving' urges of the LCC planners insisted that there should be no pubs whatsoever on the estate itself in case all the urban oiks took to drink.

Living near a Tube station is one of the defining factors of what kind of London you reside in, how you perceive and utilise the city. If you're off grid, not on the map, you're relying on buses and overground trains, so your focus is on timetables and termini. It's why South London, much of which is untouched by the Tube (partly because the heavy clay soil made digging tunnels difficult), has a very different focus and feel.

In areas without an Underground connection, people are less linked to the centre, tend to stay more locally and gravitate as much out as in. For example, Crystal Palace has a great rivalry with Brighton FC because it is easier for them to get to the coast than it is to, say, Chelsea or Fulham. It's easier today for me in Camden Town to get to Paris than it is to Palace. One train all the way from nearby St Pancras to Gard du Nord, rather than trying to work out which platform at London Bridge might just take me at some appointed hour to somewhere called Selhurst (or is it Norwood?) without stopping in every back garden in South London.

As a kid, proper trains – with doors you had to open yourself, and racks where you could put your bags – were only ever taken once or twice a year for family holidays on the Kent coast in Margate or Ramsgate. (We called them the Gits: Margit, Ramsgit.) As a result I still feel odd getting on a proper train without a suitcase, and mainline stations are a major event involving sandwiches and probably bottles of beer, certainly not for everyday journeys around town.

To my mind, you navigate round London on the Underground. You understand London via the Underground. We had the Underground a four-minute stroll from our house. If buses were the transport of my boyhood, then the Tube was the conveyance of my teenage years. I was educated above my station, a grammar school boy and later an undergraduate at the LSE.

My particular station, Burnt Oak, played a major part in every stage of my development. I was actually educated in front of my station and in front of Edgware station, Hendon, Golders Green . . . because it was the way in those days for all the kids from the different local schools to congregate at the various stations after school and in the holidays. We would rock up in the forecourt to fight and flirt, parade our latest fashion disasters, show off our up-to-the-minute musical sophistication and pledge undying love for a girl called Rebecca, who towered above you in her platform shoes. There were lots of girls called Rebecca in our part of Northwest London.

Actually, Burnt Oak station was a bit different. Only boys from the Oak itself would dare congregate there, because boys from the Oak had a reputation to maintain. I was never a fighter, but those who were, the noted Burnt Oak boot boys, did something called station duty, whereby they would wait around for hours in their Dr Martens and Harringtons, protecting the estate from would-be invaders, such as the Hendon mafia, the Mill Hill East mob and even the Camden Town tongs. Skinhead sentinels were posted for years at Burnt Oak station, which meant that the 'posh' boys from my grammar school never dared try carousing, canoodling or cavorting there, and Burnt Oak girls were strictly off limits for them anyway.

Growing up here was a perpetual learning process. Tentative shopping trips up West to look longingly in the window of Lord John and daydream about buying a jumbo collar suede jacket, but opting for Mr Byrite instead. A foray to the East End, pretending you liked jellied eels from Tubby Isaacs stall because it seemed like the correct, cockney thing to do. How can anybody eat that stuff? First visit to Wembley Stadium, not to see a game, but to stand outside pretending to be a proper horny lad, because the ladies hockey international was taking place and there were 65,000 screaming schoolgirls inside. (I believe those girls still hold the record for the loudest decibel levels ever recorded at the national stadium. It was a banshee wail you could hear all the way to Willesden.) One melancholy teenage morning waking up with a hangover and a hard-on, alone on a sofa in a place called Lonesome.

I learned to be socially and vocally schizophrenic early on, grammar school lad and Burnt Oak lad: I was the only one in my year who was both. Although I was never a scrapper, or much of a footballer, I was pretty good at trousers and tunes and had a couple of guardian angel older brothers who were faces on the estate. I always got on with the Watling boys, indeed spent a lot of time at the Watling Boys' Club, a classic rumbustious, table tennis, boxing, British bulldog and mixed disco one-Thursday-a-month youth club, whose main aim was to keep the lads from killing each other or anybody else. They did a good job, not one reported murder in our time there.

I could talk fluent Burnt Oak. The local accent and argot preserved an already slightly antiquated and exaggerated version of old-school London lingo. Burnt Oakese involved plenty of rhyming slang, glottal stops and dropped 'h's plus much contemporary talk of sorts and crews, geezers and gribos, aggro and skullduggery. I could spot a jekyll dicky or a pair of snide daisies with the best of them. But I could also talk pretty good grammar school when required.

To this day I have an accent that leaps about all over the gaff. My Radio 4 voice is distinctly more modulated and measured than my back-of-a-cab or my shouting-at-referees voice. It happens without me having to try; a completely unconscious chameleon response. I'm sure it's a London thing; this is the city of perpetual reinvention, which I've always thought is a direct result of living in those two parallel worlds as a teenager. And it was in the more refined domain of my grammar school mates that I became a station spotter, a platform soul.

I think I was fourteen the year when we went all the way. It was that in-between time, after boyhood games of run-outs and dead man's falls, but before girls and going out to pubs and clubs, when the six weeks of the long summer holiday still felt like a gaping chasm. So, for some reason a bunch of the lads from school came up with a challenge: we would attempt to visit as many last stops on the Underground as we could. Amersham and Upminster and Cockfosters (cue giggling) and Epping and Stanmore and Ongar (oh poor, dear, vanished Ongar). The aim was not really to spend any time in the ultimate destination, but simply to add it to the list, to travel rather than to arrive. We just loved riding those rails.

The only time I recall going south of the river was when we did the entire Northern line Edgware to Morden and back to Barnet. We were very much North Londoners. I also don't remember how many ends of lines we finally managed to visit in total, but I do recall the trip to Heathrow. I had never been on an aeroplane, or even seen one up close, so this was the most exciting Tube station of them all. I was mesmerised by destination boards that promised places even more exotic than Theydon Bois and West Ruislip. But bizarrely what I really remember is that it was the first time I had ever seen individual porcelain urinals rather than a communal trough in the gents' toilets . . . It's very strange how the memory works.

Quite why we were spending our days and presumably our pocket money making those trips I don't suppose we really knew, but I do know that I loved it and look back on those innocent, boyish expeditions with an intense fondness. It was part of our collective, continuing love affair with transport, with Frank Pick's vision of a civilising public transit system. It was a sign of my burgeoning, still burning, love affair with my city. Whoever said a truly developed nation is not one where the poor drive cars, but one where the rich use public transport, certainly got it right. I didn't learn to drive until I was thirty-eight, and to this day I am not very good at it and don't much like doing it; parallel parking is still beyond my abilities. But I got good at riding the Underground.

Everyone in Burnt Oak was good at bunking the fares. It was not until the late 1980s or early '90s that electronic barriers were introduced at many London Underground stations. Before that, paying for your journey was almost voluntary. Many and varied were the ways of avoiding the fare, including – for many of the local herberts – the potentially fatal trick of walking over the tracks and climbing over the fence into the back of Burnt Oak market.

I tended to employ slightly more sophisticated ruses, but was never above doing a runner past the bloke on the ticket desk. Seeing as it was often my brother's mate Victor, that was perhaps a little rude and probably unnecessary. When they finally introduced effective electronic barriers at Burnt Oak, the locals were genuinely outraged at the fact that they were now being obliged to actually pay for their journeys.

The whole system seemed much more anarchic back then, more prone to delays and breakdowns, less efficient, but more fun. It was definitely less crowded. Outside of rush hour you could usually get a seat. Trains are far too packed for much merriment these days, but back in the '70s there always seemed to be some sort of goings on going on. The presence of two smoking carriages – one from the front, one from the back of every train – was part of the party feel. Although I never took to cigarettes, I would often choose to ride with the puffers because the atmosphere was so much more rumbustious. You knew that there would be some characters in the smoking carriages, if you could see them through the fug, and the grooves in the fine, slatted wooden floor would be littered with fag butts.

There was also no prohibition on drinking on trains, so people did, but they didn't have to, because there were also bars on the stations. There were actually thirty 'pubs' on the London Underground system at one point, and as they were outside the normal jurisdiction of licensing laws you could drink at odd times, which were always the best times. The two I particularly recall were at Liverpool Street and Sloane Square. The Liverpool street 'tavern' was known as Pat-Mac's Drinking Den and was situated on the eastbound platform of the Metropolitan line, with a serving hatch that meant that you could actually have a drink while waiting for your train. If your conveyance was stuck at the station, which they often were, you could play a kind of alcoholic version of chicken, where you risked dashing out for a swift one.

But it was the bar on the westbound platform at Sloane Square that really attracted subterranean lushes, and which provokes pangs of sodden nostalgia among those who remember it, if they can remember it. Still there until the mid-1980s, it was known as the Hole in the Wall, because that is precisely what it was. It's now a sandwich bar, but back then it was a tiny, but remarkably lively, truly bohemian boozer, complete with a pub cat, who would sit on the bar by the optics.

This was a place for the kind of people who cannot go a few stops without stopping for a snorter, but was so popular that it had regulars who would buy a platform ticket just to enjoy its smoky, claustrophobic conviviality. Whatever time of day you went to the Hole in the Wall there would be a posh bloke in a camel coat and a trilby hat, an ageing thespian of either gender in far too much slap, a hairdresser and probably an old footballer hit on hard times. Sloane Square flowed with drink, which is apt as it is also the only station with a river running through it.

The reason I went to Sloane Square a lot back in the '70s was not primarily to drink in an airless underground broom cupboard, but because I liked a pair of strides and a silly haircut. The King's Road was a mecca for the sartorially extravagant, bizarrely coiffed youth of the nation. Lined with arcticly cool clothes shops, this regal thoroughfare was also a kind of catwalk for competing trouser tribes.

Every weekend in, say, 1975 to '76, Teddy Boys, soul boys, proto punks, Bowie freaks, mods, rockers, surfers, queer pioneers and the generally overdressed but unaligned, all paraded along what was then a still shabby-chic street that reeked of the stale end of the '60s. The Chelsea Drugstore was still extant, and it wasn't too hard to imagine Mr Jimmy shivering in his militaria, waiting for his man, or Mick getting married yet again at the Town Hall in a Tommy Nutter three-piece suit. Big lumbering American cars would cruise up and down the strip, their exaggerated fins and gleaming chrome drawing rounds of applause. Occasionally the cults would stage a little mock battle, usually involving getting chased down Chenies Street by a fat bloke with sideburns in a drape coat as the Teds took umbrage yet again. It was magnificent.

The King's Road was a mecca for the most zealous cultists from all across the city. We would cradle a single drink, while posing furiously inside or outside old pubs like the Chelsea Potter and the Imperial, which are now irredeemably Sloaney, but back then were genuinely rock'n'roll. The odd, old Chelsea characters were just about visible and you would occasionally see Quentin Crisp, George Best or Francis Bacon floating by or propping up a bar.

If you were particularly unlucky, you'd find yourself sitting on a stool next to John Bindon. Down at the down-at-heel, World's End end of the King's Road, there was still an air of old time SW10 villainy.

Bindon was a full-time Fulham boy, part-time actor (*Poor Cow*, *Performance*, *Get Carter*, *Quadrophenia*), gangster (protection, drug-running, murder) and Princess Margaret's minder and paramour (Mustique and Mayfair). He was also a crushing bore, who would bully anybody into buying him a drink and listening to his stories, under threat of violence, or even worse, unleashing his party piece. This involved balancing half-a-dozen pint pots on his erect penis, before whirling it round in a movement known as 'the helicopter'. He wasn't known as Big John for nothing.

We had our own crop of Chelsea characters, too. Ace faces like Jordan and Little Debbie from Sex, Rasta Don Letts from Acme Attractions, Siouxsie Sioux, Adam Ant, Boy George, Rockabilly Billy, Eric the Surfer, Pete the Murderer, Welsh Chris, the Bromley contingent, the Ealing boys, and even a little firm from Burnt Oak who had swapped skinhead gear for the outlandish trappings of mid-'70s Chelsea attire. And I was one, just about: an underage, souped-up suburban teenager with an asymmetric barnet; thrilled to be mixing in such exalted metropolitan company, in such a noted London thoroughfare.

Time would soon point both the King's Road and me in more conventional directions – the former, ultimately towards anodyne horrors, and the latter more imminently towards the unlikely fate of becoming a student.

I say unlikely, because, just like the cliché, not one of Freddie Elms's heirs had ever gone to university. Nor had a single member of my mother's family, that I know of (my mum's paternal line were a mystery – I never met them). And although I passed the eleven plus and went to Orange Hill Grammar School for Boys, I had never really contemplated what came next. Until one day my history teacher Dr Wheaton, who liked the fact that I liked his subject, asked me casually where I wanted to study for my degree. It was a question that came as a bolt from the blue, and required a little research.

It was now 1976, and I had just got to the point where I felt like I was making headway in my quest to master my city. QPR had the greatest team ever to grace Loftus Road and soul boy was rapidly mutating into punk somewhere on the King's Road youth culture petri dish. This was no time to consider dreaming spires or dreary dorms in far off towns. So I only filled out three of the six slots on the UCAS form, putting down King's, UCL and LSE. It was the London School of Economics I really wanted to go to, knowing it would make my old dead dad dead proud to hear his son was attending a famously Bolshy institution, and thankfully they made me an offer I managed not to mess up.

Back in those halcyon, debt-free days I got all fees paid and a full grant, but only if I lived at home. because our council house was within commuting distance of the Aldwych. So I became a commuter: five days a week, Burnt Oak to Holborn and back, Northern line to Tottenham Court Road, change for one stop on the Central, or even on to the now disused one-stop branch line to Aldwych. Now *that* was an education.

Doing that journey every day – and I went every day, loved being at the LSE, loved being in the centre of town, throwing eggs at Sir Keith Joseph, arguing with Maoists, feeling like I was at the centre of events, equidistant between the City and Westminster – I spent a lot of time on the Tube. So I took to playing games. I would make up stories about the people sitting opposite me, trying to imagine their lives, their work, their secrets; constructing scenarios, inventing pecca- dillos. I assumed quite a lot of S&M.

'Guess the profession' was one game, trying to garner clues as to where my fellow travellers fitted into the overall picture of this metropolis/machine going about its daily business. Another was predicting exactly which station people would get off at. I got rather good at it: I could usually determine a change at Euston from an alight at Goodge Street, and on the way home I could tell a Hampstead from a Hendon or an Edgware from a Mill Hill East, almost every time. I became a kind of mobile city sleuth.

I also managed to pick up a wanker. Most days I did the journey into college at roughly the same time, just after the rush hour, walking to Colindale rather than Burnt Oak, in order to facilitate my own particular fare dodge. The carriages would be largely empty and one day it was just teenage me, and a middle-age man who was already ensconced at our end of the carriage. We'd got about as far as Brent Cross (formerly Brent) when he began masturbating. At first behind his briefcase, then more brazenly while staring intently into my eyes. I got up and hurriedly changed into the next carriage while trying to suppress laughter. But then a couple of days later it happened again, and this time his actions were coupled with loud lascivious noises. I took umbrage and gave him a volley of abuse before moving, alerting a couple of other people further up the carriage that we were in the company of an Underground onanist.

I thought that would be the end of it. But then the very next day as I walked down the stairs at Colindale at my usual time, he was there, sitting on a bench waiting for the train/me, a big lecherous smile on his face. An elaborate game of cat and mouse along the platform followed, while we waited for the Charing X southbound. When it arrived I ran to get into a different carriage; so did he. We were together in the door of the train. A bit of argy bargy ensued, and I outed him with a variety of shouted threats and a shove. He eventually slunk away with something other than his tail between his legs never to be seen again. I rather missed him.

It was on my daily commute to college that I first learned about 'ghosts' and discovered that I went past one every day. Somebody must have told me to look out as the train sped between Tottenham Court Road and Holborn on the Central line, so I did, and eventually became aware that there was definitely something down there. For just a fraction of a second you could see the fleeting, spectral impression of a station; a platform, maybe posters, a tiled sign for a stop that is nowhere to be seen on the map, and no train ever stops at. This was my first ghost station.

Because trains did stop here until 1933, when British Museum Station, as it was known, closed down. Back in the 1970s it was still all there, and indeed a little investigation of the then-extant above ground station structure on High Holborn revealed closed but still accessible access tunnels. And in the crêpe restaurant next door, a trip to the basement toilets and a little poke about behind the mops and buckets revealed more. It was like urban archaeology, furtive exploration. I was hooked. Now, however, Museum station is all gone, wiped away by major redevelopment in 1989.

But seeking out ghost stations is a veritable industry. There are books, guides and tours, people love the idea of a shadow network, an underground beneath the Underground, pickled in dust. Back then it required real detective skills to work out where these lost stations were. I pored over old maps, marvelling at Beck's brilliance, but frustrated for once by the fact that it gave no geographical information. Where exactly was Lords station and how close was it to Marlborough Road? For years, spotting disused Tube stops became an obsession, and often it was just that, you suddenly recognised some old tile work or a familiar architectural motif, realised that a Chinese restaurant, or those dowdy offices looked like they were once a part of the network. So you did the research and added it to the list.

One summer, when I was a man in my thirties, far too old to be playing train games, I linked up with a mate, a fellow ghost hunter, and we spent a splendidly pointless week cycling round from South Kentish Town to York Road, Shoreditch to Down Street on a kind of pilgrimage to the buried past. I was fourteen again, re-affirming my teenage crush on London town.

One of the big discoveries, which had actually been there for all to see all the time, was a series of curved, Art Deco-style, pill-box-like structures sitting above ground, next to certain Northern line stations. Belsize Park and Camden Town have one each and there's a massive one just over the road from Goodge Street. It turns out that there are similar structures on the south side in Stockwell, and Claphams North, Common and South stations. These are actually specially reinforced bomb-proof entrances and ventilation shafts for deep-lying tunnels.

Beneath the existing Northern line, the tunnels were built in the

1930s and '40s with an ingenious dual purpose. Originally they were part of a plan to create a parallel Northern line expressway, a fast line with fewer stops, to ease pressure on London's most complex network. But when the Blitz started, they were converted into vast subterranean air-raid shelters, each sleeping 8,000 people on bunk beds, with canteens and toilets, so deep the bombs could never penetrate.

The Goodge Street site was used by General Eisenhower as a base for top-secret work on the D-Day landings and is still dubbed the Eisenhower Centre. The aim was that, when the war was finally won, the tunnels could all be connected up to eventually become the north–south express route they were originally designed to be. Sadly this never happened, and they are now used for corporate storage. But I've often wondered why a mayoral hopeful doesn't promise to bring them back to life and deliver the long awaited pole-to-pole expressway.

There is an interesting addendum to this story. In 1948, when the HMT *Empire Windrush* arrived in the Port of London from Jamaica, with its 492 zoot-suited passengers, many of them lured by the promise of jobs on the London Transport System, they were taken straight to Clapham South. There they were given a sheet and a blanket and each allocated a bunk down in the bowels of the old deep wartime bunker; somewhere to stay while they looked for accommodation and work. The nearest labour exchange was on Coldharbour Lane, Brixton, which is where the Jamaican community then set up home. Where you arrive is where you will stay.

I still love a ghost. I recently ventured down into what is now called Strand station with a guide from the London Transport Museum, loved the old tile-work and posters, the idea of a place frozen in time, stopped in its tracks in 1994. But primarily it made me feel very old. Because I had regularly used that stop when I was a student and it was called Aldwych. That Underground stations have died and become spectral in my lifetime was just another reminder of my rapidly vanishing London.

Being made to relive my subterranean student years here has reminded me of one of the most remarkable Underground stories, which I walked past every day without ever noticing. But then, so did millions of Londoners.

First off, it's important to recognise that there's an awful lot of stuff down there. London is lacerated with a labyrinth of tunnels and cavities and catacombs, particularly the area around Holborn, which is famously riddled with tram tunnels, train tunnels, postal tunnels and a vast former underground telephone exchange which can hold 10,000 people and played a major role in secret security and surveillance. You never know what is going on beneath your feet.

Holborn station is the deepest in central London, roughly 100 feet down, which I can personally testify to. It was a regular student prank to drunkenly attempt to run down the near-perpendicular up escalator and end up splayed across the station floor bruised and giggling. Its profundity is apparently what made it attractive to scientists, something about escaping 'radiation noise'.

Throughout the time I was arriving there every day to go and study the League of Nations and the influence of Hegelian philosophy on early Marx, and tens of thousands of commuters were coming and going, a direct forerunner of the Large Hadron Collider at CERN, was whizzing particles around beside the Piccadilly line. Honestly.

I had long heard rumours of nutty professor-style experiments taking place deep under London, but assumed they were just part of the folklore of the city. But many years later I spoke to a man who used to work at Holborn station, and he told me that every day 'the Professor' as he called him, would arrive at the station, take a set of keys out of the office, pull on his dun-coloured lab coat, and head off to his laboratory. This was set up on a disused platform accessed via a locked service door on the eastbound Piccadilly line.

'It was like something out of a Heath Robinson drawing down there, all tubes and pipes and dials stuck together,' I was told.

'The Professor' was one John Barton, a physicist from nearby Birkbeck College. He used this brilliantly British do-it-yourself facility throughout the 1970s and '80s, doing research into particle physics and dark matter of precisely the kind they now spend billions on, deep inside a mountain in Switzerland. But he wasn't the first, or the last.

The original 'cosmic ray' machine was set up down there during the war (ray guns anyone?) to search for neutrinos (whatever they are), but was hampered by rats biting through the wires. And as recently as the 1990s, experiments were still being conducted while the trains whizzed by and the office workers and the students waited just a few feet away. Who knows whether there are still boffins beavering away deep beneath Kingsway today?

There are so many more subterranean stories to impart: walking through the dripping Camden Catacombs all the way to the Round-house; the transvestite bank robber trying to escape by running through the Northern line tunnels from Hampstead Tube; the roaring alcoholic outpost of Ireland buried deep beneath Piccadilly Circus; the secret exit from the platform at Westminster, which led straight to the Speaker's chair. Some of these tales will emerge as this book progresses, others will remain buried deep. It is, indeed, the depth and age and continuity of the London Underground which makes it so profoundly fascinating. In essence, ours is an underground city.

And for most of us it is a true love–hate relationship. Love the Tube; hate being on the Tube. It is hard *not* to dislike standing crushed and contorted, your olfactory system assaulted, your sweat glands provoked, your dignity compromised, as you cram into a carriage at Leicester Square. You're just eager to get home, to get away from the world, most of which seems to be waiting on the next platform to cram into your already rammed train. But then it is hard not to love the circular uplighters at Baker Street as you ride the escalators towards the surface. Who can fail to be impressed by the geometric metal grids which sheath the steps to stop you slipping as you step down into Oxford Circus Tube from the mayhem above? Who can stand in Gants Hill's implausibly grand ticket office, like a mini Moscow, and not be enthralled? And it isn't just the old. Southwark and Canary Wharf, futurist manifestations of design excellence on the Jubilee, are equal to anything Frank Pick decreed. It is a joy to travel.

I was lucky to be invited on to perhaps the greatest Tube journey of all time. It was a one-off 150th anniversary celebration of the first-ever Underground train journey anywhere in the world. A steam-driven locomotive pulled out of Paddington on 9 January 1863, to make a three-and-a-half mile trip east, beneath and through the Victorian metropolis to Farringdon. On our twenty-first century version we would be travelling a little further, from Earl's Court to Moorgate on a beautifully restored Metropolitan 353, fully steam-powered locomotive. Exactly 100 years since the last gleaming steamer rode those same rails.

For the first and only time, I had good reason to wear my chocolate brown bowler amid immaculate black and red livery. I sat in the glamorous brass and leather trimmed teak carriage, with its gas lights and ruched curtains, smelling the coal fire, hearing the hissing song of the pistons and marvelling at the kinetic force of the traction. This is how Londoners once travelled, this is how Freddie and Albert and Reggie could have crossed the city we share.

And as we rolled majestically across town, on an ordinary workaday evening, on those same metal tracks we take every day and take for granted, there was a tangible, scalding, magic in the air. It was also in your lungs, in the tunnels, and most of all in the amazed faces of the people waiting on platforms for ordinary modern day electric trains. Their reaction as they saw this elegant, elemental apparition come steaming past was spectacular, delightful, a ghost-train indeed. Swathed in a gaseous silver halo and powered by the potency of memory, this everyday thing we do was elevated, made sumptuous and thrilling. The past was challenging the present, and for one night, at least, it was winning.

A night like that, a journey like that, can make you think. Does change really make things better or just different; is progress inevitable, a relentless move forward or is it a chimera? Is our London actually better than the one our forebears knew? Certainly theirs was dirtier, more visceral; but maybe more elegant, more intense perhaps, though definitely no less modern.

The most poignant moment of that journey was pulling into Baker

Street, a charismatic early cut-and-cover station, a beautifully over-engineered brick built, high Victorian construction, deep in the soil of our collective story, where it is never hard to imagine a city simultaneously of now and then. Now, here, steaming though Baker Street, we were deep in Arthur Conan Doyle's coruscating imagination, in a time machine dispensing delight. It was one of the most thought-provoking journeys I've ever made.

But then every time I descend into our collective underworld I think of this monstrous, wondrous London. This is a city of movement, a place of perpetual motion, restless and endless, forever pushing its own boundaries. Yet for all that frenetic, frantic energy, it manages to make moving around town considered, consistent; it cares, it takes care. London transport is the essence of our city.

The very act of urban journeying is egalitarian. Your posh car isn't going to get you there any faster; we are all stuck in this mire together. But it is also an elegant elegy to the city itself. The steely battleship light that infuses our air, making it dense and making it ours, is the best backdrop for the best view of all. At dusk, in winter, just before the lights go on, just as thoughts turn to home, stand in your overcoat and watch the line of double-decker red buses on Waterloo Bridge. There they are, solid yet shimmering, stately, connected, the same line my father saw. That is ours.

Every time I sit on a bus, especially in winter, especially upstairs, the steam inside making the windows opaque, the branches of over-hanging trees click-clacking against the windows, I am simultaneously travelling and so at home. And when I leave home and enter that vast shared space beneath us, our underground, where there are no trees or seasons, a place entirely of our own making, I am at ease. I walk with so many others along a tiled tunnel, following Beck's beautiful logic, Frank Pick's rigorous artifice. I know I can only be here. Here, where the steam spewed and electricity flows, where the bombs fell above and where so many of my journeys and our stories have begun. I know it down there; I have the Knowledge of the great subterranean facilitator. I know London by its means of transport.

*

If I ever found myself marooned on a desert island, or probably less likely on Radio 4's *Desert Island Discs*, I have already worked out the tunes I would take. I'd want songs that would transport me to places other than this godforsaken paradise prison I found myself stranded on. I want to hear a tune and instantly be in Manhattan or Havana, Sevilla or Buenos Aires, all places I have loved. So obviously the one song I would cherish above all others, is the one that would transport me back to my beloved home town.

Of course 'Waterloo Sunset' is a contender: it is our de facto national anthem. But the most evocatively London song for me is 'Debris' by the Faces. If you don't know Ronnie Lane's elegy to his disappearing city, that rich and ruined place of our youth, and his skint old dad rummaging round the 'Sunday morning markets'; a song so touching and melodically melancholy that I have known tough men cry at its opening chords, then give it a listen. It is a tune about moving on, but staying where you are, which is what we all do here in this city.

But more evocative even than 'Debris' would be my one luxury item. I thought of taking my mum's old ticket machine, the metal contraption she wore as a clippie and I played with as a boy. A Red Rover ticket would be too painful, all promise and no delivery. So I settled on the most luxurious thing I know, an artefact so wantonly handsome, yet so splendidly functional, so instantly evocative of where I live: I would take Leslie Green's Oxblood-tiled Mornington Crescent station and place it by a palm tree in the corner.

On Fridays We Ride

Every Friday at Gloucester Gate we gather. Early morning, prescribed hour, sharp as you can, look smart; I mean, look smart, ride smart too, hold your line, take your turn, stop at lights, think of others. This is a gentlemen's ride. Five laps, anti-clockwise, maybe six, not too fast, but stretch those legs, fill those lungs, feel it, feel the road, the air you're cutting through, the terrain you're rushing by, the swift dip down past the mosque, the burn as we rise up past that sumptuous Nash terrace. There's a giraffe. Feel the friendship, too, the trust. You've been riding alongside these fellows for years, close, wheels almost touching, wind, snow, rain, rain, sunshine, beloved sweet shafts of sunshine. Yes, it hurts: it hurts much more to miss it.

When we first started the Friday ride, the twenty-first century still felt new. And so did pulling on your kit, clipping into your pedals and rolling into Regent's Park to meet up with some mates on road bikes for a few laps round the outer circle, then into the inner and coffee. We had that pretty road pretty much to ourselves back then. People still looked at you askance in your tights, but it's gone mad: hundreds of riders in Rapha, peloton after peloton, chain gangs whizzing round, heads down, bottoms up, younger, faster. We're getting on now, but still we ride smart.

Birettas, bidons, groupsets, gilets, Campag, carbon, rouleurs, puncheurs . . . Learn the terminology. Enjoy the camaraderie. We start just maybe five or six of us, air always crisp, if it's winter, bloody cold, but we warm, we grow, friends merging in by the zoo, rolling handshakes as they join, 'Bonjour mes frères'.

Perhaps we become a dozen or even a score, riding two abreast, talking as we go, until we really go. Then it's hang on, catch your breath, ride hard, but never too hard, don't want to drop a comrade. We are in this together; we go as fast as the slowest rider. That'll be me.

They call me the patron of the ride, to obscure the fact that I am the man most likely to struggle, but also most likely to be there. I love Friday mornings in the park. Who would not want to see this city's most elegant space spin by: Snowdon's Aviary, Gibberd's minaret, Lasdun's exquisite Physicians, those butter-cream coloured terraces, symmetrical classical, it is the Regent's park after all. London's loveliest.

Then we sit and chat and joke in our tights and our bib shorts amid the roses in Queen Mary's Garden. Double macchiato, maybe half a pain au raisin. If you want to share your joys or woes you can, or else we'll talk bikes, or races, Boonen and Nibali, or else we won't talk at all, just ride, side by side, feeling it. At Christmas we drink champagne and make speeches.

I've always ridden push bikes. If you want to know the topography and the temper of this town, ride a bike. Your legs never lie, you feel every incline, every dip, you sense underground rivers, hillocks, mounds; you certainly know when you are approaching the edges of the bowl in which this mighty city sits. Rise up towards Highgate say or Crystal Palace in the south, and your thighs will understand the logic of the lie of the land. They will tell you this is where the ancient Thames river basin rises to an elevated, once forested ridge; great views will be your recompense for great effort.

Riding a bike also lets you know what mood this city is in. My daily commute is short but fairly tempestuous. Fifteen minutes of dodging and weaving, cars not indicating, buses not caring, pedestrians not looking, other cyclists overtaking on the inside. Of course it's never my fault. Some days it's a good ride, the tarmac feels smooth, the gaps open up, the lights change accordingly, people are polite: you arrive at work in a state close to nirvana. Other days – and you never really know why – well, it's like a war out there, and believe me nobody's winning.

If for any reason I am not on the bike for a few days, I feel a deep-down, disabling lethargy, like I am stuck: I long to roll away, to arrive at that moment of fluid transcendence when you and bike and road and city and maybe even the elements are as one, floating, fleeting, but genuinely transcendent. Then you come off.

I have had four or five accidents over maybe thirty years, and they have almost all been my fault, particularly because of carrying bizarre items. The most ridiculous involved an eight-kilogramme Christmas turkey from the

Ginger Pig butcher's, a sudden snowstorm and a badly bruised breast (the turkey's) after hitting the Marylebone Road.

The funniest occurred when I had just collected a repaired brolly from James Smith & Sons, that splendid Victorian umbrella emporium in Bloomsbury. I was on my bike, so I hung the furled stick over the handle-bars, just clearing the ground perfectly. Until, that is, I went round the corner by the British Museum, leaning as I turned, the point of the umbrella stuck in the road and I pole vaulted, flew through the air landing, at the feet of a grupetto of giggling Italian school kids. It was no laughing matter when a piece of flying glass sliced through my kneecap one Friday morning. Nor when I argued with a speed bump and broke my wrist and two ribs. University College Hospital has served me well.

But the good days make it all worthwhile. The most remarkable day was back in Regent's Park. It must have been 1998, early in the year, early in the morning, foggy, cold. I was on my own, rolling gently round the outer, anti-clockwise, just past the zoo, when I went past a small group of men walking in the direction of the mosque and thought one of them looked like Ian Paisley. I rode on, past Winfield House, the home of the American ambassador and I saw another bunch of guys walking in the opposite direction and yes, there were Martin McGuiness and Gerry Adams. I had just ridden through the Good Friday Agreement secretly in the making. Only in London. Only on a bike.

CHAPTER THREE

Up West

Let's go to the pictures. We could choose from the Rex, the Imperial, the Odeon, the Regal, the Ionic, the Astoria, the Coronet, the Essoldo, the Royalty, the Tivoli, the Gaumont, the Embassy, the Astor, the Florida, the Capital, the Lumière, the Grange, the Rialto, the Coliseum, the Electric, the Majestic, the Lido, the Forum, the ABC, the Cameo, the Rio, the Empire, the Troxy, the Biograph, the Academy, the Splendid, the Ritzy, the Ruby, the Ambassador, the Granada, the Vogue, the Belle Vue, the Paris Pullman or the Minema. But the Minema's a bit small.

If London has its ghost stations, then it is positively littered with the vanished haunts of those who favoured the flicks. Many of those grand picture palaces have been demolished, while others remain as maimed and misshapen multiplexes. But you can still play spot-the-old-disused-cinema-building as you walk along almost any high street in London. (Look out for the evangelical churches.) And what palaces these were, with such evocative, exotic names and elaborate, art deco architecture to match.

Their heyday was back in the 1930s and '40s, when my mum and dad would have gone to the Coronet at Notting Hill or the local 'bug hutch', which is now the chic boutique Electric cinema on Portobello Road, two or three times a week during their courting. She told a tale of my then teenage father getting into a punch-up at the end of the night when he refused to stand up for the national anthem, which only added to her reasons for falling in love with him. By the time I had come along, many of these pre-cathode-ray cathedrals were well past their best, but almost all were still open, and as a family, going to the pictures was what we did for entertainment.

I'm sure we must have had a television set when I was little, though I can't really remember it. I do vaguely recall liking *The Woodentops*. I know we got a colour TV at some point – rented, of course, but it was one of those where you had to put two bob bits (later 10p pieces) into a meter on the side of the television, and it was forever running out during whatever programme you were watching. There was a big, old, brown radiogram, and on Sunday mornings Mum and Dad would play their records: Ray Charles, Tom Jones, Jim Reeves, Mrs Mills, and, unfortunately, Des O'Connor's 'Dick-a-Dum-Dum'. Then in the afternoon, after dinner, it was *Sing Something Simple* on the wireless for the grown-ups followed by the chart countdown for the kids. Then it was off with the radio and let the arguing hour begin.

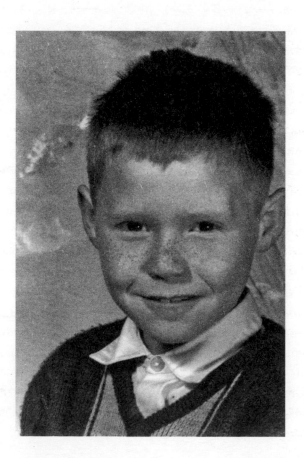

This was a family tradition, which I thought everybody had, whereby we would all sit round the table, even little me, and have a mandatory discussion on the events of the week. Harold Wilson seemed to feature prominently. We were a talking family, primarily because my dad loved a debate, and encouraged us all to have the courage of our convictions. Then, when he passed away, the talking ceased. My mum kept listening to Ray Charles, though, especially 'I Can't Stop Loving You'. We played it at her funeral.

But my primary memory of family entertainment during those early years was going to the pictures. Another bizarre tradition, but one which I have since learned was actually quite commonplace, was that we would turn up for a film at the local picture house, at whatever time my parents decided to go. I'm not even sure they bothered to find out what was on. We would simply go in to whatever was showing at whatever time we arrived, invariably halfway through the main feature, and then sit through to the next showing until we got to the point at which we had entered.

'This is where we came in,' would be uttered, at which signal we would all get up and leave, having seen the entire film, but rarely in the right order.

But when it was a big movie, an epic or an event, a *Spartacus* or a *Mary Poppins*, *How the West Was Won* or *Dr Zhivago*, starring Omar Sharif – my mum loved Omar Sharif – that was different. (My dad was blonde, but my mum definitely had a thing about dark-haired, Arabic-looking men: once, watching Saddam Hussein on the TV, she said, 'He's such a bad man, but he's so handsome'.) Then we would head 'up West'.

I do remember going to Leicester Square and being slightly scared of old-school buskers in the Max Wall mould. Ageing, threadbare men, complete with shabby, stained tail-coats, bowlers and fezzes, working the vast snaking queue, doing the sand dance and holding out hats to put your pennies in. But more usually our fancy cinema of choice was the Odeon Marble Arch, because it boasted the biggest screen in London. Size matters.

It was a dreadful shock to me to go past Marble Arch on a bus not so long ago and see that the building which housed the Odeon, that entire corner site, had gorn. My youth demolished. Going to the pictures there was a proper performance, which would be planned at great length beforehand, and would invariably involve us wearing our Sunday best for the trip up West. The staff at the cinema would be equally well turned out: uniformed commissionaires checking your tickets, usherettes selling glossy programmes in the foyer and expensive treats that you only ever saw at the cinema. There was always an interval with Kia-ora to drink and maybe even a pineapple Mivvi, and then afterwards on the bus home, long, animated discussions about how fast cowboys could really draw a gun from a holster or whether Dr Zhivago undermined the Russian revolution. The latter was an argument that clearly cut no ice with my mother, who even bought the soundtrack album and added it to the small vinyl pile by the radiogram.

Except for one pantomime at Shepherd's Bush Empire with my aunt Glad, as some sort of treat after my dad died, I don't ever remember going to the theatre. It simply wasn't part of our cultural life. Theatre was for posh people; the flicks and the football were for us. Both the footie and the films were mass, collective, bonding experiences. Neither of them was on TV, so you could only see football matches and films by actually going to the Odeon or the Arsenal, the Gaumont or the footballing flea-pit which was Loftus Road, so everybody did.

They were cheap and they were full. Nobody bought tickets in advance, which meant long, remarkably orderly, but viscerally close queues. Back then we really were a city of queues, for just about everything: banks, buses, even bread during the bakers' strike. Later, when I started going to gigs, we would stand in line on the pavement all night to secure tickets to see the Faces at the Kilburn Gaumont (a wonderful art deco cinema, now an evangelical church) or Bob Marley at the Finsbury Park Rainbow (a wonderful art deco cinema, now an evangelical church). That sense of shoulder-to-shoulder proximity to other people enjoying a shared endeavour, and the heightened expectation as you inched closer to your goal, is a largely lost part of the urban experience now that tickets are bought in advance from a machine. But then I hate queuing up now, so maybe the modern world isn't all bad.

On Saturday mornings we went to the Saturday morning pictures. By 'we', I mean just about everybody under the age of twelve, en masse, on our own, a kind of *Lord of the Flies* experience, where the naughty boys, which was just about all the boys, whooped and hollered, ran around, leaped over seating, wrestled in the aisles, and lobbed sherbet fountains into the air in front of the projector, so that it appeared to be snowing during *Tarzan* or *Tom Mix*.

A few years later, in the teenage time, the urchins from the Watling would regularly storm the ABC or the Classic. One or two of the gang paid for entry, then once inside, they opened the exit doors so that scores of ragamuffins could run in, dashing up to the Gods or hiding in the toilets. Half the time you got caught, and perhaps got a clip round the ear for your efforts, but it was all part of the jollity. Later still in life there were many all-nighters at the Scala in King's Cross, enjoying communal cinematic entertainment of a very different kind.

There were many different kinds of entertainment in the glittering West End, some of them not all that glittering, some of them downright bizarre. We always felt pulled and tied to the idea of 'the West End': it was the benchmark. Oxford Street was the ultimate destination; it was held up as a kind of paragon when we were kids, a mythologised shorthand for the biggest and the best: department stores, fashion shops, record shops, summer sales, January sales, Christmas lights – oh those Christmas lights, what a treat.

Oxford Street was a kind of working-class aspiration. We knew nothing of Bond Street, Knightsbridge and Mayfair; they were foreign lands for which we didn't have the correct visas, but Oxford Street was what you saved up for. I wish somebody had saved Oxford Street, because it has become the street Londoner's love to hate, or rather, just hate.

Like a perpetual scene from *Soylent Green*, it is rammed yet bland, barefaced and brutal in its globalised chain-store avarice. Jammed with dispirited Scandinavian teenagers desperately clutching carrier bags, who have decided to spend their entire budget on crap and their entire holiday on that hellish corner outside Topshop. London's most famous shopping parade is now a place few Londoners would voluntarily go shopping. (I accept good old John Lewis has its uses, but should always be entered via the back way on Cavendish Square, unless you particularly want a glimpse of Barbara Hepworth's exquisite *Winged Figure* on Holles Street.)

This drearily repetitive collection of the same soulless stores you would find in Manchester or Edinburgh, New York or Chicago, only with added Union Jack hats, is the city as a raw robbing machine. Money is sluiced out of the innocents abroad. Oxford Street has always been crude, but at one time it was also absolutely compelling in its gaudy, gimcrack hucksterism.

Like most of us I try not to even walk a few yards down that torrid thoroughfare, always preferring to nip into Soho or Fitzrovia to weave my way east or west. But just occasionally if I am in a particularly romantic frame of mind, I try to time travel to the Oxford Street of my youth, or maybe my imagination.

The western end was always the more glamorous. It is adjacent to Mayfair and Marylebone rather than Soho, after all, and still retains a slither of its former élan, largely because Selfridges is such an iconic building. Back in the day, even the flagship C&A up by Marble Arch was considered fancy. I vividly remember feeling like the poshest boy in Burnt Oak when I used a combination of Christmas money and Corona returns to buy a button-down Ben Sherman shirt from Mr Selfridge's elevated emporium in 1969. But I also remember being taken to the great department store at Christmas to have my photo taken with a rather threadbare and tetchy live monkey, which doesn't seem quite so glamorous and sophisticated in retrospect. And believe me, that wasn't the only species to be found on Oxford Street back in the day.

Even up at the elegant end there were signs of the width, weirdness and skulduggery to come. There always seemed to be a little team of wide-boy fly pitchers flogging hooky perfume on the pavement directly outside Selfridges' grand front doors, with its famously fragrant cosmetics section within. A trestle table, a cardboard box full of bottles of coloured water and a couple of lookouts posted to give fair warning of the old bill approaching, these shysters were masters of the rapid patter, the quick sale and the equally swift pack up and scarper. They were exemplars of their crafty craft, but in terms of street theatre they had to compete with the protein man.

Stanley Green was the legendarily implacable placard-waving, cap-wearing, anti-lust, anti-meat, -fish, -bird, -egg, -cheese, -peas, -beans, -nuts and -sitting campaigner. For years he trawled Oxford Street every day in his dun-coloured coat and cap selling his self-penned and -printed, typographically eccentric and intellectually inexplicable pamphlet, 'Eight Passion Proteins'.

Stanley apparently once worked at Selfridges, before finding his true calling as a self-elected keeper of our collective puritanical conscience, cycling in from his mum's house in Northolt every day with his sandwich board, rain or shine, to warn generations of Londoners about the libidinal danger of nibbling nuts and sitting on their butts. Stanley was a fixture, simultaneously unnoticed and largely ignored, yet integral and undoubtedly missed. And since his death, the naked lust for both protein and profit has gone unquestioned.

Stanley wasn't the only proselytiser on Oxford Street. Indeed it has been a hotbed of various persuasions of more or less manic street preaching. I recall a group of scowling bowler-hatted, Orange Orderish, hellfire and damnation Protestant zealots, who predicted the imminent apocalypse on the corner of Regent Street for a few years. The Salvation Army has the Regent Hall over on the south side and you could often hear the brass band playing their brand of old time religious tunes and even treat yourself to the occasional 'War Cry'.

The cry of 'Jesus was a winner not a sinner', barked through a loud hailer in a harsh Liverpudlian accent, from a hectoring Evertonian evangelist who seemed to appear just as Stanley passed on, was another of the sounds of the street. The 'winner-sinner' man had to compete with a much more melodious group of gospel-preaching West Indian women usually to be found singing sacred spirituals outside Oxford Street Tube. I rather liked them and occasionally joined in for a halle-lujah or two.

As you progress east, you may be lucky enough to encounter every-body's favourite bunch of percussion clanging swamis. The presence of a crocodile of benignly smiling, shaven-headed, forehead-daubed, sari-, sock- and sandal-wearing, mantra-chanting converts to Hindu mysti-cism is one of the heralds of the fact that you are approaching Soho.

The Hare Krishna temple by Soho Square is a vegetarian institution, and while I can make neither head nor tale of their belief system, I am quite fond of their lentils and very aware of the sterling work they do feeding London's hungry and homeless. Whenever I see them shimmying along the street I also enjoy having an impromptu sing along to their hit tune: 'Hare Hare, Hare Hare, Krishna Krishna, Hare Hare'. Certainly I'd rather a mantra from the Hare Krishnas than the offer of a personality test from the Scientologists round the corner on Tottenham Court Road.

There was a time when the main draw of Oxford Street was worship-ping vinyl. There may still be an HMV on the strip by the time you read this, and apparently they even stock a few records in Gap now, but this was once a mecca. Friday afternoons, a few bob in your bin, a whole list of tunes in your head, Oxford Street became the launch pad for all vinyl possibilities.

There were multiple HMV stores, Our Price, Harlequin, Simons down in the basement, and Richard Branson's first Virgin store above the shoe shop 'Ravel's Chaussures'. Then later there was the giant Virgin megastore right up at the eastern end on a site which had once been a cinema. All of these musical emporia were full of surly, lank-haired, spotty blokes in unwashed jeans and black T-shirts, and that was just the staff.

Of course the really hip stores with the really cool and splendidly stroppy shop assistants were always just off Oxford Street, in Soho itself, or best of all round in Hanway Street, the finest little urine-soaked dog leg in all London. But you could still spend many hours and a fair few quid in those giant hangars full of LPs. And what's more if you were in the Virgin store, you were next to the only pub on Oxford Street and opposite the most venal, the most enjoyable hundred yards in all London.

Sometimes back in the pre-chaingang days when Oxford Street was still wild, I would just plot up there and watch. The main focus of the action was the run-down block or three from the corner of Tottenham Court Road to Wardour Street on the southern side of Oxford Street, the Soho side of course. To this day that is still a fairly shabby stretch, although it's been so disfigured by the wanton vandalism carried out in the name of Crossrail that it's hard to tell exactly what is there behind the hoardings and the scaffolding.

What was there, many afternoons back in the 1980s, was once a wonder to behold. If the lads knocking out fake perfume outside Selfridges were wide, the chaps down this end were, in the immortal words of Barrington Levy 'broader than Broadway'. This was the place to watch three-card tricksters at their absolute trickiest and fake auctioneers who could fleece an entire flock of tourists and out-of-towners in a matter of minutes.

London has a very complex relationship with what I can only call street morality. I'm not talking about seriously bad people here. The cult of the Krays and all that Lock, Stock and two diamond geezers bollocks is quickly revealed as a fantasy if ever you spend any time among the physically active end of the career-criminal fraternity. I'm sure they can be jolly nice to their mums, but you're not their mum, and most are bullies and bores; and most crime is squalid and brutally banal. Yet who didn't smile when we read about the old boys breaking into Hatton Garden for one last heist? (Unless of course you had your own ill-gotten stored in one of those safety deposit boxes.) Who doesn't occasionally root for the light-fingered, fleet-footed, street-wise heirs of Jack Sheppard? As they sing at the football, 'He's one of our own.'

Look at the most loved fictional Londoners, and apart from Sherlock Holmes, himself a sociopathic drug fiend, almost all the others are on the wrong side of the line. Dickens's Artful Dodger is perhaps the ultimate template for the clichéd but still chirpy, cheeky, cockney street angler, bobbing and weaving, ducking and diving. Everybody loves the Dodger; everybody loves a dodger. It is in the DNA of a city built on trade, this is a port town, an individualistic place of exchange and interaction, of barrow boys and bankers, costers, scalpers and brokers, where quick wits meet fleeting opportunities, where the City of London is a paradigm and the Port of London was a source of endless possibilities.

The distinction between the Dodger and Bill Sykes, the wide boy and the psychopath, a pocket picker and a murderer, is one most of us recognise. So, we love Michael Caine's Alfie and the charismatic Charlie Croker from *The Italian Job*, Adam Faith's ebullient Budgie from the brilliant LWT series set in the seedy Soho of the '70s and above all Del Boy Trotter, Peckham's favourite 'fell off the back of a lorry' merchant. We admire an independent trader, and we all know a mush from Shepherd's Bush.

I've never known exactly where the firms who operated on Oxford Street were from. Romantically, I like to think they were the direct heirs of the eighteenth-century denizens of the Hundreds of Drury, Covent Garden's notorious criminal redoubt, or else that they had wandered over from the rookeries of Seven Dials or St Giles to work the drop, but most likely they were out of Essex. Certainly they had the exaggerated, elasticated vowels and sing-song cadences of the old East – 'Caam on daarling, git yourself a baargiin' – which are now almost exclusively the sound of the urban Essex fringes.

Having spent too many early mornings in my youth unpacking boxes of bruised bananas and soggy onions, laying out wares on that fake turf stuff with frozen fingers, then trying to flog it to Northwest London's lovely housewives, I know a little about the skills involved in street trading. My brother Reggie was a consummate greengrocer; good looking, a brilliant shouter, a flirt, a joker, a cracking convincer, quick at mental maths and for a while I was his hapless assistant.

The most important part of the job is building up an edge, attracting a crowd around your pitch. Once you've got 'em looking, you can get 'em spending. If you saw a gaggle of people on the Oxford Street pavement, peering and curious, felt a frisson in the air, you knew a canting crew were in operation. People in crowds behave differently, they go with the mob; they become irrational with communal excitement; they start to believe that they can actually win money from a geezer with an upturned cardboard box, three playing cards and an accent straight from central casting.

A three-card trick, or 'find-the-lady' team requires a lot more than three people. A large percentage of that hysteria-inducing crowd are 'shills', in on the scam: be particularly aware of the rather pretty and extremely blonde girl egging on the mug punters. Sentries will be posted all along the street to relay information of coming coppers, and a big bloke will always be present to deter anyone who wants to queer their pitch by pointing out that this is a con. The 'three-card monte', as it's known, and the pea and cup or shell game, rely on impressive sleight of hand and speed of movement. But I always found the schoolboy prestidigitation much less interesting than the psychology. Working a crowd is a city skill, it's the theatre of the chancer and some of the greatest street psychology and vagabond theatricality I've ever witnessed took place at the Oxford Street auctions.

These seemed to spring up suddenly in the '80s, and for a few years found their natural home on the very edge of the dark mile. I think it was originally an American grift, but by the time it had got to Oxford Street it had taken on a distinctly London character. And what characters were involved.

Basically a team of a dozen or so would take over an empty shop space for a day or two, fill it full of boxes and bags of gaudy gear of negligible quality and value, as well as a few genuine 'luxury' items. Although luxury back then was largely electro-tat of the Walkmans, digital watches, games consoles and flat-screen TV variety. These were prominently on display to tempt the hordes. Then the front man – who believe me had a lot of front – would proceed to build up his edge by repeating his practised spiel into a microphone, which could be heard clear across the street.

It was a mantra to outdo even the krishnas. Invariably, the man with the mic was a good-looking young guy with that real rapid patter, and the wayward gleam-in-the-eye charm of the professional barker. They were an exaggerated working-class parody of the smooth, besuited auctioneers operating up the road in the Bond Street houses. Barrow boys with loud speakers.

They certainly knew how to work a crowd, luring them in, winding them up, sorting them out. Only, rather than expensive works of art, these guys were flogging off their TVs and watches preposterously cheap. Incredible bargains sold with jaw-dropping chutzpah, great oratorical flourishes, ribald humour and corner-of-the-mouth showman-ship. Of course the original buyers getting the cheap gear were all part of the crew, and the stuff just came back in-house, but it looked like bargains were flying out. So members of the public would get suckered in, then their money would be swiftly siphoned off.

I've seen grown, presumably sane, but certainly not very sensible people hand over large sums for a sealed carrier bag of stuff. They had no idea what was inside, and even promised that they wouldn't open it until they got home, such was their frenzy and gullibility. I've seen others take orders to take all the money in their pockets or their handbags and wave it in the air in a kind of orgy of avarice and group stupidity.

Crowds of mug punters would throng round, gorging on greed, pleading to be able to give their hard-earned cash away in exchange for a bottle or two of smelly water, a ballpoint pen and a plastic trinket worth two bob at best. Large sums for big disappointments, and also big questions about morality. But then, this is Oxford Street. And while I watched those fleecing teams with a mixture of admiration and abomination, I had the added element of knowing what used to go on directly beneath their feet. We'll come to that later.

*

The early 1970s was a time when there were a series of London 'spec-taculars', big showpiece events, which captured the public imagination and every family felt honour bound to go to. The most spectacular of them all was the 'Treasures of Tutankhamun' exhibition at the British Museum in 1972, which caused an absolute sensation, veritable mummy-mania. We are used now to public galleries putting on block-buster shows which attract big crowds, but this was the first and it was different gravy. The whole country went Tutankhamun crazy and there was King Tut tat of every kind imaginable: pencil sharpeners, thermos flasks, school rulers, all inscribed with the image of the Boy King's golden death mask, which you just had to see for yourself.

Now, we were not really the sort of family who spent too much time in museums, and none whatsoever in art galleries, but we dutifully went to Bloomsbury, only to be confronted with the biggest queue I have ever seen in my entire life – and as I said earlier, this was a time of gargantuan queues. This one stretched twice around the forecourt of the museum, along Great Russell Street and round into Gower Street. It was vast, and it was cold, and it was wet. Four shuffling hours or so later we finally made it into the exhibition, but I have very little recollection of any of the priceless Egyptian artefacts. It was so packed inside, all I could see was yet more adults' backs. My abiding memory is the overpowering smell of other people's old damp overcoats and the stink bombs I bought from the magic shop opposite.

My favourite Tutankhamun story, probably apocryphal, but no less enjoyable, concerns a Scotsman, who arrived at St Pancras off the train, eager to see this sensation. He jumped into a black cab and asked, in his heavy brogue, to be taken to Tutankhamun. The best part of an hour and a fair few quid later he found himself deposited on Tooting Common. At least there were no queues.

There's always a long line of hopeful, if slightly lost-looking souls snaking along the Marylebone Road waiting to get into the myriad waxy wonders of Madame Tussauds. I see them all the time, these expectant folk from all around the globe, and like most Londoners I think, 'What the bloody hell are you doing there?' In a city with so much to offer, quite why anybody would want to pay good money and waste good time standing in line, on the most polluted road in Europe, to see a waxworks doll of David Beckham's wife and Elton John's husband is surely one of this city's greatest mysteries. I literally do not know anybody from here who has ever been to the waxworks, or at least not since the Battle of Trafalgar.

This was an elaborate tableau down in the basement of the Madame Tussaud's building, telling the gory story of England's greatest ever sea battle and Nelson's finest, yet tragically final hour. I was convinced that I'd been taken to see this by my dad, who loved history and would surely have gone if he hadn't died, just before it opened in the late '60s. So it must have been my mum or maybe an aunt or uncle or somebody who agreed to take us to this new exhibition, which was causing quite a stir and attracting big queues, because it was said to be so lifelike. Deathlike was more accurate.

I have since spoken to many other people who were also press-ganged into going to this as youngsters and never really recovered. Maybe it was the smell, an overpowering reek of cordite and smoke, or maybe the sounds, deafening bangs and cracks of cannon, and the screams and moans of injured sailors, or else the liberal use of whatever red gunk substituted for blood on the splintered and severed limbs of the dummies, but I was definitely disturbed. I was particularly upset by the fact that, among the hardened salts serving on the *Victory*, some of the cabin boys were no older than I was at the time. I vowed there and then that I would never become a sailor, a promise I have faithfully kept, despite quite liking bell bottoms.

When I bought a house in an ancient hilltop town in Spain half-a-century later, I was amazed to find that my roof terrace had a brilliant view out over the cape of Trafalgar, the exact spot where the bloody battle occurred.

Another bizarre, maritime-themed, queue-inducing event, which occurred in London in the 1970s in the name of entertainment, involved the carcass of a whale on the back of lorry. In fact there were three white whales on lorries, which toured the country for the perusal and pleasure of the masses. One of them parked up on the South Bank by Waterloo Bridge and drew large crowds. They were encouraged, for a small fee, of course, to walk inside its insides and take pictures with the poor deceased leviathan, providing they could stand the stench of slowly decaying blubber. Thankfully my family never felt the need to join that particular queue. But it clearly wasn't because they had a problem with the concept of cetaceans as a source of public entertainment. After all, they took me to the Dolphinarium.

We're now back on Oxford Street.

Just before my time, there was a cavernous subterranean nightclub at 79 Oxford Street called Tiles. This was a mid-'60s mod joint, which saw many of the famous R'n'B bands of the moment entertain a crowd of neatly dressed boys with Boston straight-edge cuts and girls with Sassoon fringes. What made Tiles unique was the fact that it boasted an entire subterranean street of shops, as well as the club itself down there; which gives you a sense of the scale of the basements under those Oxford Street shops.

'The underground city for the new generation,' they called it in the flyers. So in Tiles in 1967 you could sort yourself out a seersucker jacket, a Motown import, get your barnet trimmed and your eyelashes done and probably pick up a bag of blues in the bogs, while dancing the block or the mashed potato to Amen Corner or Cliff Bennett and the Rebel Rousers. All beneath Oxford Street.

Tiles was never really up there with the legendary names like the Scene or the Flamingo; it was always seen as something of a cash-in, a place for 'tickets', out-of-towners, rather than faces, probably because it was on mainstream Oxford Street rather than in subversive Soho itself. Tiles was short-lived, but absolutely massive while it lasted.

Over the road, almost directly opposite where Tiles had been, on the corner with Newman Street, on the slightly more upmarket northern side of the street, was another 1970s underground 'attraction', which turned out to be one of the biggest disappointments of my life.

It may say a lot about the levels of my philistinism, but I was much more excited about the prospect of visiting the Football Hall of Fame than seeing King Tut's relics. At one point I thought I had actually dreamed the whole thing up, as there is almost no evidence of the existence of this place. But it definitely opened for a few months in 1971, and I can tell you, it was pathetic. I should have known it was going to be rubbish as there was no queue outside whatsoever: my cousin Ian and myself might well have been the only people inside. But then, why would anybody but two easily excited, football-mad twelve-year-old West London exiles pay to see this motley collection of crap?

There were a couple of creepy waxworks of old, mutton-chop-wearing Victorian FA administrators, a few moth-eaten caps awarded to pre-war internationals and a scattering of dog-eared programmes. The prize display was a pair of heavy hobnail style boots on a plinth, supposedly worn by Stanley Matthews. They looked like the ones my ageing PE teacher wore. There was not a single mention of our beloved QPR, and we were deeply disappointed. The folks getting shafted over the road at the 'auctions' a decade or so later got a good deal compared to our day out at the Football Hall of fame. It was nowhere near as good as the Dolphinarium.

One of the properties occasionally taken over by the crooked auction firms was 65 Oxford Street. In recent years it has been an amusement arcade and a Union Jack crap shop, neither of which utilised the vast basement below. I would occasionally wander in and wonder if it was still down there. But in 2012 the whole site was demolished to make way for another bland shop front, and offices above, thereby wiping away all traces of one of the 1970s' most bizarre West End 'attractions'.

Opening on April Fools' day 1971 to considerable hoopla, Pathé News reported how wonderful it was and *Nationwide* did a piece for the BBC singing its praises. It was owned and run by the splendidly named Pleasurama Ltd, whose chairman was one Sir Harmar Nicholls, Tory MP. The swanky premises had an elaborate, very '70s frontage on Oxford Street grandiosely announcing the London Dolphinarium. Obviously we had to go.

I can vividly recall the excitement and glamour of it all. Actually I can't, but I can vividly recall the overpowering reek of fish in a hot, humid and sweaty basement. It was an extraordinary place, a small, swish foyer, leading down to a steeply banked auditorium at one end of a double height, windowless, underground room. It was decked out in the height of gaudy '70s taste, with a deep but not particularly large swimming pool in the middle of it.

A pair of dolphins called Bonnie and Clyde did all the usual jumping-around, Flipper-type tricks involving hoops and balls and suchlike, while seals and penguins were somehow involved as well. The male 'keeper' wore tight white Lionels, and some '70s-style dolly birds known as 'aquamaids' swam with the marine mammals and tempted them with tasty piscine titbits from a bucket. Actually, they tempted them with more than that, and it's reported that the dolphins had to be dosed with anti-androgens to stop them making amorous advances to the aquamaids.

It is always a mistake to try and impose the morality of one era on another, and I don't think too many people complained then that this was cruel. I certainly had no moral objections as a twelve-year-old, but I do remember thinking that it was all a bit squashed and squalid, and certainly wondered how on earth, or rather under it, they got the dolphins into a basement on Oxford Street. While considerably more fun than the football farrago over the road, I sort of sensed there was something fishy about the place in more ways than one.

Poor attendance figures led to them attempting a dolphin pantomime at Christmas, where a Jason King lookalike played Robinson Crusoe on Dolphin Island. And at some point the King of Soho sleaze Paul Raymond himself got involved and produced a dolphin revue, whereby the animals were trained to remove the aquamaid's bikinis by nudging them with their snouts. According to the *Sun*, who ran a picture under the headline 'Flipper Stripper', one of the girls was actually called Linda Salmon. The Dolphinarium closed a couple of years later and more regular tat took over. But it seems that the pool was still sitting there beneath the building all along, until the whole place was demolished in the 2000s.

I can't really argue that it was a better world when marine mammals performed tricks with scantily clad 'mermaids' in a sweaty cavern beneath Oxford Street. Or for that matter when every other doorway in parts of W1 lured 'tricks' with a lurid red light. But it might have been. It was certainly more interesting. I definitely wonder what tales the current West End will have to tell. I cannot imagine too many people sharing their hazy but defining youthful memories of that amazing trip to Uniqlo; the mounting excitement in the queue as they neared the cash register, or even the bitter disappointment when the puffer jacket didn't quite fit.

Cities need a slice of sleaze, a touch of chicanery, a frisson of edge. The corporate sanitisation of central London means that all the grist in the mill has been pushed out to the fraying edges, away from the now-tourist-dominated heart of town. This blandification of the centre is not a problem unique to London. Paris, when I first went there in the 1970s and '80s, was a gritty city, rich in 'noirish', 'nouvelle vague' imagery. You could still imagine a tough, but beautiful 'Little Sparrow' emerging from the dishevelled streets and Gitane-stained bars around Les Halles and Rue St Denis. It was a town of bordellos and Bains Douches, where the characters were still murky and the transactions dodgy; charismatic, slightly unnerving, rich in grimy layer upon layer of street life, but no more. The bourgeois and the bland have won the day – and the night-time, too – in the now frou-frou French capital.

And over in New York, once the world capital of sexy sleaze and exciting edge, is there anybody who really thinks that Times Square, once the dodgiest, shabbiest, most thrilling spot in the western world, is actually better now that it is an outdoor branch of Disneyland? Do you prefer *Midnight Cowboy* or *Moulin Rouge*, *Taxi Driver* or *Hannah Montana: The Movie*?

I actually watched *Taxi Driver* – for me the ultimate New York film, maybe the ultimate film – in 1976, when it was first shown at the National Film Theatre. I still haven't recovered. This was when the bar was at the front down by the river and the South Bank was still largely deserted and derided as a failed brutalist monstrosity. I loved the near-empty concrete walkways and rigorous straight lines: the quasi-Stalinist air of architectural menace, the unforgiving urbanism of it all, it made me feel like I was in A *Clockwork Orange*. Except I hadn't seen it, because by the time I was close to old enough, a bruised and critically battered Stanley Kubrick had withdrawn the film. So myself and a group of equally obsessed mates, some wearing bowlers, travelled to Paris, specifically to see it in the cinema where it was shown at midnight every night for years. Still love that movie to this day; still have my bowler.

As a seventeen-year-old boy, I had become an ardent cineaste. I was a devout reader of *Sight and Sound* and a firm believer that going to see arty and obscure movies would make me more popular with females. I had learned the word 'auteur' and learned that some girls – particularly the ones who had joined us in the sixth form at our previously all-boys grammar school – liked lads who were prepared to show their sensitive and artistic side. Which is why I also took to carrying a copy of an unreadable Scandinavian novel round in my pocket.

I also learned that even grammar school girls like other, less cerebral entertainments. This was confirmed when we went on a mass school excursion to the Hendon Classic to see *Emmanuelle* or maybe *Emmanuelle 2*. We were all a year or so too young to get into an 18 certificate, but we dressed in our best and managed to convince the not-all-that-bothered people selling the tickets to let us in. That night was an education in many ways.

Just Jaeckin's famed soft-paw corn epic was on screen one, the largest at the Classic (which had been an Odeon and is now a gymnasium), it being extremely popular and all. By this time the multiplexes had well and truly arrived, chopping up those grand old cinemas into as many separate screens as possible, with no care over architectural integrity or cinematic excellence – and of course I thought they were great.

But looking back, I actually believe that butchering the grand old picture palaces into multiple, separate boxes, was a portent of important changes to come. We now live in a much more atomised, solipsistic society. Technology has allowed us to fragment, to fill our lives with our own self-affirming choices. We watch, we hear, we experience only what we want, and we do it in our own little bubble. And that bubble began when we sectioned off the big cinemas into tiny, misshapen screens. Choice won out over shared experience, individualism over collectivism.

Along with the visits to the South Bank and the NFT, I also headed back to Oxford Street to confirm my teenage cineaste credentials. Because as tacky as the strip could be in the '70s, it also boasted one of the greatest cinemas this city has ever seen: the Academy at number 165 had been London's most important independent art house and foreign language cinema for generations. It was smart, cultured, cosmopolitan, sophisticated and preposterously pretentious.

The very act of going to Oxford Street, the epicentre of crass, yet choosing to enter the Academy and rub shoulders with supercilious academics with leather patches on their elbows, émigré intellectuals and wan-looking blonde women with too many vowels in their names, was a massive decision. I was self-consciously crossing a line. Burnt Oak boy out of Notting Dale, watching Kurasawa and all that. I was increasingly aware that my education was also schizophrenic, partly from school, but also from London. The city itself became my teacher on just about every subject from architecture to psychology, art to comparative religion. On Oxford Street, I could learn about abstract sculpture, the impending apocalypse, the three-card trick and the *Seven Samurai*.

Back in the 1950s and '60s, the basement of the Academy building had been the original home of the Marquee Club, where on 12 July 1962 The Rolling Stones played their first ever gig. But by the time I first went there in about 1976 or '77, even the Academy was multiscreen and the basement was screens two and three, while the Marquee was round the corner on Wardour Street. I was a regular there too, and over the road at the 100 Club, the sole surviving music venue on Oxford Street today. I was working on my night moves, but we'll keep those for another chapter.

I'm not telling you any of this to try and make myself seem clever, although appearing clever was certainly a desired side effect of going to the Academy and the NFT, as was the likelihood of seeing naked foreign flesh on screen. But I think I realised even then that this was what London meant to me, what London offered me and could help me to become.

Some of the lads from the Watling, quick and sharp though they were, rarely left the estate except to go to football. They felt safe in their cocoon, happy to be faces in the Bald Faced Stag. Others, like myself, were lured by the lights. Even growing up poor in a metropolis, you can still see the sea of possibilities, because of the proximities. Actors acting, musicians performing, artists doing whatever it is artists do, celebrities, charlatans, long cars, tall buildings, big stuff: that is the essence of our everyday. Out in the country, or in smaller towns, there are fewer opportunities to witness other ways, but bunk the fare on a Number 52 or a southbound Northern line train and a few stops later you hit a city bristling with alternatives. It hit me between the eyes, and opened them too.

I recently met some kids from an estate in South London, young black lads who were on the radio to talk about gang crime. They were in their mid-teens, full of braggadocio and little boy nerves, bright as Paul Smith buttons, effervescent with energy, yet clearly way out of their ends – truth be told, a little scared. For many of them, this was the first time they had ever been up West, or anywhere else for that matter, their horizons ended at the limit of their postcode. These kids, boys just like we were, had never had Red Rovers or trips to Speakers' Corner, never climbed the Monument or run shouting over Waterloo Bridge. They had on blinkers, living in a small, closed, timid, dangerous world, the opposite of a big city. Now they were at the BBC, and they could suddenly see a different universe, see people not entirely unlike themselves doing jobs they'd never even contemplated. They were excited, amazed, baffled, it was beautiful, scales were falling and London was revealing itself. Londoners were emerging

*

There was a fair amount of that going on at the pictures too – the revealing bit, that is. While most cinemas in the late 1970s early '80s had either been modernised and multiplexed, or else shut down and even demolished, there were a few which just carried on in their wondrous decrepitude. Some of them survived as specialist Bollywood houses, others as porn pits. The day of the dirty pictures is definitely done.

The best of the worst of those bug holes had been the Tolmer, a legendarily decaying venue in a truly lost part of London, which sadly showed its last cheesy double bill before I got there. Just to the west of Euston station, and backing on to Hampstead Road, hidden now behind a boxy, mirror-fronted office block, is Tolmer Square. Today it is a rather grim 1970s red-brick council estate, an insular warren of flats and scrubby grass, but once it had been a cause célèbre.

Rather like the battle to save Frestonia, this enclave of run-down but rather handsome five-storey Regency houses, with grand pillars and porticos, arrayed around a square with a cinema (which had originally been a church) at its centre, was marked for demolition from the mid-'60s onwards. (It's interesting that in the 1930s, churches became cinemas, whereas now it is the other way round). The population of what was dubbed Tolmer Village was another example of early multiculturalism, a working-class mix of Greek Cypriot, Irish, African and Indian, the last of whom who opened some of the first Indian restaurants and shops in London, just behind Tolmer Square on Drummond Street. Even the Esperanto community (is there such a thing?) had their head offices here. Of course, the plan was to wipe it all away and replace it exclusively with offices, but a combination of residents and students from nearby UCL and the Architectural Association fought a brilliant campaign to make Camden Council change their mind.

When it closed in the mid-'70s, the Tolmer was infamous as London's cheapest and grungiest place to watch films, which a high percentage of the audience were not doing. Prostitutes and their punters went about their transactional relationships in full view of students skipping lectures and a semi-permanent audience of the homeless, junkies and street drinkers seeking somewhere warm to nod off. There wasn't a dry seat in the house. By the time I went, there weren't any seats whatsoever in the house, they'd been ripped out and its auditorium used solely for inchoate dancing at squat raves. Soon after, it was demolished.

I did make it to the equally notorious Biograph – or, as it was known, the Biogrope – to see a film, but that wasn't the main entertainment. Victoria is the land of the lost. Nobody knows where they are going in this constantly stirring cauldron of perpetual revolution, a quasi-Maoist mess of turmoil and unease. There have been building works and road works and noise and dirt and digging and disorientation in the ever-shifting concrete quagmire around Victoria station throughout my entire life; never a day in repose. It is the most permanently transient of quarters, nothing is ever still, no one lives there surely, nothing survives, nothing is for us.

Victoria is a place for arriving and leaving: Tubes, trains, coaches, queues, bags, bafflement, a tour of Babel, a teeming, torrid forecourt to the city. I rather like it. I've always loved the grubby zones around the big mainline stations. In any real city worth its salt, terminal hinterlands are always turbulent and disturbing, the air is choked by fast-food fumes and taxi emissions, ne'er-do-wells, sex shops and grease-stained, red, plush steak bars on every corner. And dodgy old cinemas.

The Tolmer was by Euston, the Scala is opposite King's Cross and the Biograph, which claimed to be the oldest cinema in Britain (it wasn't), was on Wilton Road Victoria, and boasted the best 1950s Miami-style logo in all London. And for some reason it became a major gay cruising venue, which is precisely why I went there. I also went to the London Apprentice pub in Old Street, the Vauxhall Tavern, the Coleherne in Earl's Court, Bolts nightclub near our squat in Harringay, Heaven in Charing Cross and a sauna/spa/bath house thing on Endell Street in Covent Garden, where I saw my first ever, real, in-the-flesh, up-close male-on-male oral action. But the Biograph was right up there, or down there, or wherever you place 1980s down-and-dirty gay cruising culture, which I got to know better than my natural proclivities might suggest, because I shared a flat with Michael Smith. He took me to the Biogrope.

Michael is dead. In retrospect, it was close to inevitable that Michael wouldn't have made it through, but back then, in the early '80s, no one knew that his chosen lifestyle, although never exactly healthy, would prove to be quite so swiftly fatal. He was a chain-smoking, hard-drinking, drug-imbibing, poppers-sniffing, leather-wearing, rough-trade-seeking sybarite from a genteel northern town, with the most nicotine-stained fingers and engagingly smutty smile I've ever seen. Switching back and forth between New York and London, eking out a dwindling inheritance, by living as close to squalor as he could, Michael was a true cosmopolitan, a great friend and a fantastic raconteur. He decided that I should get to know his world and so made it a point of pride to take me to every sordid bolt hole in both of his towns. Nothing in London could quite compare with a night with Michael down the Mineshaft or the Manhole in Manhattan's Meatpacking District, but a matinée at the Biograph proved suitably diverting.

Quite why this shabby old picture house near Victoria station became so popular among Michael's mates I have no idea, although apparently it had acquired tabloid notoriety many years before because of the gay goings-on going on in the cheap seats. If I had actually gone there to see *Honky Tonk Freeway*, I would have been more than a little put off by the furtive shuffling and the frantic coming and going, or should that be going and coming, between the stalls and the toilets. It was a meat market indeed. Henry Cooper's identical twin brother George was the house manager, but even the threat of a tasty right hook didn't stop the shenanigans. It was the sudden appearance of the bulldozers, shortly before the building was about to be listed, that finally robbed us of this odd old institution. It was AIDS that robbed us of Michael.

I have only the haziest, trippiest recollection of a cinema that used to sit on the Charing Cross Road, backing on to Leicester Square. At the southern end, just before you get to the National Portrait Gallery, where the Capital Radio building is now. Its final incarnation was as part of the ubiquitous 1980s Classic Chain, and it was at some point in the middle of that excessive decade that I ended a typically indulgent Soho night there. It was just yet another exhausted old cinema, but one which was open at four in the morning.

I have no idea if we paid or not – I suspect we just walked in. There was definitely a movie playing on the screen, but there were also people living in the auditorium. A load of punks, of the Crass, mohican, dreadlocks and dogs-on-string variety, had set up home amid the torn and broken seats and were running it as a residential squat/cinema. Piles of their tatty belongings littered the place, domestic squabbles took place; I think there were even rudimentary cooking facilities. They definitely sold drinks and probably substances from a bar and slept in the aisles – although I don't know when, because everybody was awake during this bizarre all-nighter. It resembled a scene from *Mad Max goes to the movies*.

The time from the mid-1970s until Margaret Thatcher's free market reforms kicked in, in the mid-'80s, and we all started to go designer fancy, was a period of incredible waywardness and wonderful creativity. London had been largely left to rot, abandoned and forsaken, leaving vast spaces for young chancers to move in. These were essentially entrepreneurs, but of the piratical rather than the strictly profitable variety. Big business still wanted nothing to do with our tarnished town, government policies still assumed the flight to the suburbs would continue.

There was a band of terrible/beautiful dereliction, running roughly parallel with the river, taking in Battersea and Bankside, both of them dominated by redundant power stations and the vast deserted docklands area, starting hard by Tower Bridge and heading way out east. Only Harold Shand and the writers of *The Long Good Friday* could see any future for the docklands.

There was another swathe of former light-industrial London gone to ruin, a run-down wasteland of warehouses, lockups and would-be villains from Old Street roundabout to way beyond Bethnal Green.

Right in the centre of town, Covent Garden, with tumbleweed blowing through the former flower market, was almost serene in its abandonment, while the badlands of King's Cross's canal and railway world were extremely bad indeed.

To my mind, there are certain events, which, in retrospect, were pivotal in the transformation of these urban wastelands. Andrew Logan's fabulous Alternative Miss World extravaganza in his artists' studios in Butlers Wharf. Paul Smith opening his first boutique in Floral Street and the Blitz club starting round the corner. The first warehouse parties in 'Mayhem', Toyah Willcox's former printworks in Battersea. A designer called Willie Brown launching a shop called Modern Classics (where Spandau and I bought our kilts) in Curtain Road, when no one even knew where Shoreditch or Hoxton were. And Steve Woolley, now one of our leading filmmakers, taking over a disused cinema in King's Cross to start the Scala. When Steve moved in, King's Cross wasn't so much a neighbourhood as a jungle, and the Scala wasn't a cinema, it was the world's only ever Primatarium.

It's remarkable how many stories in this book involve animals in unlikely places. But what was most bizarre about the tale of the monkey extravaganza in King's Cross is that it didn't have any monkeys. It didn't have any punters either. Founded by a wealthy monkey nut named Cyril Rosen, the place was a disaster. If few people attended the Football Hall of Fame, it was positively popular compared to the Primatarium. Like many millions of other Londoners, I never went, and despite repeated appeals on my radio show, I have never managed to discover a single soul who actually paid to attend. One person I spoke to just wandered in off the street one day, finding nobody on duty in the lobby, or anywhere else for that matter, and took a little look round, but left after a few moments of bored bewilderment. It is on record that Michael Heseltine attended the opening party, and given that his nickname was Tarzan, there is a certain irony there, but it was a predictable disaster.

Why would anybody turn a palatial old 1,000-seater cinema into a fake jungle experience with plastic palm trees, piddling waterfalls and simian sounds, photographs and films, but no primates bar a few stuffed orang-utans and chimpanzees? And why would anybody go to see it? Clearly they didn't.

Not surprisingly the Primatarium was short-lived, and it was eventually taken over by a young Islington-born movie nut. Stephen Woolley had originally opened the Scala in Tottenham Street, over in Fitzrovia in 1979. His schoolmate Steve Dagger had put on one of Spandau Ballet's first gigs there, and I had introduced them on stage with preposterous poetry, all of which was filmed in arty black and white for LWT. But in 1981 it moved to the massive King's Cross site, still shrouded in fake jungle gear. Steve displayed his playful sense of humour by showing *King Kong* on the opening night.

The Scala was actually a repertory film club, costing 50p a year to join, in order to circumvent British censorship rules. It specialised in all-day and all-night sessions of cinematic schlock and awe; zombies, perverts, kung-fu fighters, but also avant-garde auteurs, rarely seen foreign language masterpieces and inspired art-house double headers. *Bring Me the Head of Alfredo Garcia* and *Eraserhead* is one pairing that sticks in my head. You could take in your own alcohol, smoke whatever you wanted, and party like it was a party: all this cinematic merriment, with the Northern line rattling away noisily beneath you, much of the mad jungle scenery still in place, a house cat who would jump on your lap during horror films and a raucous but seriously cineaste audience. It was the greatest fun you could possibly have in a threadbare velour seat.

The Scala was the perfect metaphor for London in the 1980s. It was the city in microcosm: anarchic, grubby, cheap, scurrilous, crumbling, still hungover from a former age, yet blessed with a wayward, gutter creativity; all of which operated on the very edge of illegality and occasionally toppled over it. The Scala closed in 1992 after it was fined to the point of bankruptcy for showing the still-banned *A Clockwork Orange*, advertised as *Mechanical Fruit*. But by then Steve Woolley's mind was not on his picture palace, as he had started Palace Pictures and had begun producing a slew of brilliant British films, including *Mona Lisa*, which is probably the best representation of old King's Cross in all its deeply dodgy glory.

And today? Well, the Scala is a nightclub and music venue (it was always more like a nightclub with films showing) and King's Cross is a swanky neighbourhood. As for going to the pictures, well it's never been better. Sadly we have no more flea-pits, but along with the myriad chains we have got Secret cinema, Rooftop cinema, Hot tub cinema, Floating cinema, boutique cinemas, cine-clubs and live soundtrack events; London still loves films, and films still love London.

Come on, let's go to the pictures, we could choose from: *The Long Good Friday, The Lavender Hill Mob, Blow-Up, Quadrophenia, Meantime, Dirty Pretty Things, Hue and Cry, Notting Hill, Alfie, Oliver, Babylon, Nil By Mouth, Mary Poppins, My Beautiful Launderette, My Fair Lady, To Sir with Love, Repulsion, Poor Cow, Party Party, Up the Junction, A Clockwork Orange, The Blue Lamp, The Krays, Layercake, Lock Stock and Two Smoking Barrels, Passport to Pimlico, Piccadilly, Gangster No. 1, Bend It Like Beckham, Withnail and I, The Ladykillers, The Red Shoes, The Blue Lamp, The Elephant Man, Hope and Glory, From Hell, Prick Up Your Ears, The Small World of Sammy Lee, Mona Lisa, Life Is Sweet, Bedknobs and Broomsticks, Bullet Boy, 28 Days Later, 84 Charing Cross Road, 10 Rillington Place, Wonderland, Somers Town, Frenzy, The Ipcress File, The Omen, A Kid for Two Farthings, Kidulthood, Performance, Sliding Doors, Deathline, Jawbone, An American Werewolf in London, The Lady in the Van, Bridget Jones* or *Steptoe and Son Ride Again*, I think you can see our old house in that one.

Do You Fancy a Schvitz?

While sitting naked, flushed and sweating on a marble slab, or being pummelled by a hirsute cab driver in a scalding fog of steam, I occasionally wonder if I am somehow communing with my ancestors, reaching back to recover lost memories of a never-known shtetl. Do I like a schvitz so much because of the Jewish blood that flows from my mother's ancestry? Or perhaps it's an unconscious recollection of the old Lime Grove wash house, where generations of Elmses would have soaked away the grime and the blues, when a tin bath in the kitchen wasn't sufficient. Maybe it's just the second best fun you can have with no clothes on?

A schvitz is a Yiddish sweat; sitting, lying, lounging naked, letting it all flow out in a hot room. A Turkish bath, a Finnish sauna, a Moroccan hammam, a Russian banya – so many different cultures can lay claim to the tradition of communal perspiration and ablution and you can find every variation here in London. You can find them all at Porchester Hall.

It seems fitting that the first person who ever took me to the baths to open my pores and pour some tea was a second-generation Irish hairdresser and punk rock memorabilia dealer from Clonmel via Finchley, called Ollie O'Donnell. Mr O'Donnell is not notably Jewish. You definitely don't have to be 'of the faith' to go to Porchester Baths; a grand but gloriously decaying Edwardian edifice in Bayswater. But you can't really immerse yourself in either the 'frigidarium', the freezing plunge pool, or the coruscating culture of the place unless you learn a little Yiddish.

Men's days at the baths are not for the faint hearted, and nor is schmeissing. When you first arrive at the baths, unaware of its complex traditions, elaborate rigmaroles and hierarchies, you are a pisher. Literally a bed-wetter, a know-nothing new boy, and you are probably also a schlump, a schmuck, a shmendrick and a schlemiel. Not to mention a bleedin' goy, which will become obvious because you are tuchas naked and everyone can *see your schlong hasn't been circumcised. But I wouldn't worry about all that.*

One of the most endearing things about the baths is the rigorous egalitarianism. Half of the week is dedicated to women and I'm sure ladies days have their own arcane rituals. When the guys are in, Jew or gentile, gay or straight, rich or poor, black or white, Tottenham or Arsenal, it makes no odds. You may well find yourself sitting with Terence Stamp, Frank Bruno, Damon Albarn, Wayne Sleep, Ian McShane, a blagger, a plumber and a card counter, a Lord, a judge, a journalist and a bevy of black cab drivers, all naked, and all complete cunts according to Morrie over in the corner.

There used to be scores of Turkish baths around London, especially in the East End where they were a vital part of the social and religious life of the Jewish community. They brought the custom over from Eastern Europe and used the baths to get suitably spruce before going to synagogue. The famous old Russian Vapour Baths at 86 Brick Lane, known as Schewzik's, after its owner, was for years a Bengali supermarket, but is now a hotel. Therein lies a London tale.

There is still a sign set in the pavement, near my old flat on Russell Square, pointing to a long-gone hammam which stood on Southampton Row. Jermyn Street once had two, including a particularly palatial place, which got bombed in the war, and a smaller one that lasted into the '70s and was favoured by dandies, politicians, West End actors sweating off post-play hangovers, Lord Boothby and the Kray twins. Another was on Leicester Square but was demolished when the famed Alhambra Theatre went.

These days only a couple of old-school schvitz's remain, and my favoured one is under threat. There are proposals to make Porchester Hall plusher, in accord with the gentrification of the area it serves. More of a modern 'spa' with all the connotations of scented candles, soppy music, serenity and expensive treatments. There is not a lot of holistic 'omming' or quinoa at Porchester Hall, but there are plenty of eggs on toast, strong tea and schmeissing.

I am technically a 'schmeiss ponce', which means that I enjoy being given 'a bath', as it's always called, but haven't acquired the skills to give one back in return. Basically, teams of men gang together to take turns lying in the hottest steam room with a wet towel over their heads waiting to be pummelled. The others rub you vigorously with a raffia brush, called a besom, dipped in a big bucket of soap, raising the temperature to diabolical, working your muscles and your soul simultaneously with tough forearms and palms. It is unbelievably hard to give a bath in the pulsing, burning heat, but great to get one. Followed by a dip in the icy plunge pool, it is the perfect end to a sweating session. Then the fun begins.

The word banter has been horribly debased by lads' mags and Twitter twits. But the first time I ever sat upstairs in the 'tepidarium', the cooling-off area, and meekly listened to the verbal volleys ricocheting off the marble pillars, and the often lewd, ludicrous stories being told, I was knocked sideways by the dexterity, the humour, the obscenity and the sheer volume. Loud, rude, crude, cutting, but also clearly, deeply loving. Blimey, that was banter.

Here were big, naked, flabby men, adoring this time they spend together, revelling in their concept of community. To me, sitting in a robe, clean and scrubbed, eating toast, listening to Jimmy Two Baths joust verbally with Harry round the corner, laughing out loud at their rotten jokes, was London life at its very best, and I was hooked.

For a few years I went every Wednesday, got to know some of the characters, maybe even earned a little respect in the cauldron of quick wits. One of the guys I used to see there was a voluble North London cabbie called Mitch. A big, loud, dapper man with his clothes on, prone to a spot of crooning, who was very much part of the inner circle. They all got to know what I do for a living and would occasionally rib me about getting them on the radio. But with Mitch it was different, he wanted me to get his daughter on the radio: 'She's a great singer,' he would say, 'She's going to be big. Her name is Amy.'

Lord of Lord's

What is the most luminous, numinous space in all London? St Paul's is clearly the main contender: born of flames, its dome shrouded in Hitler's fire, yet still here, dwarfed now and aged, but still the vision we carry of our collective continuity, the capital's eternity. St Pancras Old Church is a personal favourite, a humble jumble of a prayer room overseeing the now secreted Fleet, whose patchwork history stretches back to the baptism of the first Christian Londoners in Vale Royal.

Number 19 Princelet Street, just off Brick Lane, is heartbreakingly special, a crumbling Huguenot house with a spellbinding private synagogue at the back; spare, silent testimony to the narratives of arrival and survival, a prayer in the night. But as a non-believer in all and any faiths, bar a faltering trust in my fellow man, the most awe-inspiring space in this city, replete with so many monuments and so much reverence, is Lord's, ladies and gentlemen.

I've always adored the great sporting icons, temples of will and suffering, joy and dreaded hope. I've seen games at the San Siro, the Bombonera and the Bernabéu, boxing at Madison Square Garden and the Royal Albert Hall, baseball at Fenway and cycling on Ventoux. I've watched sombre men in suits of lights parade and dance and kill and die in Seville's unequalled La Maestranza, undoubtedly the most sumptuous arena of them all. (Arena, now the word for all sporting venues, just means sand in Spanish, the sand where the matadors walk.) But in a whole world of beautiful, historic cathedrals of sinew, there's none that can compare to the cricket field in St John's Wood.

If I could treat a treasured friend to any one special day in my city, it would be the opening day of the first Ashes test at the home of the Marylebone Cricket Club: the tradition of eggs and bacon, the crackle of verdant anticipation, Old Father Time, the W.G. statue, the stature of the pavilion and the modernity of the media centre. Like all truly special spaces, it is an accretion of moments and mythologies, but it is also a love song of England, a paean that touches even my cynical metropolitan soul. If you can allow an idea of perfection into your heart, even just for a few hours, then this is the perfect setting.

No grass is greener, no silence quieter, no buzz buzzier than that contained within the confines of the cricket ground. It doesn't have to be the Ashes; it doesn't have to be a test: any day when the sun shines upon NW8, arms are turned, shots are played and drinks are poured, is a pretty good day.

I am not a cricket nut – football is my true affliction – but I first went to HQ as a local kid and was instantly entranced. Back then you could sit by the boundary rope in your school uniform like something from a 1940s film and watch the men in white toil and swipe, dreamy green hours folding upon themselves. Later at county games I stood in the tavern with the noisy boys, holding a pint and self consciously chanting 'middle, middle middle, sex, sex, sex'. Today, whenever I can, I blag a ticket for a test or sweet talk my way into the pavilion with a member; being in the inner sanctum holds a definite sway. That majestic room is certainly long on atmosphere.

I think I understood straight away that Lord's is a place to suspend disbelief, cast aside prejudice and immerse yourself in the myth, revel in the spell. Once through the Grace gate, traditions that would grate elsewhere are great here: bells are rung, tea is taken, snoozing is almost compulsory. Old codgers in blazers are venerable sages, corporate suits in boxes are firm aficionados, grown men mark cards, small boys seek signatures. Sportsmanship is celebrated, milestones by either side are applauded, draws are honourable, champagne is available, life is enjoyable. If it's not cricket, it has no place at Lord's. But they don't make it easy.

I like the fact that they have standards. One of my true London disappointments was going to the Royal Opera House for the first and only time to see a portly person warble, putting on my bestest bib and tucker, only to discover that most of the crowd were in casuals. Jeans for a night at the opera, what have we come to? Mastering appropriate attire for all occasions is an essential city skill: Covent Garden is not an allotment. One of the pleasures of a day at the cricket for me is getting suitably suited and booted, pale linen and loafers.

I opted for just that ensemble when I and a couple of mates decided to attend a Middlesex versus Yorkshire county game on a Monday after a languid, liquid lunch. One of our party is an MCC member, so we knew to sport jackets and ties, even though it was that rare beast: a swelteringly hot day in North London. We needed to be suitably suited as we intended to partake of the pavilion and rules is rules.

Three immaculate, middle-aged men in whistles and Peckhams, in 80 plus degrees of heat, in a ground with maybe a few hundred hardy souls present. We paid the exorbitant entrance fee and strolled towards the pavilion, confident that for once we would make it past the sentinels and into hallowed space. But as we went to walk in, eyebrows were raised, heads were shaken, entrance was barred. 'Socks,' is all the stern looking security man said, and we all looked down to see that my mate Richard was indeed without the aforementioned garments. 'You cannot enter the pavilion without socks, this is not Italy.'

I could not have loved them more.

Except perhaps when I heard a story from Sebastian Coe. Lord Coe, Baron Coe, aristo Tory MP, head of the IAAF Coe. He arrived for a test match at the big gate to discover that his tickets were awaiting him round the other side of the stadium. He tried to reason with the doorman, insisting that he had an important meeting with MCC bigwigs inside. Exasperated, he finally played the 'Do you know who I am?' card.

'Indeed I do my Lord,' said the humble chap barring his entry. 'Therefore I also know that you should be able to get round there to collect them pretty quickly.'

Even a Lord can't beat Lord's.

CHAPTER FOUR

Dinner Time

On Friday I had a bender. For the rest of the week our daily eating pattern went like this: breakfast was cereal with milk, fresh from the silver-topped bottles left daily on the doorstep, or else a slice of 'holy-ghost' and jam, sometimes eaten with your feet in the gas oven to keep warm; dinner (which was what we called lunch) was served at noon in the hall at school. I got it free when my dad died, and I liked everything about it except the semolina.

The evening meal was called tea and was taken at about 6 p.m. Cooked by Mum, it invariably involved meat in some form, usually minced, vegetables boiled to the point of suppuration, and fruit from a tin – mandarin segments were best, served with Bird's custard or Carnation condensed milk. Occasionally – and I realise now it was when we were particularly skint – something grim from the war, like ox heart (very St John) or tripe and onions, would be put on the table. The kitchen would smell like an abattoir, and we would all grimace as we ate. But we ate.

Later on, when '70s culinary futurism and E-numbers really kicked in, Cadbury's Smash, boil-in-a-bag fish and Angel Delight – butterscotch flavour hopefully – became staples, washed down with a bottle of lurid pink Cresta ('It's frothy man'). Snacks were of the chocolate variety: Penguins, Club biscuits, Tunnock's wafers, but occasionally, if the cupboard was bare, sugar sandwiches. Yep, white sugar poured liberally between slices of Mother's Pride bread.

My mum was never much of a worrier about nutritional technicalities, nor much of a cook, love her. But she made a decent spotted dick in an old muslin cloth, we were never hungry and there was always some form of roast on a Sunday with Brussels sprouts you could drink through a straw. But on Fridays, after a hard working week, she opted out of standing by the stove to make our tea, and instead we all got a takeaway. I had a bender.

Traditional Friday evening fare was fish and chips, and we would sometimes still patronise the local chip shop for our takeaway tea. I would be dispatched to go up to Watling Avenue to ask for cod, or rock and chips four times, a couple of wallies and a ha'porth of crackling, just possibly a saveloy, lashings of salt and vinegar – wrapped in newspaper of course – run back to keep it warm. To this day I cannot eat chipped potatoes, in any form, no matter how fancy the restaurant, without applying sour wine, ideally malted; certainly not balsamic.

It is also interesting how fried fish, particularly served with a pickled cucumber (why is that a wally?) comes from the Jewish food tradition. But though I love fish and chips now, as a young boy I was seduced by the more snazzy delights of a juicy bender with thin, crispy chips, and maybe even a knickerbocker glory, if mum was flush. Oh the wonders of the Wimpy Bar.

Burnt Oak in the late '60s had three dining options. Opposite the station was the Beta Café, always pronounced the Better Caff. A classic, nicotine-shrouded, Formica-topped, greasy spoon run by a lovely Italian family, the Miglios, who had moved out of Clerkenwell to dish up strong tea, sausage and mash or liver and bacon to the good folk of the Oak. Actually quite a few of the bad folk went there too, but no one ever took liberties in the Better Caff, as old man Miglio was always assumed to have 'connections', plus he usually had a very sharp knife in his hand, and he took no lip.

The chip shop was a little further up the Watling, and the young girls who worked there were considered quite a catch, despite the lingering smell, because it was said they always gave their boyfriends extra chips. But five minutes further away, round the corner, on the Edgware Road, near the bowling alley, which undoubtedly meant it was posher, was the Wimpy Bar. This was an exciting place indeed: a destination restaurant.

The Wimpy Bar was often my mum's destination when she finished work on a Friday, first at Woolworths, later at the nearby Green Shield Stamp offices. She would stop off and get a takeaway to bring home for our tea; burger and chips for my brothers, but a frankfurter for me, with notches cut into it so that it curled round in a circle to fit in the toasted bun, hence the retrospectively risible name, the bender. They were usually almost cold by the time she got them home, but it didn't matter. This was a real treat, which we looked forward to all week, and I could smell them as she opened the door. But even a kinky sausage eaten in front of the TV while watching *Here Come the Double Deckers!*, was as nothing compared to the rare event of actually 'eating in', which is what we called eating out.

I recall eating in at something called the Golden Egg once or twice. This was a chain of egg-based eateries, which we went to on a trip with my dad up West, where they somehow pulled off the trick of making egg and chips seem glamorous. To be honest any meal taken sitting at a table outside of our little kitchen was exciting, especially the Burnt Oak Wimpy.

We didn't exactly eat in at the Wimpy all that often, but I definitely remember the thrill of sitting in a booth, with menus coated in plastic, the red plastic seats and the red plastic, tomato-shaped tomato sauce dispenser, with American music playing, while a Greek bloke in a funny uniform cooked the food. It was a chain, which seemed exotic and exciting and apparently American and therefore modern. (Wimpy was actually owned by the very old fashioned and deeply British J. Lyons & Co of corner house fame). If we were in the Wimpy it was probably somebody's birthday, so we would definitely push the boat out and get a coke float or glory in a Knickerbocker, perhaps even a frothy coffee for Mum, confident that there probably wasn't a more sophisticated dining experience in all London. And truth be told there weren't very many.

The quality, quantity and diversity of eating places in this city now: restaurants, cafés, bistros, takeaways, fine-dining institutions, gastro-pubs, pop-up experiences, gourmet vans, vegan joints, tapas bars, tavernas, trattorias, teppanyakis, ocakbasis, etc. etc. etc. is incredible.

The transformation in our communal eating habits and the amazing explosion of culinary options is, I believe, the biggest single change in London in my lifetime.

On my radio show, during the 2014 World Cup, we did a listeners' inventory of the number of distinctly different national cuisines you can find in London, and we stopped when it came to considerably more than the number of nations in the world. You want a Kazak restaurant, well there's one just off the Old Kent Road, fancy a Burmese feast, it's on the Edgware Road, Ghanaian Food, that'll be Cricklewood, there's even an Afghan place in Burnt Oak now. And if you should want to consume raw fish wrapped around cold, vinegared rice, dipped in soy sauce served with pickled ginger, well you can get it on just about every high street and in every supermarket in town. Who could possibly have predicted that?

We didn't have many restaurants when I was growing up, certainly not for the likes of us. I wrote in the introduction to this book that I don't believe my mum had ever been to a proper restaurant, with tablecloths and waiter service, before I took her to one in the 1980s. And if you don't count the Wimpy Bar in Burnt Oak, Lyons Corner Houses with their uniformed nippies, and the occasional pie-and-mash shop, I think that is probably right.

My dad might, perhaps, have splashed out and taken her out up West when they were courting, but I doubt it. The kind of fancy, formal, usually French establishments with snotty waiters and snooty manners that constituted fine dining back then would have made her deeply uncomfortable, and her initial reactions to 'foreign muck' when we first tried edible exotica in the '70s certainly suggested she had never been exactly experimental in her tastes.

Londoners like us did not have restaurants, but we did have blokes with bells. The ice-cream man with his charming, chiming van is the last remnant of an entire economy of mobile campanology merchants. We still occasionally have an ice-cream van turning up outside our house in Camden Town in the summer. Our kids, now grown-up, will still respond to the pre-recorded peeling of his bells by rushing out to buy a 99 with sprinkles in a conditioned Pavlovian response. And it all started in Burnt Oak. Sort of.

There was an absolute cacophony of ambulatory vendors and street hawkers in Victorian London, all armed with bells, whistles and elaborate cries to attract trade. From the muffin man to the pigs' trotter man, girls with cakes and sherberts, pie people aplenty, and the ubiquitous oyster boys who flogged bivalves for pennies to the poor.

My own great-grandad Albert was a milkman, selling dairy products of all kinds from a hand-cart he pulled along Ladbroke Grove. There's a great photo of him with a vast handlebar moustache and a crisp uniform, standing proudly with his newly acquired horse. But unfortunately he died not long after, aged just forty-one (the exact same age my own father Albert passed away) in a horrific accident when the cart toppled over on him. Later on, my brother Reggie spent years as a milkman, and I regularly helped him on his round, which we both survived despite me crashing his electric float into a lamp post in Hendon one Christmas eve. We've got milk in our blood.

'Stop me and buy one' was the slogan of the original purveyors of 'penny licks'. These tempting Italian émigrés were the first ever ice-cream men, flogging gelato in thick glasses, which would be handed back to the vendor once the frozen delicacy had been consumed: tasty, but none too hygienic. The first recognisable, motorised ice-cream van, however, complete with chiming tune and wafer cones, was started in 1937 by a London Italian called Toni Pignatelli, operating out of his cassata-coloured ice cream parlour on Watling Avenue, directly opposite Burnt Oak station.

It was still there, next to the Beta Café, when I was growing up and buying the occasional cornet or a vanilla block to take home. The shop was called Toni's, and his company Tonibells boasted the largest fleet of vans in the entire country. Throw in the fact that the first ever Tesco store, started by market trader Jack Cohen, also opened on the Watling in 1931 and humble Burnt Oak played a remarkable role in our high street history.

But you didn't have to go the high street to get comestibles: they came to you. In these days of Ocados, Amazons and Deliveroos we are used to goods being brought to our door, but it certainly isn't new. There was a positive armada of craft cruising the streets, delivering everything from laundry to bread, burgers, paraffin and fizzy pop.

As well as a weekly wet fish man in a white coat, there was a mobile fish and chip shop that came round, tempting you with the combined waft of chip fat and diesel. But my mum was convinced it was deeply insanitary and the burgers he sold were never likely to compete with a Wimpy. The smelliest van was the one selling paraffin, which parked up on the corner of our road belching noisome fumes you could see hovering in the air. People would queue up to fill plastic containers with noxious pink or blue liquid for the parlous old heaters in their parlours. For some reason the same bloke also sold big tubs of vinegar. We all got through lots of vinegar.

But it was the equally vividly coloured liquids proffered by the Corona man that I waited for with thirsty anticipation. This was a system of delivering bottles of lemonade, limeade, orangeade and my personal favourite, cherryade, to your door. He had crates full of the stuff on board, clinking and clanking together temptingly. And once you'd drunk the pop and experienced the considerable sugar rush, there was money back if you returned the bottle, and a fierce competition ensued between us kids, trying to find old Corona bottles to get the pennies back to spend on sweets.

The Corona man, with his bright, pop art livery and the accompanying television ads with the strapline 'It's Fizzical' felt positively modern. But it was a chap pedalling a weird tricycle contraption and peddling all manner of ancient fare who really took us back to our collective culinary past. I remember him as the toffee apple man, a grizzled old fellow with the air of a morbid Victorian novella, a sonorous bell on the front of his three wheeler and a mournful, elongated cry of 'Tooffeee Aaaapples'.

The melancholy toffee man rolled slowly through the estate with a big box on the front of his trike full of Cox's pippins dipped in bright, thick, glossy red toffee, which could crack the most resilient enamel. As kids we loved eating them despite the rumour that he made them in the same tin bath he occasionally washed in. He also sold bags of monkey nuts, peanuts in their shell, which were primarily football food, always flogged at matches by blokes running round the touchline before the game. But in the winter the toffee apple man mysteriously morphed into the faggot man, an even more ancient, arcane figure, wearing an old First World War greatcoat, flogging these strange, steaming rissole things to be eaten with pease pudding, always pronounced peace pudding. It's a beige mush made out of split peas, a kind of cockney hummus, which my mum found weirdly irresistible.

It's amazing that we were ever able to sit down for a few minutes without rushing to the door, because as well as all of the above-mentioned traders there was a constant stream of callers. There were coal men with black-smeared faces and those leather hats down their backs humping heavy sacks of carbon, and their allied and equally sooty trade of chimney sweeps. Italian/Swiss mobile knife sharpeners knocked on your door, offering to refresh your kitchen knives and garden shears with a grinding contraption on a push bike.

French onion sellers also on bikes, laden with alliums, laundrymen bringing back bedding, potato men with sacks of spuds from the Dickensian potato depot behind St Pancras station, where the British Library now is. There were Kleeneze men selling dusters, Avon ladies proffering smelly products, the pools man come to collect your coupon, the man from the Pru to collect your premium, the rent man, the meter-reading man and the dreaded provident cheque chap, knocking ominously demanding you pay the overdue instalments you owed on that loan you got for a new pair of Levi's.

But it wasn't just agents of Mammon who disturbed the peace. The Boys' Brigade would wake us up with their holy trumpets on Sunday mornings, the Jehovah's Witnesses would occasionally venture into the Oak trying to save some souls by interrupting your tea, and one Catholic friend remembers there was even a mobile altar wheeled round in a pushchair by a group of nuns, so that you could hold mass and say a few Hail Marys in your own front room.

One evening something remarkable happened. I think it must have been 1970 or '71 and my eldest brother Barry, by then a working man earning a decent wage, asked me to run an errand for him. Perhaps he'd come home too late for tea, or maybe he didn't fancy my mum's usual fare, but either way he asked me to head up to the Edgware Road to get him an Indian. I honestly had visions of bringing back Geronimo. Indians for me were still connected to cowboys, and I had no idea that a new, proper, sub-continental restaurant had opened almost opposite the Bald Faced Stag. I certainly had no notion that the world was about to totally change in just one mouthful of food.

Once Barry had explained what it was he actually wanted and written it down on a piece of paper so that no mistakes were made, I struck a bargain. I would go and get his dinner providing he would let me have some. So on that night, having run home as fast as I could with a bag full of worryingly pungent foodstuffs, I had my first ever breathless taste of prawn dhansak, sag aloo and stuffed paratha, pickles and chutney. Blimey. I'll say it again. Double bleeding blimey.

I know precisely what we ate that night because my brother Barry has ordered precisely that combo almost every time I have eaten with him for the last thirty-odd years. He moved to America in the 1980s and the first thing he does when he occasionally returns to London is go to an old-school Indian restaurant. Ideally with the flockiest wallpaper, the floralest carpet, the coldest lager and the spiciest food, to get the kind of curry that just doesn't exist in New England. I'm not sure that food really exists very much in old India either, but it has of course become an absolute staple of the British diet.

For me that first mind-blowing, mouth-exploding experience of Indian food was a life-changing event, a personal epiphany and a portent of incredible culinary things to come. It was comparable only to the jolt of seeing David Bowie on *Top of the Pops* performing 'Starman' with his arm draped lasciviously around Mick Ronson a year or so later, when we all saw the world change in a song. Sitting on the sofa, mouth agape, Bowie opened our eyes to a whole universe of wonderful, dangerous, mouth-watering possibilities. In the same little room in a council house in Burnt Oak, prawn dhansak opened my taste buds to the same. When my mum saw David Bowie on the telly she said dismissively, 'He's a "weirdo".' When she smelled Indian food she said it was 'filthy foreign muck'. Which just confirmed how good they both were.

And it wasn't only me. Just as an entire generation of people can remember the eye-opening electric shock of the Starman on that epochal Thursday evening, so our entire city was about to be transformed from a bland, stodgy, culinary backwater to perhaps the most open-minded, cosmopolitan food capital in the world. Perhaps it's because we did not have a great indigenous food culture in this country, or great restaurants in this city, that we were so eager to try new things, greedy for the good stuff whatever its provenance. Soon every high street had an Indian and a Chinese and even my mum deigned to try a spring roll or two.

The next stage on my own personal journey of culinary enlightenment involved George Michael's dad. It is difficult now to imagine the humble kebab as a memorable experience, but again I can recall exactly where I was when I first ate one. Which is surprising given that I can barely remember anything about any other evenings spent in the company of a kebab. I had been to the pictures in Edgware with a group of boys from my grammar school and afterwards one of them suggested we go and get a kebab. I didn't want to reveal my ignorance by saying I had no idea what that was, so went along with them, to this Greek Cypriot restaurant, with a glass takeaway counter at the front. I spent every penny I had, including my bus fair home, on a lamb shish in pitta bread with everything (I already knew from my Indian food experiences that I liked spicy). Yet again, I loved it immediately, savouring every last meaty, greasy, umami-drenched morsel on the long walk home.

I became a positive proselytiser for the wonders of the kebab, and the next weekend led a small group of herberts from the Watling on an expedition to Edgware, way out of their geographical and culinary comfort zone, to try this exotic delicacy. They all loved it. They all lived on kebabs for the next few years.

It was only many years later in a conversation with George Michael, whom I had known from his early days as a podgy, pretty young North London soul boy on the fringes of the trendy Soho nightclub scene, hanging at the back of the Blitz with a look of desire in his eyes, that I discovered the connection. I had been asked to work on the script of a documentary about his life and in a series of conversations with this now very self-serious and clearly uneasy superstar, with an obsessively neat beard, and a whole host of neuroses, one of the few light moments came when I mentioned the saga of my first-ever kebab. Those big anxious eyes lit up, he beamed a very welcome smile and said, 'That was my dad's restaurant.' Further probing around dates revealed that he may well have been sitting in the back of the shop the night I lost my kebab virginity, as he habitually used to do as a young boy.

While we are on the subject of kebab houses, permit me to muse a little on the nomenclature of high-street eateries. Who decides which terminology gets applied to which type of cuisine? I'll explain. In the old days London was awash with chop houses, and pie shops. Today it is always a kebab *house* and a curry *house*. But tradition dictates that it's a burger *bar*, a noodle *bar*, and back in the day a Jewish nosh *bar*. Whereas it's always a fish and chip *shop*, a chicken *shop*, and a sandwich *shop*. But if you fancy something Italianate you visit an ice-cream *parlour* and even a pizza *parlour*, while for Chinese or Thai it is simply a *restaurant*. Is there a secret committee who decide which linguistic appellation contrôlée we are going to use?

I am very aware that my journey through London's gastronomic past has thus far been extremely parochial. That's because the idea of travelling across town to go and eat was absolutely unthinkable. I now know that there were chic little bistros aplenty on the King's Road complete with gingham tablecloths, candles in wine bottles and wait-resses in mini skirts. I first heard about Lee Ho Fook's and its famous chow mein from Warren Zevon in the song 'Werewolves of London'. I have since been regaled with tales of Schmidt's German restaurant on Charlotte Street with its splendid sausages, bellicose waiters and Weimar mores, though sadly I never made it there before it closed in the late '70s. I have eaten in such long-term London institutions as the Gay Hussar in Soho, Simpson's in the Strand and Rules in Covent Garden, which has been there since 1798. But these were the excep-tions that proved the rule.

Today we all know where to go to get the best of everything. Acquiring geo-culinary nous is part of contemporary London life, at least for the restaurant-going classes, which is an infinitely broader demographic than it ever was. My eldest daughter Alice, in her mid-twenties, spends her money on food, and her time and social life is played out largely in restaurants. Almost no one her age did that back in the 1970s or '80s. Restaurants then were for old, stuffy, wealthy people, while the young went to pubs and clubs. Where I was in the Wag Club in Soho searching for excitement, Alice is in the same street with her mates consuming Szechuan spice.

As a family we've always eaten out, so my kids have a detailed mental map of where to go to consume what. Vietnamese pho and those gossamer summer rolls made by the original boatpeople in Shoreditch. Turkish food, the sweetest lamb chops charred and rich, grilled onions in pomegranate juice and crunchy salads with sumac in Dalston. (We've been dining in the same splendid Kurdish ocakbasi next to Gilbert and George for decades. When Alfie was about ten he tried to sell a school raffle ticket to the pair by asking them 'Would you like to win a flat-screen TV?' George answered 'Not half' and bought a bookful.)

Chicken soup with kneidlach, sweet and sour pickle and a latke, from Harry's in St John's Wood High Street. The best dim sum on Baker Street, but always Lisle Street for Cantonese roast duck and char sui. Fish and chips means queuing up with the gobby cab drivers in

Lisson Grove. Three kinds of Bengali kebabs and the best Peshwari nan from a tandoor in Whitechapel. The finest shawarma this side of Beirut, washed down with freshly squeezed juices from a brightly lit café on the Edgware Road. What an education they've had. What a world they enjoy.

The seismic shift in London's dining tectonics really started in the mid-'80s when the likes of Alistair Little and Rowley Leigh opened up funky, independent restaurants in Soho and Kensington, and the whole foodie concept emerged. But my own personal food journey began in the late '70s. Eating was still way down the list of priorities in terms of consumption, but I did manage to visit some of the famous names of the time. Perhaps notorious names would be more appropriate. There were three places in particular, each from a distinctly different culinary tradition, each vying to win the title of rudest restaurant in all London.

Bloom's Kosher restaurant on Whitechapel High Street is simultaneously one of the most reviled and yet revered food memories this city carries. It was an institution in the way that Bedlam was an institution. The closest we got to Katz's, the noisy, shabby, vibrant New York deli on the Lower East Side, where Meg Ryan famously pretended to have an orgasm. But the only loud moaning in Bloom's came from the phenomenally grumpy old blokes in stained and frayed white jackets who constituted the staff.

Bickering, grumbling, confronting, insulting, seemingly affronted by the very fact that you had chosen to eat there, it was like being served by a coterie of particularly stroppy cab drivers who you've just asked to take you to South London. One Jewish friend, taken to Bloom's as a boy in an act of pilgrimage and a rite of passage, which seems to have been universal among North London Jews just one generation away from the streets of Whitechapel, was told 'Bloom's is horrible, you're going to love it.' And it was and I did. Especially the salt beef. I loved Bloom's, loved heading East.

The East End has always exerted a mesmeric pull on Londoners,

even a confirmed Westie like myself. It is ingrained deep in our collective mythology as the great point of entry, the start of so many stories.
Oriental, exotic, edgy, yet full of the palpable energy of upward traction
and trajectory. But by the late '70s it was all but broken. Mired in
grainy black and white, looking like a war zone, windows missing, doors
boarded up, its grimy streets festooned with dribbling winos sitting
round burning braziers in the middle of the road, angry, sad. The
markets were dying, the Hebrews were leaving, happily handing this
crumbling slum over to the newly arrived Bengalis who would fill up
the sweatshops, take over the food shops and cram into the tenements
and garrets to bring back life.

The more secular, cultural Jews had done well and headed east and
north, but there was still a fading air of old Ashkenazi culture; bearded,
side-locked, over-coated, insular yet garrulous. Rabbinical Hassidim
talking Torah on street corners, dusty synagogues echoing with aged
cantors, Katz's twine shop with just one ball of string in the window,
the Schmutter brothers sitting on rolls of fabric, Roggs's deli with
barrels of brining pickles, Fishberg's jewellers, Grodzinski's bakers.
Yiddish signs, Russian names – it was fascinating and foreign, yet
absolutely intrinsic to the fabric of our city and the mythology of the
East. I first knew the East End through staying at my cousin Ian's prefab
on Fish Island in the '60s, but a decade later I was regularly exploring
its anarchist alleys and Hassidic haunts, which were all the more
enticing as they were so clearly doomed. As was Bloom's.

My favourite story of Bloom's hideous rudeness concerns a man who
had ordered mashed potato with his chopped liver or tongue, but
instead received boiled potatoes. Upon politely pointing this out to
Lou, the famously ferocious head waiter, Lou picked up the man's fork
from the table and proceeded to crush his spuds while shouting 'You
want mashed potatoes, I'll give you mashed potatoes.' It was all part
of the pantomime of terrible service, overpriced food yet deeply attractive authenticity. And oh the salt beef. Bloom's is now a Burger King.

It was the hot-and-sour soup at Wonkeys, or Won Keis as it is officially known. This was Bloom's main competitor in the rank rudeness

stakes and it is still there in Chinatown, but it has cleaned up its act and stopped being so spectacularly aggressive as to be legendary. The tales of meat-cleaver-wielding waiters, shouting and swearing at customers who took umbrage at being moved to a different floor halfway through their meal are legion. Small tips left in coins literally being thrown back at you was normal. The rancid toilets and the communal tables with people smoking in your face were famous features, but the hot and sour soup and indeed all the standard Hong Kong Cantonese dishes were fantastic, and I developed a real Wonkeys jones back in the 1980s. Perhaps it was masochistic, maybe I was subconsciously preparing myself for marrying into a typically loud and pugnacious Cantonese family many years later, or else I just enjoyed this down and dirty, cheap and spectacularly charmless Soho experience. Until the day I didn't have enough money.

I'd supped my soup and stripped a dead duck, only to discover I had less cash in my pocket than I thought. I was only a pound or so short, but I was petrified as I tried to explain to the waiter that I would go out to the bank and come straight back. His face went bright puce and it took him a few seconds to find the correct terminology. 'YOU FUCKING CUNT' delivered in a heavy Hong Kong accent. Those were the words ringing in my ears as I left. When I returned a few minutes later as promised, I thought he might be pleasantly surprised by my honesty, but he called me exactly the same thing again.

Jimmy's couldn't possibly compete with Bloom's or Wonkeys in terms of out and out hostility. The geriatric staff at this antediluvian Cypriot, somewhere beneath the streets of Soho, could even be civil, occasionally jolly if they had drunk enough ouzo, but what it lacked in venom and vitriol it more than made up for in old fashioned ineptitude and decrepitude. And it was certainly old-fashioned, even back then.

No one ever really knew where Jimmy's was. Partly because it had moved a couple of times from when it first opened in 1948, also because its subterranean setting meant all you saw from street level was a small sign and a doorway down, but mostly because nobody ever went to Jimmy's sober. Trying to find it would require a drunken hunt round the streets until you literally fell upon it. It was one of those much-loved Soho institutions, like Jeffrey Bernard, which is forever associated with excessive alcohol. But I can confirm that my research has revealed that it was actually next door to the Bar Italia on Frith Street, and when you stumbled down those steps you entered a time-travelling troglodyte taverna.

Stuck firmly in the grim austerity of post-war London, the thick white undulating walls were grimy and grey with age. There were a few decades-old tourist postcards pinned up for decoration and a bizarre Hellenic mural clearly painted by one of the waiters, who were now so old they could barely navigate round the fusty smelling warren of little cave-like rooms. Jimmy, a rotund man, sat in the corner smoking a cheroot and sipping something potent, while his wife or possibly even his mother, a truly ancient crone, perched permanently on the till silently glaring.

The food was also deeply grey, though filling and fabulously cheap, but the place was burdened with bizarre stipulations. The meze could only be ordered by groups of four, and for some reasons chips had to be served with every meal. It was questioning these arcane rules which would prompt heated rows with the staff who would come close to the plate smashing Greek eateries are famous for. Wrong dishes would be delivered, trays dropped, wine spilt, curses exchanged. It was great.

There was sometimes a musician propped up on a stool in the corner playing mournful rembetika, and as the night wore on he would slide into drunken oblivion like everybody else and sometimes literally slide off his stool. Losing Jimmy's along with the loss of the Pollo (catchphrase, 'You ordering food or mucking about?'), the Stockpot where I first had spag bol not from a tin and the Café Espana, which served nothing Spanish whatsoever, all on Old Compton Street, really did mark the end of an era of dirty, dirt cheap, charismatic old Soho institutions. But perhaps Jimmy's hasn't really closed, maybe it's in a basement somewhere and we just can't find it.

Greek Cypriot food was the mainstay of both the West End and

Camden Town back in the 1970s. The community had settled along-side their Irish neighbours (who opened pubs not restaurants) in the southern end of Camden, so Mornington Crescent and Fitzrovia were awash with Domestica, which tasted like Domestos, and littered with the shards of intentionally cracked crockery. There was the famous late night carouser's kebab house Dionysus on Tottenham Court Road with the bouncers on the door and the eternal flame outside, until it burned down.

There were half-a-dozen 'bubbles' on Charlotte Street alone, almost the only places in all London where you could eat lunch outside on a sunny day, pretending you were still on holiday. Names like Anemos, Aphrodite and Athena, Zorba's and Hercules, and the supposedly upmarket but impossibly crusty White Tower, all serving identikit dolmades and rubbery rings of calamari. But it was only at Anemos where the head waiter doubled as a table magician, whose top trick involved magically removing the bras of female diners before dancing on their dinners. It was the 1970s.

So we weren't very good at sophistication either. The most elevated dining experience in all London had been just around the corner from the Charlotte Street Greeks, atop the Post Office Tower. The famous revolving restaurant on the thirty-fourth floor was spoken of in whis-pered, reverential tones in our family, so unbelievably posh was it. Dinner-jacketed diners and their taffeta-encased consorts choosing from French menus and sipping French brandies as the city whirled away romantically beneath them.

Of course we had never actually been to eat there, despite the fact that my dad had worked on the iconic building shortly before his death. But such was the potency of this undeniably phallic symbol that we always spoke about going to dine there one day. Then one day we were robbed of even the remote possibility of sampling such sophisticated delights. I remember them saying on the news that 'The Kilburn Battalion' of the IRA had blown it up in late 1971 and we were genu-inely sad to lose such a beacon of elegance. (It now seems more likely to have been the anarchist Angry Brigade who placed the explosive device in the men's loos as an overt act of class war.)

But actually I did eat up there, though only a sandwich from Pret. I spent three hours presenting a live show from the revolving room, so I can attest that the view is spectacular. I would go as far as to say that despite the proliferation of viewing towers and sky diners, it is still by far the best vantage point in town, an incredible panorama. But I certainly didn't feel like boeuf bourguignon and a bottle of claret after going round and round and round or else I might also have deposited something nasty in the toilets.

And when I discovered who ran this most exalted dining experience back in its supposedly glamorous heyday that also put me off my food. Because the Top of the Tower restaurant, the apogee of swinging '60s élan, was actually a branch of Butlins. It was opened by Billy Butlin himself, accompanied by Tony Benn no less, and the happy campers (or maybe it was 'delirious diners') were given a tacky 'certificate of orbit' to prove they had eaten there. Hi de Hi.

Pizza was the next major high-street sensation to broaden our collective palette, and I was amazed one afternoon when my mum came home and pronounced that she had been to a restaurant in Edgware with the girls from work to try this Italian delicacy. I was rather relieved when she pronounced it Pizzer, to rhyme with whizzer, and also pleased when she said, 'That pizzer, it's just cheese on toast.' Mum wasn't yet ready for her own culinary Damascene conversion, though it would come, and besides, she had a point. I've always preferred her Welsh rarebit.

My own first taste of Italian cheese on toast was from Pizzaland on Tottenham Court Road. (Owned by Associated Newspapers and United Biscuits of course.) It was somewhere up at the northern end, near the lap-dancing club where I first mourned my mother's imminent death. I do remember it had a texture close to cardboard, but also that it was called a Pizza Platter and came served with coleslaw and a baked potato. Quite how many Neopolitans have ever tried pizza and jacket spud I do not know, but I wouldn't really recommend it.

Soon though there were numerous variants on the pizza theme including a horrendous, though strangely popular, place called the Chicago Pizza Pie Factory off Hanover Square, which sold some bizarre American pizza pie so thick and gloopy it was basically a quiche. But still there were queues outside. In the late 1970s and early '80s there was still a long way to go on our journey to culinary cosmopolitanism, as evidenced by the fact that the next big thing to emerge was indeed a potato.

Boxer Billy Walker, the Blonde Bomber from West Ham, had the first chain of London-based spud emporiums under the name Billy's Baked Potato. (I always thought they should have served a side of cauliflower ear.) But it was the launch of the horribly monikered Spudulike that elevated the humble potato to a brand name and surely constituted a nadir in our collective taste. My mum seemed genuinely pleased that an indigenous dish was fighting back when one opened in Burnt Oak, but even then it seemed to me to be a sorry indictment. It was like something from the end game of the Soviet Union to fetishise a baked potato, made even more tragically mundane by the fact that Spudulike was actually owned by the British School of Motoring. As a city we valued food so little that we were fed by a company of driving instructors.

Food and the infernal combustion engine can go together, as evidenced by the fact that there was actually a Formula One-themed restaurant in London briefly in the 1980s. All roaring engine noises, chequered flags, podium girls and overcooked burgers. I hate car racing, and I soon learned I'm not too fond of themed restaurants either.

This was the age of the 'concept' and just about every idea, except serving good food in a convivial environment, was tried. A few still exist: the Rainforest Café is a sweaty concoction of jungle noises, waterfalls and fake wildlife (eerie echoes of the Primatarium there) which is part of the terminally tacky experience that is the Trocadero in Piccadilly. Planet Hollywood is still flogging the notion that we want photos of lardy old American film stars with facelifts served up with our dinner (more burgers). But these places are aimed at desperate out-of-town families with easily impressed children. Back in the 1980s it was universally assumed that grown-up Londoners also needed such frippery to be enticed into an eatery.

So we had Magic Moments, a basement place in Mayfair entered via a 'secret doorway' accessed by pulling a book from a 'library' to reveal a room where table magicians would thrill you with close up prestidigitation while you ate burgers. There was Old Kentucky, where you would be served by riverboat gamblers and cathouse kittens in low-cut tops, and be regaled by live barbershop quartets warbling far too close to your ears while you ate more burgers.

Most of these places were direct American imports, which shows how London was still in thrall at this point to all things Stateside. There were though some spectacularly naff and profoundly embarrassing home-grown concepts, featuring beer and wenches, or in one case mead and wenches. It was 'Carry On Up the Restaurant Trade'.

The Tudor Rooms was a large space on St Martin's Lane where failing thespians, including the ultimate brassy blonde Diana Dors, tragically eking out a living towards the end of her life, entertained stag parties and bewildered tourists to a Henry VIII-themed evening of overcooked beef, rotten table manners and bawdy serving girls flashing their cleavages.

School Dinners was in High Holborn and very much aimed at exploiting the juvenile fantasies of the City boys and ill-suited businessmen of that barrio. Young girls in revealing St Trinian's-style outfits were encouraged to flirt and tease the punters, goading them on, then caning them while everybody cheered and flung about their shepherd's pie. A friend of mine, known as Dangerous Jane, worked there for a while and actually enjoyed thrashing those tossers. It certainly hurt them more than it did her, especially when they gave her big tips for an extra swish. But they loved it and more branches opened across town.

Some of those sexually starved City boys would also have gone to Casper's Telephone Exchange, another burger joint in Mayfair, whose

USP was the fact that they had telephones. Big clunky old white plastic jobs on every table, so that you could call up the attractive occupants of table ten and flirt or joke, or whatever might hopefully lead to a leg over at the end of the night.

Next door to the London Palladium on Argyll Street was a place called the Video Café, where the cutting-edge technology was such that they could show these exciting new things called pop videos while you ate. What's more, they had cameras present, which honed in on the punters and actually projected them on to the big screens so that you could watch yourself eat, a horrible foretaste of people taking selfies in every restaurant in town.

Apart from one night watching Kate Bush warble at the Video Café, I can honestly say that I never tried any of these places, though I am extremely partial to a shepherd's pie. Food in the early '80s was still a low priority on a night out, but I had already developed my Londoner's collection of cheap, ethnic staples to keep me fed. I had my Indian, my Chinese, my kebab and I had also become fond of a Malaysian place in deep Soho called Rasa Sayang on Windmill Street, which sat below a brothel, next to a junior school and opposite the last surviving Soho nosh bar with pictures of boxers on the walls. Perfect setting.

But if I had to choose food, or drink and fun, it was bring on oblivion every time. For a while it was all about cocktails, as day-glo coloured concoctions complete with swizzle sticks, umbrellas and preposterous names, 'a long slow comfortable screw up against the wall', were all the rage. Hairdressers loved cocktails and everybody loves hairdressers.

Peppermint Park in St Martin's Lane, Zanzibar in Great Queen Street, that place above Widow Applebaum's, opposite Browns in South Molton Street. West End cocktail bars in the early '80s were where the fashion crowd and the wide boys entwined. Minor villains from Bermondsey and street traders from the Angel, in baggy Woodhouse whistles, flirting with the girls who worked at Sassoon's or Fiorucci over a mai tai and a Luther Vandross tune.

Rumours, just up from the Lyceum in Covent Garden, was the epicentre of the London cocktail scene. Always busy with a smattering of lithe local ballet dancers, the elegant black kids who hung out at the Pineapple studio, the coolest bouncers and club runners, the staff from Paul Smith and even the occasional famous thespian, sipping a tequila sunrise and discretely scoring some charlie before dining round the corner at Joe Allen's or Orso. Throw in a couple of old bill from Bow Street for good measure and you had the perfect London cocktail set. The measures at Rumours were really good.

The problem was I suffer from a pusillanimous constitution and simply could not stomach cocktails. Especially on an empty stomach, and I could rarely afford both food and a night of Long Island iced teas. Rumours was great fun; sexy, noisy, throbbing with desire, and with none of the oh-so-serious mixologist bollocks that obfuscates cocktails today. But after a night of gulping gloop and trying to impress a stylist from Streatham, I usually ended up throwing up over my Comme jacket and probably sitting alone in a doorway somewhere near the Strand. I was rather glad when the Soho Brasserie opened, and we suddenly went sophisticated. Cocktails became passé, and I could finally drink fizzy water.

I honestly believe that the opening of the Soho Brasserie in late 1983 was the pivotal moment in London's dining story. Not because the food was especially good, although the calves' liver and bacon was lovely, much better than my mum's. It was sensational because they had those chunky tumblers for your Badoit or beer, because they had green opalescent tiles on the walls, and the zinc-topped mahogany bar at the front where you could see everyone and everyone could see you. It was a roaring success because they had good-looking young waiters of both sexes wearing white shirts and black aprons, because they had citron pressé and jazz and Nick Logan, the editor of *The Face*, having lunch with Julie Burchill in the back.

The Soho Brasserie changed everything because they had that bustling, yet cool, easy-going vibe we'd all enjoyed in Paris or Barcelona, but thought was impossible to replicate in stuffy old London town. Until they did just that on Old Compton Street, next door to a peep show, which smelled of spunk and disinfectant. Suddenly London did dining out.

You should always be careful, of course, what you wish for. With hindsight this was the first sighting of the kind of gentrification that has transformed Soho from the sleazy, shady tenderloin we all loved so dearly to the slick urban showroom it is today. Though it was more accurately described as trendification; not too many members of the gentry were involved. The Soho Bras became the epicentre of a whirling emerging medialand, full of thrusting young turks with flat cockney vowels, big hair and even bigger padded shoulders, angling for advances on record, film or book deals, before going to have sex or drugs or ideally both in the toilets at the Groucho Club, which opened round the corner a few months later.

The Soho Brasserie was zeitgeist in a bottle, with a wedge of lime in the neck. There was the 'spend it like money' conspicuous consumption of Thatcher's now roaring free market wonderland. There was the laid back, al fresco, *Le Monde*, El Tel, watch the world go by, would-be continentalism of a European street café. There was also a newfound, about time, terribly un-English egalitarianism.

The Soho Brasserie and the legion of similar joints that soon joined it were not stuffy-old-bloke, old-school-tie affairs. This was not Simpson's in the Strand, but a young, anything-goes-as-long-as-it's-hip hangout. Gay, straight, black, white, male, female, didn't matter as long as you looked decorous draped over a double macchiato. Nobody was going to test you on which fork to use, but they might just use you in their latest pop video. This was a fulcrum of urban theatre with crème brûlée.

If you wanted cutting-edge cooking you went round the corner to Alistair Little's appropriately mini, minimalist place or the revamped, rag-rolled eau de nil coloured L'Escargot for a spot of nouvelle cuisine. But if you wanted to feel you were at the centre of the universe, you pulled on your Gaultier and ate goats' cheese at the Soho Brasserie. Nothing in this city would ever be the same again.

The Soho Brasserie is long gone and also largely forgotten, but it opened the dam. Corbin and King were simultaneously doing what they still do so brilliantly over at Le Caprice, and later the Ivy. Terence Conran joined in by reviving Quaglinos, a restaurant Bryan Ferry had sung about in 'Do the Strand', and everybody nicked the ashtrays. The Criterion Brasserie, one of London's most glitteringly opulent rooms, was literally rediscovered hidden underneath a layer of '50s Formica, and briefly became the place to nibble on cornichons and pretend to read La Gazetta dello Sport.

Later still, urban archaeology uncovered the giant art deco gem that became Oliver Peyton's roaring Atlantic Bar & Grill in the basement of the Regent Palace Hotel, which had recently been a knocking shop with rooms to rent by the hour. Going to a good-looking restaurant with good-looking people suddenly became the thing to do, the places to see and be seen. We'd gone continental. But we were also turning Japanese.

It was in a Japanese restaurant on the corner of Endell Street in Covent Garden, one of the earliest I remember appearing in London, that I had my Joe Gargery moment. By now I was doing all right, making a few bob, living in a flat in Bloomsbury and pretending I'd had a sophisticated palette all along. I even started drinking wine. (I haven't yet stopped.)

I decided that my mum should be introduced to the delights of fine dining. So I took her first to L'Etoile in Charlotte Street, a real old-school institution which still had the legendary Elena taking care of hospitality, and after a few nervous moments fussing over the cutlery Mum began to enjoy the attentive service and the starched white tablecloths and the fact that they took her coat and called her Madame and gave her beer. She even liked the food although was quietly insistent that the vegetables were undercooked. It was taking her to a Japanese which turned me into Pip.

Quite why I thought raw fish and steaming sake might be a good idea I'm not sure. Though I suspect to my shame that I was simply trying to show off my newfound sophistication and cosmopolitanism to the woman I wanted to impress the most. Japanese food was still very formal, exotic and extremely expensive, and I was displaying the fact that I'd come a long way from Burnt Oak and the Beta Café, and so had London.

I dearly wanted my dear old mum to be impressed by how far we'd all travelled. In retrospect I'm not sure she had ever quite forgiven the Japanese for what they did in the war, so she was a little on edge, thrown further by the bowing waitresses and the shaven-headed chef with the razor sharp sushi knife. When she nearly retched at her first taste of hot rice wine I realised I had probably pushed too far, too fast in my quest to broaden her tastes.

My mum would never dream of doing anything to cause a stir or a scene, but even surreptitiously spitting out sashimi because they haven't cooked it is not technically considered good manners in Japan. Then when they brought a bowl of rice she turned to me and said 'Robert where's the sugar?' She had only ever eaten rice pudding and honestly thought that these sneaky orientals were trying to rush us out by bringing the dessert at the same time as the uncooked main course. I realise now that it was my showing off which made for a rather uneasy meal, and that my embarrassment was gauche in itself. But I was glad the chip shop over the road was still open, and I could actually feed her something she liked. She definitely preferred her fish fried.

We never ate a Japanese meal together again. But when I got married to my Mancunian Manchurian wife, we took to taking Mum out with us on Sundays for dim sum. We wanted our kids to see people who looked like them and know a bit about Chinese culture, which in large part means Chinese food. So we went every other weekend for the traditional feast of tiny steamed or fried morsels that are dim sum, plus big plates of dead birds and bits of pigs – and Grandma came with us.

After a slightly wary start she became an absolute enthusiast for cha siu bao and ha gao, roast duck and even steamed rice. The sweet, earthy, salty flavours of Cantonese cooking appealed to her, but so did the noisy, steamy atmosphere of big bustling Chinese restaurants. She loved the fact that families gathered en masse, generations sharing food and love, the elders sitting at the head of the table, kids running around, babies on laps, her own grandchildren arrayed around her.

Wielding chopsticks like a Hong Kong maven, she became a real fixture at the Oriental Plaza, a massive pan-Asian centre that opened on the Edgware Road, really close to her house. She loved the fact that they knew her name as she walked in. She also loved trips to Chinatown followed by a beer or two on the sofa in the Groucho Club, where they always made a fuss of her. She'd come a long way too. This wasn't her London but she loved it.

Just how far we'd all journeyed, both in terms of food and also food as a metaphor for life in London, was displayed when I unexpectedly popped by her house one Friday afternoon. This was the same house I had grown up in, devoured benders and drunk Brussels sprouts and Cresta in, but it had changed. She lived directly opposite a junior school, and in her later years took to looking after kids after school had finished – a bit of child minding for which she charged something like a pound an hour, and probably didn't even take that. She just loved having young children around. This particular afternoon she had dozens of young children around because it was a birthday party for one of her charges, so noisy chaos prevailed.

It was like a council estate version of a Benetton advert, with kids of every conceivable colour and a smattering of their mothers helping out. They had obviously brought food, because our little kitchen table was laden with offerings; there were heaps of Malaysian noodles, samosas and pakora, fragrant Middle Eastern pilaufs, chicken legs in a Caribbean style and a variety of dips and sweets. As I walked in the room my mum was standing next to a Somali woman in traditional garb, with hennaed hands. They were nattering together and my mum had some sort of unleavened bread in her hand with a big dollop of hummus about to enter her mouth, which was beaming a massive smile.

'Help yourself to some food Robert,' she said, gesturing to the United Nations feast in front of us. 'The girls have put on a lovely spread.'

Every Day I Take Coffee
with the Portuguesers

*The finest little corner shop in Camden Town is run by a pair of charming
brothers from the banks of the Douro. One reserved, slightly serious and
kind, the other much more garrulous, jocular, prone to air guitar: both of
them call me Mr Roberto. I talk to them in Spanish, which is clearly silly
but it allows me to practise my second language; and they are Iberian after
all, so they indulge me. Especially as I am often the first person in the shop
at 8 a.m. looking for my breakfast shot.*

*We talk football, music, wine, have a good old gossip about local affairs,
or just lark about. They make good and remarkably good value sandwiches
on terrific, rustic Portuguese bread and get through vast piles of those fabulous pasteis de nata, the flaky custard tarts, which have become part of the
London diet. But they are not monocultural; they stock other non-Portuguese
urban essentials like baklava, samosas and hummus.*

*It's the sort of jumbled, overstocked shop where you can get just about
anything you need, and somehow the staff know where everything is. The
Fereira delicatessen, for that's what it's called, is open every day, starting
early, closing late. You can even sit outside, and people do; tourists on the
way to Regent's Park, regulars who take a cup of something and a cake at
the same time every day.*

*The coffee, made in a big old espresso machine, is served just as I like
it: short, dark, sweet, cut with just a little hot but not frothy milk. In Spanish
it's called a cortado, so that's what I ask for. My daily cortado, usually
taken while chatting away, is one pound, it's always been one pound and I
hope it will always be one pound. This is definitely not a chain.*

*While I'm standing sipping from my polystyrene cup, families come in
and pick up their vital supplies of bacalhau, that dried salt cod which looks*

skeletal, tastes fecal and no one but the Portuguese can stomach. Along with their smelly fish, they stock up on fresh figs, a baffling variety of tinned sardines, vinho verde wine, boxes of Omo and magazines devoted to the torrid love lives of Brazilian telenovela stars and pictures of Cristiano Ronaldo.

On a Friday afternoon, the occasional bottle of Sagres changes hands, tuna patties are eaten out of serviettes; it's something of a focal point for a community, which is otherwise largely invisible. If it wasn't for the fact that they talk their strangely sibilant tongue I would never have known there were so many Portuguese people nearby.

But the brothers don't just cater to their quiet, unassuming country folk. The Eastern European builders queue up to get those sarnies, often eating two at a time. Cab drivers from far and wide drop in to get some nutrients. Coppers, road-sweepers and school kids all in their respective uniforms *wander in and out. The local elders, Irish and Greek Cypriot mainly, often nip in for a natter and maybe even a nata too: it's where the street meets. You can get an onion or a bottle of bleach; you can run a tab and enter a raffle at Christmas, which I won one year. I gave them back the bacalhau.*

Places like the Fereira are what put paid to the lie that London is somehow cold, anonymous, unfeeling. I don't know most of my neighbours by more than a nod, which is just fine, prying eyes and knowing glances have no place in my town. Others, a few, are firm friends, but we all know that the corner shop is collective territory. If you do want to feel part of something larger, dare I say a community, then nip over for a cake and you may see Suggs or the shabby Indian bloke who lives down the street, drinks far too much rum, loves Cliff Richard and quotes the Bhagavad Gita. If I ever move, I would dearly miss that shop.

I was in there for my coffee on the morning of 8 July 2005, when the English newspapers on the stand in the corner were obviously full of the barbarous, murderous events of the day before. I was speaking English on this occasion. It definitely wasn't a day for jocularity, and I commented on the bloody outrage, which had been visited on the Tubes and buses just a stone's throw away; the pitiless, pointless placing of bombs to kill randomly in the name of somebody's God.

'What a truly terrible crime,' I said, quietly, as much to myself as my Portuguese friend behind the counter. I wasn't really expecting a reply, but I certainly got one. He too spoke English, his heavily accented voice, quavering with a mix of indignation and pride, 'Yes Mr Roberto, it is a terrible thing: but you know us Londoners, we do not give in.'

In that moment, I was so proud of us Londoners.

CHAPTER FIVE

Kicking Off

It was already smouldering on the Sunday. Reports filtering through of trouble up Tottenham way, something about a rude boy getting gunned down by the police, stuff on the news, stuff in the air, making it thick, harder to breathe. My boy, Alfie, much closer to the streets than me, reported back that the gutters were filling up with bile; it was getting slippery out there. I told him to be watchful, but didn't think much of it, pulled on a whistle – linen, because it was hot – and headed into town.

I was meeting up on the Monday night with one of my musical muckers, Robert Ryan. He's a thriller writer – which, given what came next, is pretty apt – and is one of the few people who shares my taste for difficult atonal jazz of the kind my wife dubs 'nervous breakdown music'. Which is exactly what we were going to Soho to see: a very nervous breakdown indeed.

We rendezvoused in Bar Italia and I remember glancing up at the big TV in the back, where they normally show Serie A games. But they had rolling news on, and it was definitely rocking and rolling, kicking off, scenes of rebel youth, hoods up, trainers rampant, glass smashing – Croydon or somewhere, still a long way away, another world. We wandered over the road to Ronnie's for some spirituals. It was Matthew Halsall, a laid back Manc trumpeter with a lovely tone, and his fluid, fiery sax man Nat Birchall, blowing a tribute to the Coltranes. They even had a harp player for 'Journey Into Satchidananda', right up my ashram. Then the lights went out.

I loved power cuts back in the '70s, everybody did: the old 'uns got all misty eyed about blackouts in the war and us youngsters thrilled to the shadowy potential for mischief. And as Ronnie Scott's was slammed into pitch black, an air of communal nostalgia, with just a mere hint of menace, descended upon the place. Apparently this was a localised shutdown of all electricity, just in a few Soho streets, but it took out theatres, restaurants, bars and our famous music venue. So candles were lit and the band played acoustically, and we all listened intently, which, given the intensity of the music, made it even more potent. A great set, but walking out into the heavy, lightless West End air afterwards, a truly eerie atmosphere had descended upon the darkened, made-medieval streets. Agitated and edgy, people talked quietly, conspiratorially, whispers about sedition, fears of a contagion and a conflagration engulfing the town.

You could literally feel it in the air, as if the encroaching flames had made the summer evening hotter still, scorching the darkness, burning off the oxygen. Perhaps the power cut was part of some larger, even scarier series of events controlled by the rioters or maybe the state, shutting down, closing in. Rumours were flying; some said a column of the sans-culottes intent upon blood were heading towards us, marching down the Tottenham Court Road to sack Soho in the murk. Others said police marksmen had gathered atop Centre Point, and maybe they had. In its original '60s incarnation, the top floor of London's then tallest building was designated for use by the security services, the best vantage point in town. A helicopter appeared overhead, its deafening rotors blowing blasts of paranoia downwards into the W1 darkness.

I remember saying to Rob that it felt like something cataclysmic was occurring, so we headed a few streets north and dodged into a pub, which had electricity and a TV. There on the screen we saw our city aflame, rioters amok. The Clash came to mind, the song, which always started the set way back when, Joe Strummer taut and sprung, fists clenched, shouting out the title before a burst of drums . . . LONDON'S BURNING! So it was happening again.

Rob and I split, wishing each other well, a safe journey. I jumped on a bus headed north, a Number 29 or 24, saw some windows gone just past Euston. A few straggling youths with strides around their arses, looking forlornly for more; more trouble, more trainers. Then we got to Camden Town, my town, and I jumped off by Sports Direct to see, in the distance, a small bunch of boys with armfuls of booty, smiling maniacally, shouting gleefully. It felt like a rather jolly mass hysteria, a *Beano* for the bad.

But in NW1 we were lucky, relatively unscathed, minor skirmish. I got home to hear terrible tales of Hackney and Walthamstow, Peckham and Croydon, Ealing, Woolwich . . . out of order, out of control, in flames. Another song from even further back leaped into my head, a reggae tune from Skinhead days, 'Dem a loot, dem a shoot, dem a wail, a shanty town . . . all the rude boy bomb up the town.'

The London mob was back: the unseen, unled militia living always in our midst, in our margins, the spectre in the shanty. This is our resident poltergeist, a force, which springs forth whenever chaos is summoned, and once again they had claimed the city for themselves. The lords and ladies of misrule had risen from the cracks and the dreary, broken places and were on a spree. A wanton revelry that ran for days and spread to towns and cities across the land. War in a Babylon, burning and a looting, dem bring sorrow, tears and blood.

They have a history; we have a history. Spa Fields, Grosvenor Square and Red Lion Square, the Gordon riots, the Poll Tax riots, Broadwater Farm and Brixton, Notting Hill and Southall, Lewisham, the Battle of Cable Street, the Battle of Waterloo station, the Brown Dog affair, Grunwicks, the Angry Brigade, the IRA and the SPG, Headhunters and Bushwhackers, NF and BNP, Red Action, Blackshirts, black bloc.

Despite the usually accurate image of ours as a civilised city, level-headed, calm, there has always been a backbeat of turmoil and tribulation; an unseen undercurrent of aggro and strife, trouble on the streets. This was trouble aplenty. Lashing out and cashing in, a convulsion of consumerist chaos, but were the mob ripping it up for good or bad, rioting for right or wrong?

Certainly there was a cause, the death of Mark Duggan under police fire, a fatal pool of young London blood in a car. Yet another black man gone, another young life lost, too many, too much. Black lives matter, poor lives matter. Questions need to be asked and answered. But some of the youth on the streets smashing windows and grabbing armfuls weren't challenging authority, they were accruing booty. It felt disconnected, disrespectful to the events up in Tottenham. For the first time in my life I did not know whose side I was on, where my sympathies lay, and it vexed me. Mine is a tribal town, red or blue, left or right, North or South, Irons or Lions, us or them. 'You've gotta decide which side you're on.' And I didn't know.

I've always considered it lily livered to sit on any fence whatsoever. I cannot watch a sporting event, an election or a war, no matter how distant, without having a team to root for. This need to select my side and stick by them has meant cheering on Benfica against Man United in 1966 and the Russian Basketball team against the USA in 1972. The MPLA, the ANC, and the YPG/YPJ. I support the Cubans at baseball, boxing and embargoes, the Druze Militia in Lebanon (Oh Walid Jumblatt), Euskaltel–Euskadi in cycling and the West Indies in cricket.

I was there at Lord's in '76, sitting by the boundary rope whooping when that Boer and bore Tony Greig said he'd make the great Windies grovel. I turned out for the Grunwicks workers, the striking miners, the Fleet Street printers and backed a whole series of rather dodgy 1970s liberation movements and eternally useless sports teams. But I could not work out whether this nameless, shapeless, shameless mob causing mayhem on our streets on a steamy night in 2011 were on the right side of history.

I wondered if I was now too bourgeois a burgher, too invested in the status quo to feel their pain, understand their anger or even their joy. I could not see their point, didn't even know if they had one. And maybe I was, maybe I am. For all the lefty ideology of my background and my youth, I am now a property-owning, profoundly middle-class, middle-aged Londoner who prefers his high street not in flames thank you.

But despite that, I knew those ragged-arsed rioters embodied a forgotten, or rather conveniently overlooked London, ignored as much as ignoble. We know they are there, but we avert our gaze, we float past without wishing to see, put combustible cladding over the stained and cracked concrete. Perhaps the point is this: the London mob, an apparition made manifest whenever the city boils, are what we are.

During the civil war, the mob were the London apprentice boys, cropped-haired round heads flocking to the Parliamentarian cause. In the Gordon riots they were rabid anti-Catholic bigots. In Notting Hill in 1958 they were racist Teddy Boys; in Notting Hill in 1976 they were enraged Rastafarian rebels. In 2011 their rage was inchoate, inarticulate, indiscriminate.

The people kicking in windows and torching cars are always there, but usually a mute presence, a voiceless, aimless golem hovering in the shadows, lurking in the alleyways as you walk home. This wasn't so much about government or policing or race, it was about the mess we've made, the crap we've brushed under the carpet. We are all guilty of neglect. We have turned a blind eye, given a cold shoulder, allowed things to fester, to ferment and stink. Store up flammable materials in unsuitable conditions, then neglect them and eventually they will burst into flames.

These herberts, nicking high-street crap and burning down furniture shops, were us. Our crassly materialistic, de-politicised, de-moralised (literally stripped of its core morality) and horribly divided society in the flesh, in our faces. Sometimes looking in the mirror is not particularly pleasant. As befitting an urban beast, this rampaging gang were not so much a force of nature as nurture, they are what we have created. Every age gets the mob it deserves.

Our rampaging twenty-first century London rabble was not heroic or even artfully nihilistic, they have been stripped of all dignity as their culture has been shredded, their history denied, their collective values undermined by crushing materialism and crude individualism. This was not Railton Road in 1981, when the righteous flames licked the racist Babylon. They were not Ho Ho Ho Chi Minh chanters, or staunch Cable Streeters, ensuring they did not pass. Not all the people on the streets on those nights were vicious and vacuous. Some were genuinely enraged by racist policing, but many more were just enjoying the headless adrenaline rush of a city turned temporarily on its head. It's fun to be bad.

The potential for badness and abandon has been severely curtailed in our video-surveyed, closely monitored, hard-working, censorious, controlled, well-behaved city. So steam builds up. The London of my youth was a much more unruly, much more raucous place, regularly bubbling over, but rarely in so cataclysmic a fashion. These rioting twenty-first century youths, in all their ugly emptiness, were a potent and timely reminder of two things. If you ignore something for long enough, it doesn't go away it just gets worse. Oh, and London loves a row.

Trafalgar Square is simultaneously the very centre of our London universe and a profoundly foreign land. In its every day, the vast, soulless expanse is exclusively for tourists to loiter and litter, but we collectively reclaim the Square in moments of extremis; joy and cele-bration or trial and tribulation. My mum and dad were there on V.E. Day, the most gloriously righteous knees up this city has ever seen. I was there demonstrating against the Poll Tax, the most terrifyingly violent protest I have ever seen. I spent a few dreary, but satisfyingly self-righteous afternoons in Horatio's shadow in my student days, pick-eting the apartheid South African Embassy. I was also there on Wednesday 6 July 2005, when I accidently became the first person in Britain to learn that London had won the Olympics. I was broadcasting for the BBC and the radio feed from the IOC meeting in Singapore, announcing whether London or Paris had got the vote, reached my headphones a fraction of a second before it reached the giant TV screen.

However, I was definitely nowhere near Trafalgar Square in 1907, for what was perhaps the most surreal riot this city has ever witnessed.

To tell this story, we first need to go on a detour to Battersea Park, where, almost hidden away among the rhododendrons, you'll see the second-most-intriguing canine memorial in all London. It is actually a risibly twee casting of a cutesy little terrier on a plinth, but the story told in its inscription is fascinating. This is the tale of 'The Brown Dog Affair'. It's a saga of blood on the streets and on our collective conscience: vivisection, suffragettes, medical students, class warriors, toffs with dogs on sticks, and a communist council estate.

The original statue of a brown dog, a much grander, more ornate and upstanding affair was commissioned by anti-vivisection campaigners and paid for by public subscription in 1906. It was the likeness of a poor hound who had been used for grizzly experiments by student doctors at UCL, and who became the subject of a court case and a cause célèbre. It was a truly contentious issue, which enflamed passions on both sides, and caused much debate in the press. Because it was so controversial, no council would agree to have the statue on their turf until Battersea said they would take it. That's how the bronze mutt ended up on the newly built Latchmere Estate, suitably close to the dogs' home.

Currently the focus of the most febrile outbreak of luxury apartment mania in the entire city, Battersea back then was very different. Often dubbed the smelliest spot in London because of so many pungent factories, it was described as 'full of belching smoke and slums'. It was also a notorious hotbed of radicalism. At various times Battersea boasted London's only communist MP and its first black socialist mayor. So these rampant South London lefties agreed to give a home to the statue, which included a seven-foot plinth, a drinking trough for thirsty pooches and a vehemently anti-animal-experimentation inscription. George Bernard Shaw even spoke at the unveiling. Little did they know the trouble that would ensue.

Medical students, exclusively the male scions of upper-class families, objected to a monument which seemed to impugn their profession and so decided to go and smash it up. The Battersea council estate dwellers were having none of it. Nobody was going to bash their statue, so they gathered to defend it and a rather lively bit of class war heave-ho ensued. This went on for weeks, becoming more and more vitriolic and ended up with a permanent twenty-four-hour police guard around the brown dog and countless injuries and arrests.

The would-be surgeons were not giving up though, and on 10 December 1907 roughly one thousand of them marched along the Strand, some of them wearing white coats and surgical masks, some of them carrying canine effigies and even stuffed pooches on sticks, until they got to Trafalgar Square. There they ran into an equally large group of suffragettes and trades unionists, who sided with the statue, objected to the doctors and all hell broke loose. The image of purple-clad women and militant working men in flat caps going toe to toe with junior medics armed with taxidermy is intrinsically funny in a Mary Poppins kind of way, but this was a serious affray. Around four hundred police were needed to help quell the trouble and plenty ended up in local hospitals being treated by presumably fully qualified doctors.

Meanwhile Battersea Council had a change in political control. The Tories were now in charge and one night, without any consultation, the brown dog suddenly disappeared. Rumours suggest that it had been unceremoniously dumped in the nearby Thames, never to be seen again. No remaining reminder of one of London's most surreal violent convulsions survived, but the story never entirely went away. In 1985 the Anti-Vivisection Society commissioned the new pooch, who sits now, not in the old council estate, which is still there, but in the nearest park. Shame it's such a ropey statue.

While we're doing dogs and statuary, will you allow me a little diversion into an alternative, and completely unreliable version of the tale of the most celebrated London canine of the twentieth century and his part in the story of the stolen statuette? Pickles was the pooch who famously found the World Cup. He discovered the Jules Rimet trophy, wrapped up in newspaper and hidden under a hedge in Norwood in 1966. The elegant golden winged figurine had been nicked from a stamp fair just a couple of months before we were due to stage the tournament. The most famous trophy in the world, the one destined to be held aloft in Bobby Moore's hand after the game against Germany at Wembley (or was it?), had been put on display on a Stanley Gibbons stall at a philatelist event in Westminster Central Hall. It was guarded by a single seventy-four-year-old bloke with a weak bladder who required frequent comfort visits. While he was relieving himself, somebody simply pinched it from the open display case and had it on their toes.

For over a week the mysterious case of the missing World Cup kept the nation enthralled and appalled. Until it finally turned up under the aforementioned South London privet. And that was also because of a pee stop. Pickles, a black-and-white mixed breed collie, sniffed it out while on his morning ablution walk, saved the blushes of the nation and became a star. Fêted, photographed, featured in films and even on *Blue Peter*, the name of Pickles still resonates. He is buried in a South London back garden, a canine superstar. But I was told a slightly different version of events.

I had reason to get to know a chap who dealt in tickets. I've always (with a whole suitcase full of caveats) rather enjoyed the company of London's 'entertainment brokers' as they now dub themselves. A funnier, broader bunch of blokes it would be hard to imagine. This one was larger than life in all sorts of ways, though charming as all hell, a self-appointed heir to the notorious and portly Stan Flashman, the 1970s 'king of the ticket touts'. My fellow's family roots were in the Italian community in Clerkenwell, and the conversation one evening, oiled of course by Comos of Chianti and Apennines of pasta, got round to the World Cups (for which he could get any briefs you wanted) and the story of Pickles and the missing trophy.

Now I have no way of knowing if the story he told is true. But what is undoubtedly beyond doubt is that this fellow's father's family knew people in low places. They were privy to the whole Little Italy, Sabini shebang. What is equally true is that my man could certainly tell a tall tale or two, so everything he said to me could well be extremely fantastic. But the way he'd heard it, the trophy had indeed been lifted by an opportunist thief, a low-lying member of the mob, who had nicked it for the self-same reason dogs lick their bollocks: because he could. But then he had no idea what to do with it. Who wants to buy the World Cup? (Don't mention Qatar or Russia.)

Obviously the heat was on the Met to find this thing, but it was also a little embarrassing for the firm, positively unpatriotic. So phone calls were made and a deal was struck. The World Cup would be handed back, but to avoid embarrassment all round it would be done in such a way that everybody involved could keep well clear of the transaction. Like perhaps sticking it under a hedge in some distant bit of South London, a long way from EC1, where it could be fortuitously found, perhaps by a hound.

This (shaggy dog) story doesn't end there, though. There have long been rumours that the trophy, so famously held aloft by our captain at the end of the game, might not have been the real thing. When the World Cup went walkabout, the FA, against the strict instructions of FIFA, had purportedly made a copy just in case it never came back. Spooked as they were by having lost the thing once, it was the replica that was given to Mr Moore to celebrate with. Which might not have been such a bad thing. As folklore also has it that it was left that night in the house of a bloke in Leytonstone, where Jackie Charlton had ended up kipping on a stranger's sofa, paralytic drunk. The real Jules Rimet was finally given in perpetuity to Brazil when they won it for the third time in 1970, only to be nicked again and melted down. Or so they say.

All right then, once more unto the breach and all that. I often find myself shaking my head when I hear it said that we live in a violent city, in violent times. No we don't. Thankfully we don't. Definitely we don't. Or rather most of us don't.

Occasionally the city explodes into wanton violence like the riots of 2011, sporadically it always has. Yet despite such spasmodic paroxysms, I would argue that – for most of its inhabitants – daily life in London has rarely, if ever, been safer. Compared to the randomly violent, tribally troubled, frequently dangerous London of my youth, this is a quiescent, rather placid era. The streets are calmer, the pubs safer, the dance halls quieter, the football terraces duller. Yet paradoxically and tragically these are the deadliest of times for some.

There are among us a group of usually young, all too often black males, afflicted by the curse of knife and even gun crime. Locked in an ever-diminishing cycle of poverty of expectation and poverty of example, and the temptations of the get-rich-quick drug trade. Trapped by a claustrophobic, postcode cage and lashing out. Robbed of positive role models and the cultural solidity of community and force fed a live-fast, die-young gangster mythology, they are all scared; they are all victims. Often the brightest and the sharpest, denied a vision of the future, the best become the worst. Again we live in parallel Londons. Streets that are secure and serene for me may be terrifying and ultimately deadly for a kid from the estate round the corner. He lives and maybe dies in his tiny, scary world.

Every time I hear of a lad stabbed in a stairwell on his estate, or fatally shanked in a shopping precinct by a gang after school, my soul seeps and weeps at the cruel stupidity of it. What a waste of precious young Londoners. What is to be done to stop such futile carnage? But the reality is if you are not in their claustrophobic and dangerous world, hemmed in by ingrained institutional racism, poverty and paranoid adolescent machismo, egged on by a braggadocio of bad-boy gangster glamour, chances are you live in the safest, most pacific London ever.

Despite the outrages, despite the knives and the guns, we live in largely peaceable times, in an unusually well-behaved and non-violent city. The statistics support this argument, but it's less about crime figures, more about a sea change in attitudes. The London I grew up in was much more casually, randomly, pointlessly prone to rucks and rumbles, punch-ups, bootings and head-butts, and it always had been.

My mum used to tell us how, when she was first married to our father, if they had no money to go out on a Saturday night, for entertainment they would sit on the window sill of their one-room flat and watch the brawls and bust-ups which routinely took place outside the Monkey House, the pub opposite in W10. The police were so used to this ritual of pissed-up blokes having mass fights in the street at closing time that they were armed with strait jackets to wrap up the combatants before they dragged them off to the cells in waiting black Marias. Just a normal night in old Notting Hill.

The Bald Faced Stag in Burnt Oak was just as spectacularly rowdy forty years later, when I was a lad, a boozer so wantonly wild it was an entertainment in itself. No band or comedian could possibly compete. It was not uncommon for the chaps of the Stag to capture the governor, lock him up in a cupboard and help themselves to the bar. Outsiders would often be welcomed by a volley of flying beer bottles, and drunken duels between regulars would regularly take place in the car park out back, chair legs at closing time. It was a perpetual mini riot. It was also great fun, but like so much fun it was dangerous, and you never quite knew when it would turn.

Growing up in London in the 1960s, '70s and '80s, we learned to navigate our way through violence from a very young age. You didn't have to go anywhere near a pub to find yourself assaulted for such everyday sins as looking at somebody in the wrong way ('You screwing me out?'), wearing the wrong pair of trousers, or the wrong colour football scarf. Sometimes even such minor provocation wasn't necessary, and you could end up in a ruckus for no discernible reason whatsoever. Trouble was part of everyday life and this city was also perpetually torn with sectarian, sporting, political, cultural and tribal strife and division, regularly brimming over into affray and physical confrontation.

For one thing, the Second World War was still rumbling on. If I want to make myself feel particularly old I remember that I was born less than fourteen years after the global conflict officially ended – sometimes it felt like it never did. The scars and wounds in the fabric of London were still raw. There were flattened bombsites all over town, colonised for car parks, markets and makeshift playgrounds, rows of prefabs where bombed-out houses had been and pot marks and surface damage on buildings everywhere. (Cleopatra's Needle still carries the scars of First World War Zeppelin raids.) People had Anderson shelters in their gardens, gas masks in their cupboards and ration books in their handbags.

Us kids made Airfix models of Spitfires and Heinkels, and staged mock battles with plastic desert rats. For 'show and tell' at school, boys and girls would bring in medals or bits of shrapnel. Army surplus stores were still flogging khaki killing kit and on Lisle Street in Soho, where the Chinese restaurants now are, there were rows of shops selling ex-military technology. Every now and then an old undiscovered bomb would be located and families evacuated. Armistice, what armistice?

There were Nazis everywhere: in the TV shows we watched, in the films we saw, particularly in the comics I read. The war was still there in the songs the older generation sang, the stories they told, and deep in the mentality of people who had not yet forgiven or forgotten. They certainly mentioned the war. My poor Uncle Ernie, who would undoubtedly now be treated for PTSD, walked round my nan's house reliving the torment of being on a torpedoed ship. Another uncle devoutly hated Japanese people after his time in a camp. Every family member had a tough tale to tell.

The ultimate violence of total war, albeit one where Londoners could be rightly proud of the part they played, was a backdrop to just about everything. This was a battle-hardened, maybe still shell-shocked city and the potentially cataclysmic shock of nuclear destruction hung over us all: duck and cover, kids, duck and cover. Armageddon time.

As small children we would walk arm in arm round the infant school playground chanting, 'Who wants to play war?', and we knew exactly which war we meant. We were nine-year-olds shouting 'schweinhund', 'hände hoch' and going on Kamikaze missions up the Edgware Road. By the time we got to junior school, the game of war had morphed into mass bundles of bruising, sometimes bleeding intensity, often followed by a set-to between two boys with everybody else standing round in a circle egging them noisily on, 'fight, fight, fight'. And if you came home with a bloody nose, your mother wanted to know why you didn't win and may well send you back out for another go.

Now can I point out here that I rarely won. Thankfully I rarely had to. The fact that I had two elder brothers of some standing gave me a certain latitude in matters of machismo: wise souls knew not to pick on Reggie Elms's little brother. I also became aware early on that aggro was not my forte. I had neither the stomach nor the fists for the fight;

I was no good at it. But that realisation didn't stop the fighting.

Because I didn't have the bottle (which is of course rhyming slang, bottle and glass, arse) for the battle, it just meant that I got pretty good at sidestepping. Keeping your cool and your distance while all hell is going on around you is a street skill, which has served me well. And it was first learned in the playground, then honed in teenage years when pretty much every night out and every trip to football seemed to involve friction and a fracas of some kind.

One of the great myths of the 1960s and '70s is that London was the centre of some sort of swinging hippy love-in, a groovy, trippy town draped in crushed velvet. Well not round our way it wasn't. I have spoken to people who were in cool, patchouli-scented scenes in Powis Square, and Pont Street with various stoned Stones, and as one of them said, 'Swinging London involved 22 people, 16 of whom had rich parents.' For most of us, peace, love and flower power were some-thing hairy people from San Francisco sang about.

Just about everyone I knew had cropped hair and big boots, not necessarily made for walking. I don't want to make it sound as if I spent my youth terrified of the next ruckus; it was more that you accepted that a degree of violence was a normal part of everyday, and certainly everynight life. And providing you were light on your feet it was usually easy enough to swerve. Occasionally though it really did get out of hand.

The two most spectacularly unruly and downright vicious events I was involved in during my teenage years took place in the two least likely parts of London imaginable, Barnet and Dollis Hill. Yep, High Barnet; the verdant, affluent suburb on the very limit of the northern fringes of the city, which is said to be the highest point between London and the Urals. And Dollis Hill, a drearily mundane Northwest London community of humble Edwardian homes that doesn't have any noted high points whatsoever. Also both of the venues for these clashes have since ceased to exist. Barnet football club no longer play at Underhill and the Grunwick photo-processing plant is now a housing estate. But they are both seared on to my memory.

Enough words have been written about football hooliganism in its 1970s and '80s heyday. But unless you regularly stood on those decaying old terraces watching attack teams of kamikaze youths trained in 'Who wants to play war?' and British Bulldog, kicking lumps out of each other, pretty much untroubled by any police intervention or safety consideration, you cannot know how wild and wanton it was. If working-class lads like kicking lumps out of each other let them get on with it, seemed to be the rule.

At Loftus Road, I regularly witnessed huge firms of hundreds of lads, from bigger, tougher teams try and 'take' the Loft, our humble home section; routinely saw pitch battles occurring while the game continued unaffected on the pitch. Watching Cold Blow Lane's finest clad in butchers' coats, tooled up, pissed up and riled up, heading for your end, can certainly put the fear of SE1 into you.

But it was also true that unless you specifically wished to get involved, the violence had a remarkable way of dancing neatly around you. I was yards from the action on numerous occasions, indulged in a fair amount of baiting and banter, but never really got hurt. Football hooliganism was a sport for consenting juveniles, most of the people involved loved it and you could usually opt out while staying close by. But not at Barnet.

It was 1973, I was fourteen and already a war-wary football fan. I was used to being alert to the myriad dangers of a game, but not expecting too much trouble at a non-league ground where my team had to go for a cup replay. Burnt Oak is the black sheep of the London borough of Barnet, a tough working-class enclave, but this was up in the proper posh old county town. Famed for its charming little sloping ground, I went with a group of mates from school expecting a gentle night watching my team. I should have remembered from history that the Battle of Barnet was one of the fiercest of the Wars of the Roses, and part two was about to commence.

Both big North London firms, Arsenal and Tottenham, plus a fair few fighters from every other crew in the capital, joined forces to defend the little local non-league team. They forged an unholy alliance against

QPR's relatively small but still game gang of fighting boys from Ladbroke Grove and Shepherd's Bush. The Westies were led by Ellie, a lad with polio who dragged his leg, but swung his fists, and turned up maybe two or three hundred strong, to be met by this large, unexpected alliance in wait. All this at a ground with no segregation, no fences and very few police.

No exaggeration, for two hours, a pretty much non-stop, no-holds-barred assault occurred. I had somehow dragged my nice grammar school mates into the QPR crew and we found ourselves hemmed in under the one stand with a roof, which was being dismantled from above with the slates raining down on the blue-and-white lads below.

It was Rorke's Drift with a football match going on a few feet away. I saw people carried off, bleeding from head wounds, only to get patched up by the St John Ambulance and return to the fray. Others laid out in lines on the side of the ground in improvised triage. There were charges and counter charges, pincer movements, and all out attacks, it was absolute mayhem. The few police present were overrun and battered too.

I have witnessed Millwall's Bushwackers running riot round the Blue and Chelsea's Nazi Headhunters Sieg Heiling and smashing up Loftus Road. I've seen decades of football violence close up but never have I been so terrifyingly close to such constant, hand-to-hand, boot-to-head, head-to-nose, toe-to-toe combat, as that night in sleepy suburbia.

Then we went home. Not a word in the papers, not a TV crew in sight, just a few young boys, battered but boasting in the playground next day. QPR won.

The next time I was involved in a major North London affray, not only were the TV cameras present but I ended up on the *Six O'Clock News*. In October 2016 there was an exhibition held at Willesden Library to commemorate forty years since the start of the Grunwick dispute and thirty-nine years since my first ever appearance on national television. Grunwick was a grim and grimy, breeze-block photographic processing plant in Chapter Road NW2, where an almost exclusively

Asian, female workforce faced Dickensian conditions and appalling racist treatment, so went on strike. For the first time the still largely white, working-class TUC supported an ethnic-minority-led strike, and a major, protracted dispute began.

The dispute started at the end of the deliriously long hot summer of '76, and it was still rumbling on a year later. Over that time the staunch Asian women attracted increasing support from trades unionists, socialists, bearded, paper-selling Trots and grumpy old-school 'tankies'. This motley collection of '70s lefties, visionaries and malcontents turned up every week in those crowded residential streets to try and stop the 'scab' workers bused in by the management from entering the plant, and to argue noisily among themselves.

Because it was only a bus ride away from Burnt Oak, I went along a couple of times to see what was happening and to bolster my credentials among the cadre of sixth-form agitators who had become my mates. Then on 22 June 1977 it was announced that a national mobilisation and mass picket had been called for Grunwick: the big push, the final showdown. The proletarian heavy cavalry – the National Union of Mineworkers, led by the legendary Arthur Scargill, Yorkshire's own Che Guevara with a comb over – would be coming down to Northwest London to save the day and shut the plant. Exciting is not the word for it.

I distinctly recall getting up in the dark before dawn and donning my then de rigeur leather bikers' jacket and heading for Dollis Hill with my comrades. A skinny, ginger fashion punk about to be thrust into the forefront of the class struggle. All too literally.

The scene was extraordinary. Crammed into these mundane, tightly packed, slightly shabby residential streets, ordinary people's homes, was the usual picket line of striking workers, dignified and proud in their saris with placards in English and Hindi, plus tens of thousands of protesters. On the other side, just feet away, were rows and rows of police, most notably a stern-looking phalanx of riot shield and baton-wielding SPG.

These were the dreaded Special Patrol Group, a terrifying paramilitary mob whom I had last encountered in August 1976. Then they had been lined up across the Harrow Road ready to wade into the Carnival and play their part in provoking the trouble which followed, trashing the Grove and prompting The Clash to write 'White Riot', their first single. On that day they had stopped me and my nice white mates as we had headed towards the carnival and asked us a question. It was, and I quote: 'Why do you want to go in there with all the niggers?'

That was the 'enemy' we were facing that day. Their job was to make sure that the bus, literally an old Routemaster, full of strike-breakers, could make it through the picket lines into the plant. Ours was to stop them. The very language of the time – scabs and scum, filth and pigs – gives you an indication of how embittered it all was. And arrayed against us were a collection of shadowy far-right ideologues like the NAFF (National Association For Freedom) and the Monday Club, funding the strike-breaking operation. This was serious business.

But I just remember loving the excitement and drama, especially when word went out that the flying picket of miners had arrived. To the sound of huge cheers, this column of tough, northern men, led by Comrade Scargill barking instructions into a loud hailer, came marching towards us from up Willesden way, flying their banners as if to war. Which is pretty much what it became. Here in these tightly packed suburban North London streets, on a sunny summer's morning a no-holds-barred, no-prisoners-taken, no-quarter-given battle commenced. It was bloody mad.

You must have seen the scenes from the Battle of Orgreave, the massive clash between miners and coppers during the strike in 1984. Well, this was a dress rehearsal for that, but in the backstreets of Dollis Hill, with local residents trying to get to work and take their kids to school. In fact I recall one moment when a group of miners and old bill were literally exchanging blows, only to break off to let a family go by, then resume hostilities after they had passed. There were bitter little side tussles going on all over, big grown men just openly fighting in side streets and people's front gardens, using dustbin lids as shields and plant pots as ammo; blood on the doorstep and the dahlias.

Then the scab-laden bus came, and the SPG tried to smash their way through our lines. Somehow, at this pivotal moment, through the unstoppable momentum of the crowd I found myself in the very front rank. I was arm in arm with fellow protesters, faced off by a copper with his baton drawn, hovering over my head, but also by a cameraman from the BBC pointing at my face. I suspect his lens saved me from a whack.

But it was all to no avail, our lines couldn't hold, the bus got in. We lost. Almost all the sides I've picked over the years have lost. Though history has undoubtedly decided that the striking Grunwick women were right; steadfast strugglers for equality and decency. Like so many apparent defeats it was actually a vital step on the path to victory and the recognition of everybody's rights, regardless of race or gender. But on that fateful, fearsome day, and in the coming months as the strike petered out, we lost.

That evening I sat down to watch the TV with my mum and there I was on the news, an eighteen-year-old boy, the self-same age my lefty, agitator dad had been when she first met him on the strife-torn streets of W10. Apparently I looked very much like him too. When she saw me on the TV I saw her smile and cry simultaneously. Caught perhaps between her two Londons, her past and her future, her husband and her son.

'You take care, Robert,' is all she said. 'You take care.'

By the end of that summer I had taken my place at the LSE, where being a veteran of the Grunwick dispute gave me a certain cachet on the steps of Houghton Street. I plunged into the alphabetti spaghetti of student politics, trying to disentangle the IMG from the WRP and the SWP from the CPGB. I was never more than a fellow traveller, bunking the fares at that. But I could at least claim proper proletarian status, whereas most of the resident revolutionaries were middle-class Marxists, convinced that the great leap forward for oiks like the Elmses was just around the corner.

There were sit-ins and occupations, pickets and protests almost every day if you fancied it. Politics was an integral part of a lively student social life, which invariably involved roll-up fags, pints of beer in subsidised basement bars, girls with CND haircuts, benefit gigs at Conway Hall in Holborn and trips to Collet's bookshop on the Charing Cross Road. This was a tatty labyrinth of proselytising pamphlets, Soviet posters and Gramscian tracts next door to Foyles up near Tottenham Court Road Tube. Every self-respecting student revolutionary went to Collet's to browse books and buy badges. Power to the people and pass the pot.

The GLC, once famous for knocking things down, went from villain to hero, building an anti-Thatcherite bastion at County Hall, just over from the LSE. There were numerous benefit gigs there and at Islington Town Hall, which proudly flew the red flag. Indeed there was a whole alternative network of left-wing life in which LSE students were deeply involved. I dipped in and out depending on which outfit I was wearing that day.

My favourite of all the many slightly mad lefty bookstores, which once littered the city, was the Albanian Shop in Betterton Street, Covent Garden. This was a musty treasure trove of Stalinist statuettes, key rings, badges, flags, pickled fruit and the collected twenty-four-volume speeches of Enver Hoxha, the dear leader of the Socialist People's Republic of Albania. For years it sat next to a launderette in what was still a run-down and cheap part of town. It was a hoot until the Iron Curtain and the Soviet Union fell and the shop vanished, along with Collet's and so many others almost overnight.

Over in Whitechapel, up Angel Alley, redolent with layers of East End sedition, the Freedom Bookshop and printing press, the fervid home of British anarchism, thankfully still survives. The Soviets would never have subsidised raging Bakuninites, so it rages still, a lasting tribute to the dreams of generations of libertarian visionaries and plotters.

If the term loony left was applicable to anyone, it was the certifiable lunatics who supported the various Maoist groups, who somehow saw the LSE as their spiritual home. One lot were ardent followers of the Sendero Luminoso, the Shining Path, a wildly violent Peruvian guerrilla group, who plastered the campus and much of WC2 with stencilled posters singing the praises of Chairman Gonzalo, their bearded guru. But they were positively mainstream compared to a bunch of wild-eyed, exclusively female Maoists who would stand on the steps of the main LSE building trying to convince us that the revolution was indeed just around the corner. I mean literally round the corner. One of them actually told me that the glorious Red Army had dug a tunnel from China and would be emerging, little red books and AK-47s in hand, somewhere near the Strand at any moment.

I laughingly told this story for years, until in 2015 it was all over the news that a group of females had been held as virtual hostages and sexual slaves for decades in a house in Brixton by one Aravindan Balakrishnan, leader of 'The Workers Institute of Marxism-Leninism-Mao Zedong Thought', a charismatic charlatan who had studied at the LSE. It was them.

The most chilling moment of my student political shenanigans came when we were preparing to occupy some building or other. One of our comrades was an older guy called Richard, with a bona fide South London accent, a pair of Dr Martens and an intense commitment to overthrowing the state. He was very unlike most of the posh Trots and no one ever quite knew what he was doing at the LSE – he seemed to be a sort of semi-professional agitator. Before we set off he took me to one side and asked conspiratorially if I wanted anything for the operation ahead. I didn't quite understand what he meant until he said openly: 'If we need any guns I can get them.' (I have since wondered whether Richard was actually an undercover cop infiltrating our ranks.)

'You take care Robert. You take care.'

The real irony of this raging revolutionary milieu – 'the final push, brothers and sisters, the final push' – is that yet again I was watching another London on the edge of extinction, though nobody realised it at the time.

One of my tutors was an Australian political scientist called Kenneth

Minogue (I never thought about this before, but I love the idea that he could possibly be related to Kylie), who was part a new breed of brash 'neo-liberal' ideologues based at the LSE. He preached what seemed at the time like far-out free market economics and neo-con politics. I remember a heated debate between Professor Minogue and a group of us undergrads, in which we mocked his assertion that this upstart milk-snatching woman he was advising would change the world. The meteor was about to hit.

Just how much London and the universe would change in a few short Thatcherite years can best be illustrated by spending some time in Stoke Newington. I did that because one of my best friends from the LSE had somehow wangled a council flat there, as you could in those days. Even by the shoddy standards of the late '70s, N16 was a remarkably run-down neighbourhood. Grimy, grotty and seemingly stuck in a forever February of murky half-light and constant drizzle. But there were compensations.

We spent many hours getting disgraceful while wrongly thinking we were putting the world to rights in a series of mordantly unreconstructed Stokey boozers. Nicotine-stained, sticky-carpeted, cheap, warm, rollicking boozers with great old jukeboxes and a clientele that divided into three elements; Irish, West Indian and revolutionary. Oh and there were always exemplary kebabs on every corner.

The Irish and West Indian lads reminded me very much of my Westie roots, but the Hackney reds were of a different order. These were proper hard men (and a few hard women) plotting the violent downfall of almost everything. There was an exiled Basque reporting gleefully back on the latest ETA outrage. There were decidedly post-peace-and-love Class War anarchists, including some near-insane Italians, intent on incendiary insurrection. And most terrifyingly a group of home-grown 'squadists', shovel-wielding, building-site warriors, who would later form Red Action. They were a militant working-class anti-fascist, street-fighting cadre who regularly came to blows with Combat 18, and gave honour guards to IRA marches. Stoke Newington was the epicentre of tough, radical London. And who would know it now.

Stoke Newington went through a transitional period in the 1990s when it was largely lesbians, kite shops and dreadlocks, but Stokey today is the very model of a modern well-mannered inner-city community. Clissold Park, Church Street, the Gothic cemetery, the gastropubs, the pilates, the artisan bakers, everything from the tabbouleh to the mummies is yummie. Walk down Amhurst Road now, or Milton Grove or Walford Road, all prime slices of gluten-free N16 loveliness, and you would never know that those three addresses were the scene of three of the biggest terrorist busts of the twentieth century. All within half-a-mile of each other, but a million miles from the pleasant, pricey Stoke Newington of today.

Six members of the Angry Brigade, anarchist activists who blew up the Post Office Tower among others, were nicked in a flat full of explosives in Amhurst Road. The rampaging IRA cell behind the Balcombe Street siege and numerous bombings and shootouts were captured in Milton Grove. While one of those Red Action hard men, an English guy who progressed to full membership of the Republican Army, was lifted from his flat on Walford Grove, after he planted the Harrods bomb (which ruined my hair: I was having it cut in Smile in Knightsbridge and was evacuated with half a haircut when the blast occurred).

But it wasn't just lefties and it wasn't just Stokey that harboured political turmoil. I will talk in detail about the extraordinary changes that have been visited upon the Cross, but suffice it to say that back in the 1980s when I lived nearby it was seething. Argyle Square, a potentially beautiful rectangle of large, but neglected, Georgian houses opposite St Pancras station, was the single most seedy place I have ever visited, anywhere in the world.

The square itself was smeared with drunks and junkies: Old White Lightning imbibers and young smack- and crack-heads in a rambling, mumbling, shouting intergenerational intermingling of the eternally damned, splattered with vomit and blood. The drearily decaying houses around were all dirt-cheap hotels offering rank rooms for those in despair. Knocking shops, shooting galleries, beds by the hour and places of last resort for homeless, hopeless families. Except for number 21, the Ferndale.

I used to wonder why you saw so many nasty skinhead revival types in King's Cross. All big boots, MA1s and bleached jeans, tattooed and ugly, robbed of the minimalist élan of their 1969 progenitors. These were clearly skins of the racist, National Front, BNP variety, and it turns out it was because the Ferndale Hotel was a fascist safe house. Which didn't make the area particularly safe. The Ferndale in the early '80s was run by a man named Maurice Castles, who was convicted of supplying guns to a cell of local NF fanatics, based at his grotty gaff.

These racial warriors went on a spree of sulphate-fuelled armed robberies, turning over local sub-post offices and banks to further the white nationalist cause. The Ferndale was a magnet for far-right fanatics from across the globe. It was rumoured that the two Italian terrorists who went on the run after the Bologna bombings were hidden at the Ferndale, and it was definitely the long-term home of Ian Stuart, leader of Skrewdriver and the whole neo-Nazi Blood and Honour movement, and a bolt hole for swastika-sporting boneheads.

So the 'commies' went and fought them. The IRA placed a small bomb in Argyle Square and Red Action led numerous sorties upon Stuart and his cropped-haired cronies. Every weekend, just up the road in Chapel Market, there was a rampaging set-to as the two sides sold their inflammatory tracts and tried to take control of the streets of North London. Old biddies going to do their shopping in the market and families bound for double double at the pie and mash would have to run the gauntlet of political gangs kicking seven shades out of each other outside the Agricultural pub, as the aggro ebbed and flowed. Right or left, right or wrong, you gotta decide which side you're on.

Which was definitely an issue for the Irish lads. Anyone who tries to tell you that multiculturalism is new to London, or that suspicion and prejudice against an ethnic minority because of terrorist outrages is unique to the current Muslim community, clearly wasn't around in the '70s. On my first day at Orange Hill School in 1971, I would estimate that 'indigenous' white English was a minority in my class. There were a large group of Jewish boys, a pair of brilliant Nigerian twins, an Italian whose dad ran the local café, some Indians, Greek Cypriots, a Maltese lad, a Polish kid from RAF stock, a Grenadan and just the one Irish boy, Patrick, or Padraig to his mum and dad. But if he had gone to St James's, the Catholic school directly opposite, he would have been among hundreds of his first-, second- and third-generation country folk. Burnt Oak was full of O'Keefes, Kellys and O'Neils, and of all the cultures that made up the patchwork quilt of our city, the Celtic strain was the strongest.

London working-class life was absolutely streaked with emerald. Irish dancing classes in the local scout hut, the *Sligo Champion* and the *Leinster Express* for sale in the newsagents, hurling and Gaelic football games in the park. Men gathered on high ground to hear the All-Ireland Final on the crackly radio; diddly music and bacon and cabbage every time you entered your mate's house. Confirmation gowns, priests smoking at the bus stop, pints of Guinness settling on the bar, mass on Sunday morning followed by a session in the best dark suit and tie. Summers spent in Mayo, shovels, poets, Hail Marys and the craic. Bombs.

As soon as we could get served in pubs, which pretty much meant you could see over the bar, we migrated up the Edgware Road to Cricklewood and Kilburn and the roughhouse Irish taverns full of the boys on 'the lump'. These pubs were almost exclusively male, almost exclusively Irish, accents as thick as doorsteps. Big Tom and the Mainliners, racing tips and teary Tipperary memories from sentimental stakhanovites on stout, heroic, occasionally tragic fellows, who left home to build this town, then possibly help to blow it up.

As the night wore on in the Cock or the Crown, the lyrics of the songs became more and more bellicose, the anti-English feeling more belligerent, and all my Irish mates knew all the words. But I never felt threatened, it wasn't aimed at me, their argument was with the British establishment, and their generosity and warmth (until a fight started) were palpable. But then at the end of the night, as the bell for last orders sounded, so the strains of the Irish national anthem rang out and those who could still stand had to do so and sing. A bucket would be passed around, collecting for 'Irish orphans', and you just knew that it would be for making them rather than helping them. None of my young mates were exactly IRA sympathisers, they were Londoners; it was our city, us they were blowing up, but some were perhaps IRA understanders.

Putting aside folk memories of Guy Fawkes, the first terrorist attack on London was a Fenian bomb, which exploded in Clerkenwell in 1867 killing twelve people. Bombs and bullets have been part, if not of the everyday life of London, then certainly of its nightmares, ever since. The only decade without major terrorist incidents was the 1950s, when London was unusually quiet after the traumas and exhaustion of the war.

Irish Republican attacks have certainly been the most persistent and by far the most deadly, but it was the anarchist outrages, which raged throughout Europe and the USA roughly 100 years ago, which bear most similarity to our current situation. Young men, mainly of 'alien' extraction, often living in poor, excluded communities, driven on by a fanatical, nihilistic, millenarian creed, radicalised in secret meetings in dusty halls or by inflammatory pamphlets in unreadable tongues, were convinced they could make the world better by blowing it up.

The siege of Sydney Street in 1911 was one example, when a group of Latvian revolutionaries, including the notorious Peter the Painter, were holed up in a house in Stepney after a spree of murders and armed 'appropriations'. Winston Churchill (Winnie the Painter) turned up to oversee the deadly shootout that occurred. But one of the most incredible stories of London's perpetual terrorist past took place two years earlier and takes us back to where this chapter began. The Tottenham Outrage.

You still occasionally hear the area up towards Edmonton, around Lorenco Road, called Little Russia, but back in Edwardian times this poor and tough part of Tottenham really warranted that moniker. It was full then of eastern émigrés, asylum seekers who had fled the repressive Tsarist regime, including scores of anarchists and Bolsheviks, many of them Jewish. Two of those – Paul Hefeld and Jacob Lapidus – attempted to rob a rubber company on the High Road next to Tottenham police station, and it was the ensuing chase and firefight which has gone down in history.

Zig-zagging for eight madcap miles across the Lea valley towards Chingford in Essex, it took hours before the final felon was fatally shot at Oak Cottage, Hale End. Four people died, including the Russians, a ten-year-old boy and a police officer. A further seven PCs were wounded along with seventeen members of the public, many of whom joined in the pursuit, which involved sequestered motor cars, a horse and cart and perhaps the only ever tram chase in history. At one point the two alien desperados were being pursued across the marshes, through a football match, where the players stopped the game to join in. At the funeral of PC Tyler, it was reported that 3,000 police officers and half-a-million civilians lined the route to pay their respects as the cortège went by. (Echoes of the heroic PC Palmer, perhaps.) He is buried in Abney Park cemetery in fashionable Stoke Newington.

Wherever you look in our city there are reverberations of a violent past, and occasionally an explosive, horribly flammable present. London isn't always burning, but the potential for a conflagration is always there, just a spark away.

There Are Dead People
All Over the Place

Ours reside mainly in Mortlake, a verdant, affluent suburb of Southwest London, where the living people all drive cars all the time, so the traffic is forever terrible. They also follow rugby and wear polo shirts with their collars turned up, or at least the male ones do; the female ones have blonde hair and lots of vowels in their names. Both have wax jackets and go to pubs by the river, which is nice. Going to see Mum and Dad, which I don't do often enough, feels a little like going on holiday, so different is the leafy London they now rest in.

I do wonder sometimes what they make of it down there, but then my dad, deep in an Elms family plot with his own mother and father, has had plenty of time to adjust and my mum is merely dust. Every year on my mother's birthday, we meet up with Reggie and his family for a little cere-mony, followed by a spot of lunch in a lovely spot overlooking the Thames. When we do the commune, I always say a few words, tell them about the kids and stuff, how we're all getting on. I remember how much I miss them both, how much I have always missed him, every single day since the age of six.

Then I get to wandering among the graves and wondering about all the other, no longer living, Londoners. How many there are, and where are they all? I've also increasingly taken to discussing where I am going to go, when the great day comes. I waiver between ashes scattered on the river and an elaborate eternal mausoleum in one of the magnificent seven, ideally Highgate or Kensal Green, where the Mason's Arms pub has a special space for coffins. Definitely not Brompton, too close to Stamford Bridge; I wouldn't rest easy.

As I get older, I enjoy a touch of Victorian funereal melodrama; love it when a villain gets a horse-drawn hearse, mutes and plumes and all. Little Bernie Katz's big day in Soho was perfect. Equestrian elegance, marching band playing 'When the Saints Go Marching In', and a glass-sided coffin parading down Dean Street with the Prince on board and the mourners processing slowly behind, not a dry eye in the street. That was the best afternoon of the century so far.

The London Necropolis Railway, the black-draped line of the dead, which ferried cadavers, coffins and criers from a special terminus in Waterloo to

Brookwood Cemetery would have been a good way to go. (Though I don't want to be buried in South London). Certainly makes sense of the word terminus. And in typical Victorian fashion they had three classes of funeral. I quite like the idea of a first-class ticket to oblivion.

The grandest emporium in all nineteenth-century London was Jay's Mourning Warehouse; an entire, ornate block of Regent Street, bigger than the current Apple Store, selling just the jet-black paraphernalia of grief.

I do think we collectively underplay death now, try to deny its dominion. When I lived in Harringay in the 1980s, when it was still a resolutely Greek Cypriot neighbourhood, they knew how to do funerals. Masters of lamentation, the whole street would go in for public weeping and wailing, quite possibly gnashing of teeth, women prostrating themselves over coffins, men arm-in-arm in floods, and there would be excellent food, dolmades and all.

I like dead people, and I like the places they are interred. I'm not a grave-botherer or anything, I just enjoy the stories those cemeteries and churchyards tell. Abney Park's tangled abundance. St Giles-in-the-Fields, where the gallows fodder were laid. Bunnhill Fields behind Old Street, full of famous non-conformists – surely they have to be more interesting than conformists. The mournful Sephardi cemetery in Mile End, which backed on to my mate Graham's house. Old St Pancras, with Sir John Soane's sepulchral masterpiece; the upright Moravians off the King's Road; Postman's Park near Cloth Fair, where plaques celebrate Victorian Heroes who died pulling lunatics from train lines and the like.

I enjoy a little homage to the Winchester Geese at the Crossbones grave-yard by Southwark Cathedral, which for years was a municipal car park full of dead whores. You can meet them after a chorizo sandwich from Borough Market. I once spent a freezing winter night in the chilling Crypt of Kensal Green with Sting, hearing tales of necrophilia among the sarcophagi. But my favourite grave of all is the resting place of Giro the Nazi Dog.

Whether a canine can actually be a Nazi is a moot point, and technically this particular pooch was originally a Weimar Republic terrier. His gravestone sits by a tree, next to the Grand Old Duke of York and up the steps from the ICA – although his bones are actually next door in the garden of 9 Carlton House Terrace, which was the German Embassy until war was declared in 1939. (Originally a Nash mansion, now the Royal Society, its interior was redesigned by Albert Speer in 1936, and rumour has it a huge swastika mosaic is still hidden beneath a fitted carpet in one of the grand rooms.)

The beloved pet of Leopold von Hoesch, the famously dapper German ambassador who predated the fascist regime, Giro died after Hitler came to power in 1934. He was buried in the back garden and given this headstone by his doting master. Hoesch himself expired two years later and was afforded a full state funeral including a swastika-draped coffin and Nazi salutes from the terrace above the Mall. Years later, when the garden was being redesigned, Giro's monument was moved to its current spot by a tree, the only Nazi plot in London.

There is one other burial I would like to bring to your attention, though no mortal remains remain, because there never were any. This is the saga of Butty Sugrue, a Kerryman, showman and publican, who once pulled a bus across Westminster Bridge with his teeth, and the burial of his barman, Mick Keane, 'the human JCB' from Cork. Mick was entombed alive in a builders' yard off the Edgware Road for sixty-one days in 1968. This is my favourite tale of the rollicking old-time county Kilburn.

So splendidly potty is this yarn that I'm glad a typically patronising Pathé newsreel exists to prove it is not just another North London Irish shaggy dog story. Thousands turned out in dark suits, white shirts and ties to watch the specially adapted coffin, with the living, breathing Corkie inside, being ferried on the back of a builder's lorry, in search of a world record. They went from Butty's boozer, the Admiral Lord Nelson (now sadly deceased) to a deep grave dug in a yard a few hundred yards up the Kilburn High Road. A bit of plumbers piping acted as an air vent and Keane was lowered down and covered with soil.

For sixty-one days people paid to peer and marvel as food was passed down the pipe, and at the other end waste went out of a trap door into a layer of lime. The BBC covered the event, questions were asked in the House of Commons, Butty the showman did a roaring trade and Mick the Barman kept on breathing. Henry Cooper came to have a word and world boxing champ Joe Louis talked on a phone passed down to the buried barman.

Some suggested that Mick secretly nipped out at night for a pint of nourishing Guinness in the Nelson, but no skulduggery was proven, and he broke the existing record.

The day he emerged, a world champ himself, thousands stopped the traffic on the Kilburn High Road. Girl pipers played, grown men wept, the coffin was put back on the truck and ferried to Butty's pub where the lid was raised and the triumphant if hirsute Mick Keane emerged to huge cheers and copious rounds. They say that night in the Lord Admiral Nelson the craic was so loud it woke the dead.

Down By the River

Where is the epicentre of our city? Officially, the midpoint of the metropolis is marked by a small plaque in the pavement on a traffic island outside Charing Cross station, by the statue of King Charles I just down from Trafalgar Square. So all distances to the capital are measured from that precise point: twenty-five miles to London, twenty five miles to there.

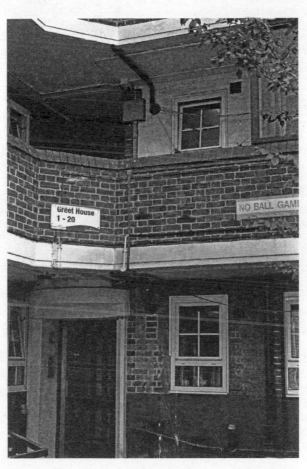

But as this city keeps morphing and moving, so its axis shifts, and clever people with computers have recently calculated that its geographical centre is now technically further south, over the water in an anonymous spot in SE1 – specifically in a pleasingly plain council estate called Greet House on Frazier Street, close by Lambeth North station. If you've ever tried to drive from town to Gatwick Airport (a very bad idea) you'll know that the South London sprawl goes on forever, dragging the centre of gravity down with it.

Individually, we will all have our own version of the location of the heart of the city. Mine, as a Northwest Londoner who holds Soho and the West End dear, is pretty close to Seifert's soaring Centre Point. Emerging from Tottenham Court Road Tube, at the teeming crossroads where the four historic neighbourhoods meet – Soho, St Giles, Fitzrovia and Bloomsbury – feels like being deposited right into the belly of the beast.

For some, the City itself is the core, for others maybe Mayfair or Marble Arch. But collectively in our heart of hearts, we know that the soul of our city resides in the breeze that blows across the Thames as you stand on Waterloo Bridge at sunset. Ray Davies got it right.

We all live by the river. No matter where you are in London, even if you are ensconced in a suburb many miles from the great grey torrent, you dwell in a city by the banks. The Thames is the reason we are here, our raison d'être and our perpetually flowing source of nourishment. And if you haven't seen and felt the water flow for a while, you have to get yourself down to the Thames to sense its mighty power and purpose. Ours is a port town, a trading town, a water-born town, and as soon as you hit the river-side and see the open vistas, sense the rush of ions and feel the distant lure of the open sea: all that history, two millennia of maritime London stories, flows swiftly past and through you.

The Seine is a slow-flowing, elegant river, meandering and inviting, rendering romantic Paris lush and feminine, whereas the Thames is a brute of a waterway, tidal, tough to navigate, hard to handle, difficult even to cross, making this a more prosaic and masculine city, a sailor's town. The Seine joins the two halves of Paris, linking left and right, those pretty bridges inviting you to amble back and forth, whereas the Thames divides London north and south, a huge barrier we all recognise and many of us keep to.

I have lived in many places in London, but always on my side of the divide, still feel out of kilter when I cross it; could never be transpontine. A friend of mine who had grown up in a tight London family, less than a mile from the Thames in Holborn, was once discussing a relative of his who was now a black sheep, rarely seen. When I asked what he had done to be cast out he said, 'He married a girl from over the water.'

But what we share as Londoners, whichever side of the great chasm we are from, is the river itself. Our common ground is not ground at all. We all have our favourite bridges: Hammersmith might be mine, Bazalgette's low-slung suspension bridge, verdant and handsome, sitting solidly just above the flow, great boozers on its banks, plaques and adornments on its structure, confident yet ultimately fragile, forever in repair.

A cold and misty morning by lovely Albert Bridge is a fine thing, as the Pogues so poetically reminded us. Tower Bridge is a preposterous, yet perfect, symbol of our city, a film-set, set-piece of a bridge lying about its age, a Victorian fantasy of medieval London, a music hall entertainment: 'How's your love life? Up and down, like Tower Bridge.' Contemporary Hungerford Bridge is a poseur, a tart's boudoir of a crossing, festooned with fairy lights, but the wobbly bridge is a good 'un, svelte and sharp, our shiny new London incarnate.

The governor is Waterloo. Not by any means a beautiful structure, though I like the fact that the current iteration was built by women. It is known as the Ladies' Bridge, because a largely female workforce constructed it during wartime. But in this case you don't want to see the bridge, you stand on the bridge to see the view. Sitting at the perfect point of the curve, it is positioned equidistant between the twin forces, City and State, which have shaped our town and our destiny. It is said that Londoners first look east when they arrive on Waterloo Bridge, towards St Paul's, and the City, because we know that London began there, whereas visitors initially look west, seduced by Big Ben, the Wheel and Westminster's tourist lures. Either way is magnificent.

London is an autumnal town, so November light is ideal to see the river: flat battleship skies, rendering our city serious yet ethereal, muting colours, yet amplifying grandeur. You also want brisk autumn air, to feel it in your hair, the breeze blowing one way, the tide flowing the other; elemental. The River Thames, father of the city, flows below you on this bridge, yet soars above us all on this journey. When my children were small I went through a ridiculous, quasi Kunta Kinte ritual involving holding them on Waterloo Bridge and showing them their birthright, our town, telling them all this is theirs.

One time my wife's friend asked if we could show two fifteen-year-old Mancunian girls who were staying for their first-ever weekend in London around. The first place I took them to was Waterloo Bridge. We walked together to the centre, turned to the east and I began to give them my spiel about this Roman ford growing into the greatest metropolis known to man, a city of scholars and scoundrels who between them built so many monuments, which have been bombed and bashed, but never beaten. I showed them St Paul's: domed emblem of eternity and the National Theatre; angular symbol of modernity. I sung my love song of London and they listened for a few minutes until, as one, they said to me: 'Robert, where's Topshop?'

CHAPTER SIX

At Night

It began by moving the furniture. The sofa and chairs would be shoved to the side, rugs rolled up to reveal the floorboards, nick-nacks put away upstairs. If it was going to be a particularly big shindig, the front room might be cleared completely by putting the whole lot, except the radiogram, out of the window, into the garden, but more likely a bit of humping and shifting to the corners would make enough space for a knees-up.

There were often parties. Usually they were just impromptu; grown-ups back from the pub of a Saturday, continuing the fun with a few friends, bottles of beer clinking, sing-songs, maybe a dance or two. Ties loosened, shoes off, Dad doing a rendition of 'King of the Road' before giving of his party piece, jumping over a broomstick held in his hands. Mum, proud in a floral dress, still young, I realise now, in love and lovely, earrings glittering. Sitting together on the sofa singing with friends, me sneaking downstairs, bouncing on a knee to Al Martino's 'Spanish Eyes', crooned by all concerned. The bitter taste of stout on smiling lips, big men with big hard hands honed on girders. Drowsy, dreamy memories of the nights before Dad died.

Those nights were intimate, familial, fun, but wedding receptions were a different order of nocturnal intensity. Usually held in draughty back rooms, in pubs heavy with the astringent aroma and wafting fug of adulthood, the rarefied air of anticipated revelry. Best would be worn; for me it was shrunken versions of that svelte, early '60s silhouette, sported by older cousins and uncles from Paddington or Acton. They would gather by the bar looking admirable, if slightly menacing, in dark sharp suits with thin ties, black lace-up shoes polished to conscription perfection, smoking cigarettes from the back of their hands, telling stories of spivs, sparring with Terry Downes, running with the Notting

Hill boys, flirting with concomitant women with beehive hair. One had a Humber Super Snipe bought from Warren Street.

In another corner, an older generation still, born before both wars, men in collarless shirts and scratchy demob suits with fob chains with large brassy kettles, heavy boots and silk scarves. There were rinsed and set old women keeping their coats on, drinking port and lemon, sitting down, looking stern. These were people who'd kept nags in yards behind railway arches, celebrated the relief of Mafeking, cursed the Kaiser and maybe seen that monkey jazz band down Latimer Road. They were closer to Freddie than to today. They'd been young Londoners once, too.

The young ran riot at weddings. Scores of little cousins from White City, that ruddy-faced, blessed-by-the-blarney blush, buzzing round the room, getting in people's way, getting a clip round the ear or a ruffle of the hair. Nicking cake, guzzling coke, dancing the twist to Chubby Checker with an aunt who had those bow legs that were a sure sign of rickets. (My mum's only attempt at sagacious life advice consisted of telling me, 'You have to be very careful when you do the twist or else you could split your spleen.' So I have been severely hampered at weddings ever since.)

As the night wore on, the adults, inflamed now by beer and chasers, maybe carrying ancient grudges, hit the dance floor, and then someone hit someone, there was always a to-do at a do, a scuffle and a kerfuffle. But then they made up, put their arms round each other and sang the old songs. We sang them too, no generation gap, no embarrassment. I still know all the words to all of the following: 'Roll Out the Barrel', 'My Old Man Said Follow the Van', 'Bye Bye Blackbird', 'Bless 'Em All', 'Down at the Old Bull and Bush', 'It's a Long Way to Tipperary', 'Pack Up Your Troubles' and 'Doing the Lambeth Walk'.

The Lambeth Walk is not much of a dance really, more of an exaggerated bowl, and no Elms had ever walked much in Lambeth (strictly wrong side of the river) but we did their dance anyway and sung their song with a big booming old 'Oy' at the end. The finale of a wedding night, the finale of any good night, was a proper knees up and 'Knees Up Mother Brown' was inevitable, the old girls flicking their skirts in the air like Marie Lloyd, who they may just have seen at the Empire.

There was always a lusty rendition of 'Maybe It's Because I'm a Londoner', our cockney accents notched up for that one, ending with a loud 'Get Off Me Barrow', followed by a cheeky 'Get Off Me Sister'. There was no maybe about it: we were Londoners and we told ourselves so loudly at every party. I liked parties. I started to realise that I liked the night. But somehow, even then I knew the night is a dangerous place.

*

Cities are designed to defeat darkness. One of the reasons I have never been able to settle in the countryside is the lack of light at night. I'm not so much scared of the dark as annoyed by it. Nature has never really struck me as a particularly good thing, creeping and crawling, biting and stinging, shitting and the like. I don't care for fields or mud, and I don't much like the fact that out there, in the woods and the wilds, the setting sun is an injunction, it is ordering you to go to bed like a bossy parent. In civilisation, which means in cities, the night is an invitation, a time of infinite possibilities, day is for work, night is for play.

London draws you out after dark by lighting your way with lamp posts and shop signs, the pulsing promise of neon, the taxis' glowing golden insignia, signalling a ride to wherever you want to go. The bright light, floodlit lure of music and laughter, narcotics and stimulants, good company, bad people, sex: London at night is sexy. Better dressed than during the day, dandified and prettified, garrulous, glamorous, more relaxed, less business-like and serious, more frivolous and aban-doned. I've never been remotely frightened of the night in London, but energised and enthralled by it, tempted and teased by it. Though I am well aware that the night is a dangerous place.

The best nights when I was a boy in Burnt Oak were the ones when my elder brothers threw a cabbage. That particular piece of obscure rhyming slang is now just about moribund, but back in the late 1960s, early '70s, it was definitely the chosen word for a party. (Apparently it was costermonger's lingo from the cry, 'I've got cabbage all hearty.') When Barry or Reggie had a cabbage at our drum, (drum is a much more commonplace piece of slang, but not of the rhyming kind, it's from the Romany for road or home) I was beside myself with excite-ment, as it meant a glimpse of all the wonders and possibilities of the night that the future might hold.

Having two brothers considerably older than me, two boys who had exemplary shoes and a certain standing, meant that I was surrounded by the myriad delights and temptations of teen age way before my time. As an eleven-year-old in 1970, I proudly sported a number two crop with a razor parting, a pair of Levi's Sta-Prest held up by narrow red clip braces and – most proudly – owned my own import ska record by Laurel Aitken: 'Mr Popcorn' on the New Beat label, purchased with birthday money from Webster's in Shepherd's Bush Market. I knew far more than I should about Harrington jackets (named after Rodney Harrington, the character played by Ryan O'Neal in *Peyton Place*, which my mum watched assiduously), Solatio box-top loafers and button-down Ben Shermans.

I would sit at home after school playing not just my single, but working my way through the large pile of 45s, and a few LPs my brothers owned: *That's Soul* with the jigsaw puzzle cover, and *Motown and Reggae Chartbusters*, volume two was best. I became an instant, infant expert on the difference between the shiny Detroit sound and the deeper southern soul of Stax, could tell Marvin Gaye from Wilson Pickett within a note or two. I was a particularly annoying, precocious little know-it-all on the finer points of the Jamaican music that made up the core of their collection: Pama, Trojan, Studio One, Blue Beat, R'n'B; ska, reggae and rock steady.

This was the premier London soundtrack of the time, the staccato rhythm and shuffling backbeat of our streets. *The Return of Django* as you strolled past a market stall, Slim Smith seeping out of flats, Pat Kelly blasting out of cars, 'The Liquidator' on the terraces, *1000 Volts of Holt* in every household. Reggae flows through all our veins, marks our step.

If jazz is the sound of New York and chanson is Paris, then the rhythms of the Caribbean have resounded around and been incorporated into the rhythm of our city since the HMT *Empire Windrush* first blew into dock. Heavy dub bass lines anchoring our feet to the floor, righteous roots and culture lyrics telling our collective story, 'Police and Thieves' indeed, dancehall slackness like bawdy old-time music hall, soaring lovers' rock harmonies on a summer's day. Reggae is one of the reasons we walk with a shoulder-rolling swagger.

One of the most delightful tales of London's totally organic blending and blurring of cultural lines is the story of RnB – Rita and Benny Isen – a middle-aged Jewish couple who started out flogging platters

on Petticoat Lane. They then ran a record shop called Rita and Benny's at 260 Stamford Hill, amid the Glatt kosher butchers and wig emporiums of deep Hassidic country. This little shop had such a great stock of the various island styles that it became a mecca for the local skinheads and the Jamaican musicians who made the sides they sold. Heavyweight JA producers would head straight to Rita and Benny's from Heathrow with their tunes.

Benny was apparently a wiry little man while his wife was a big voluminous woman, and between them they became perhaps the greatest London authorities on and purveyors of reggae music. They regularly flew out to Kingston to do deals with the toughest studio bosses, perhaps bonding with the Rastas over a shared distaste for pork products, securing exclusives of the latest import hits. They then started their own record label called RnB which put out and even produced and pressed some of the most cutting-edge rocksteady, ska and reggae of the era. If you went to a club in London in the late '60s you were dancing to records made by a nice Yiddish couple from N15.

Although I had obviously never been anywhere near a nightclub, I knew the names of all the places to go from eavesdropping on my siblings talking to their mates about nocturnal adventures, making mental notes for future reference. There was clearly a two-tier structure when it came to going out. Local, suburban Northwest London dives like the Beehive or the Birds Nest were the midweek staples, usually attached to pubs in places like Harrow, Wembley and Hendon, where the tribes would gather to skank and moonstomp and Burnt Oak's crew demanded and received utmost respect. But there was a whole other layer of places to go after dark, which were spoken of with a muted mix of reverence, awe and maybe even fear. Shrines of the night.

Up West were the Scene and the Flamingo, super-hip, super-cool clubs where you had to be a face and Georgie Fame, the very best of the white boys, could be seen with the Blue Flames; moddy, moody, groovy, the tastiest looking 'sorts', the best-dressed geezers, pills and promises. Then there were the black clubs; the Four Aces in Dalston,

Count Suckle's place in Paddington and the Ram Jam down in Brixton where you might see Geno himself, hand-clapping, foot-stomping funky but live. But you better step lightly, take no liberties. The West Indian boys were held in esteem, high esteem indeed. All this I knew by the time I was ten.

But it was only when my brothers had a cabbage that I could really study the finer points of night-time teen behaviour. The room already cleared of extraneous clutter, adults banished, the pile of records from the collection would take centre stage, joined later by others brought by their mates, six to a spindle. Boys would start to arrive first, their hair cropped just for the occasion, their Royals reflecting, steel combs in pockets, bravado in abundance, crombies and sheepskins piled on the bed. Bottles of light ale and those big Watney's Party fours and sevens would amass in the kitchen, packets of Players No. 6 were proffered.

Then came the girls. Flat shoes, A-line skirts, feathered hair, giggles and swaggers, shy, confident, fragrant, flagrant. Lorraine from over the road. Some would say I was cute, maybe ruffle my barnet. I wasn't sure if cute was good.

I did a deal, which was that I would be allowed downstairs for the first hour or so, then it was off to bed, before the action really started. But obviously I learned that the more the night wore on, the better, the hotter, the more intense it got, ratcheted up. So I got good at sneaking down, never actually undressing, still wearing my prized Ben Sherman, so that I could try and slide and sidle into the front room or the kitchen and observe unnoticed, or just stand in the doorway and spy on proceedings.

I noted how the faces held themselves, self-contained, tidy, a presence, an aura. I saw dance steps, groups of three or four lads skanking in unison, sharp neat shuffles to 'Double Barrel' by Dave & Ansell Collins, or a lone boy throwing self-conscious shapes to 'Hard to Handle' by Otis, catching his reflection. I saw girls in a row doing formation moves to 'Groovin with Mr Bloe', sending signals, the sexual semiotics of the night.

Unlike the middle-class parties I went to later where people sat around and talked, words were kept to a minimum, the music was loud and there was perpetual movement, agitation, inebriation, dancing and occasionally fighting. Teenage angst had not yet been invented, at least not round our way, but teenage aggro was all the rage. I witnessed arguments, which came to blows, but always outside – sort it out outside. Inside, in that hot little room, lights down low, I smelled desire, saw flirting, snogging, sobbing and the kind of heavy petting which is specifically prohibited at swimming baths. I saw people getting out of it and out of hand, others rising above. I saw and understood the way that the night-time and its attendant temptations can lift you up or knock you down. I was mesmerised. I was waiting.

As I got a little older, Watling Boys', the local youth club, held monthly discos, when girls were let in and boys were let off the leash. *Three Plus Three* by the Isley Brothers was the album of the moment and Patrick Kamara, a half-Irish, half-Jamaican lad with great grace and balance, was our premier hoofer, the look now flared and dervish twirling, soul boy swagger. I learned there and then to respect superior talent and only go on the dance floor if it was very packed or you were very sure. I also learned that the way you dance, the way you walk and move and hold yourself, your demeanour, is your main weapon in the strobing, noisy, non-verbal world of the night.

Watling Boys' was a training ground, but we all knew it was not the real thing, too early, too soon, too early in our paths, too early in the evening. A youth club disco at 6 p.m. in a room where we habit-ually played ping-pong was not going to cut it. Going out had to mean going out of your comfort zone, a leap in the dark, the big step into the other London.

Red Rovers, excursions and explorations by day were one thing, always home in time for tea. But specifically leaving home to venture forth after the day was done, when others were travelling in the oppos-ite direction, bound for TV and bed, curtains pulled, was a different order. Crossing that nocturnal line is still one of the great coming-of-age markers; it is your graduation into the other dimension and all it offers. Except today it happens much later, kids cannot get into clubs and pubs and bars in London anymore, we've become prissy and puritanical, demanding ID on every door; but when I was fifteen, the time had come, the night was ours, the city was available.

London looks and feels different after dark. The molecules vibrate more slowly, more space around them, making the air rarer, sharper, your visual senses heightened by the crisp contrast between black skies and bright lights, your hearing attuned to pick up sounds on muted streets, your awareness of danger, but also of potential pleasure is piqued and honed. The night is expansive.

Back then London after the curfew was much quieter than it is now, there was no concept of a twenty-four-hour city or the night-time economy. There were almost no night buses, certainly no night Tubes and night czars, shops and just about everything else shut at five, pubs at ten-thirty, there were far fewer restaurants and amenities, far fewer souls to be seen once the curtain of darkness came down. Middle-aged people, middle-class people, nice people, hurried home and stayed there. A Clockwork Orange time.

This city's nocturnal affairs hadn't yet been gentrified, monetised and commodified. The unconstrained streets of the 1970s at night were dark and anarchic, feral and great fun. Certainly out in the dormitory suburbs where we lived, only the eager and the desperate ventured forth, the night was harsh and wild, it was the time for wanton teens, and we desperately wanted to make the most of it.

Standing at the bus stop mob-handed outside the station on a Friday night in 1975, we were 'the little Oak'. Not yet ready for the serious rough and tumble of the Bald Faced Stag and beyond, but bound for the Bandwagon. Our high-waisted, flared strides from Wembley Market flapping round skinny ankles to reveal a pair of platform shoes. Waiting for the bus to Kingsbury for a night of fun, funk and maybe even a fumble, felt like the biggest ever thrill, like you had taken your place in the lineage.

My mum and dad met as teenagers jitterbugging at the Hammersmith Palais, my brothers had come of age skanking in the Tottenham Royal, and I was now going to my first-ever nightclub. The music in my head was already pulsing, the rhythms rocking, the Fatback Band singing 'Bus stop, do the bus stop, people are you ready to do the bus stop.' I was ready.

The frisson in the queue in the car park outside a hall attached to a pub in deepest, darkest NW9 on a Friday night more than forty years ago, is one I can still feel now. Excited, hyped, anxious. Despite the fact that clubs were not too particular about underage punters, I was one of the youngest and there was always a chance the bouncers might make an example. So I learned to stand tall, front it out, make like you belonged. And once inside I quickly grasped the geography and pin-table geometry of a nightclub, the hierarchies and battle lines, the dancers and the dressers, the flirters and fighters, how to navigate the fluid, rhythmic flow of energy around a crowded room where pleasure is the sole purpose of your performance, but myriad dangers lurk.

I studied the peerless ones; the most beautiful girls and the most desirable boys with their routines and retinues. I kept an eye on the dodgy ones, growlers and brawlers, shams and scammers. I could see, despite all the distractions – throbbing music, flashing lights and the air saturated with stinging pheromones – that, like the city itself, a nightclub is a constant interplay of fleeting transactions. London is perpetual motion, showing off and putting out, creating and consuming, buying and selling; it is a dance – do the hustle. Master the night and you have mastered the metropolis.

The Bandwagon was our local Xanadu, serving disparate tribes on different nights. Funk for us on Fridays and Saturdays, heavy metal for the hairy gribos on Thursdays and Sundays and never ever the twain shall meet. That would have been very ugly indeed. This was a strictly teenage pleasure-dome fabled in four postcodes, and it certainly wasn't the only one.

Every far corner of the sprawling city had its local equivalent, all with splendidly terrible names: the Lacy Lady in Ilford, Cinderella Rockefellers and Tiffany's in Purley, the Purple Pussycat in Finchley, Manhattan Lights in Muswell Hill, the Bon Bonnie in Herne Hill, the

Bali Hai and the Cat's Whiskers in Streatham, Elton's in Tottenham, Cheeky Pete's in Richmond, Barbarella's and America's in Southall, the Pink Toothbrush in Raleigh, Flicks in Dartford, Tudor's and Bogart's in Harrow, Scamps in Sutton and Croydon, which also boasted Sinatra's, Dr John's and a disco called Boobs.

Naff as the names may sound, these places featured top DJs like Chris Hill and Robbie Vincent and attracted ardent funkateers from all across town. (Though probably not Boobs in Croydon.) The suburbs held sway, and soul was the sound of young working-class London. Black and white in equal measure, male and female alike, excellent hair, fine attire, Cortinas to travel. And travel these posses did, beyond the boundaries even, to the California Ballroom in Dunstable, the famed Goldmine in Canvey Island, Caister and Bournemouth, mobile funkateers in search of the beat. But they rarely ventured into town.

The mid-'70s funk scene was peripheral, a southern equivalent of the northern soul stompers in such exotic outposts as Wigan and Cleethorpes. But as I claimed my place in the soul train, located my tribe, grew my wedge, wore my pegs and plastic sandals, I began to hear whispers of an exalted, sacred place. Every club had its ace faces, those chosen children graced by the dancing or dressing Gods, and our top ranking Bandwagon boys and girls spoke quietly, discreetly, in the same way my brothers had done about the Scene and the Flamingo, and the word they whispered was Crackers.

The first time I ever went to a nightclub in Soho it was in the middle of the afternoon. Friday lunchtime in late 1975, bunk off school, bunk the fare to Tottenham Court Road, stand amid the shoppers and moochers at the grotty end of Oxford Street, where it meets Wardour, with 50p in the pocket of your jungle greens. In a line with a bunch of the most dauntingly hip black kids and a smattering of good-looking girls and tough camp guys from the hairdressers and fashion stores on South Molton Street, to filter into a grotty basement smelling of burgers and sweat. A disco designed to hold 200 but with double that already present, jazz funk pumping and it isn't even 1 p.m. I was about to enter urban heaven, the greatest ever nocturnal experience by day. I was also about to truly experience and maybe even grasp London for the very first time.

I wrote about Crackers in my previous book *The Way We Wore*. About how it contained the most wonderfully, rhythmically, terrifyingly cool kiddies; the sharpest, most agile, joyous and righteous young Londoners. Pretty much no one present was over the age of twenty-one, gathered from estates and comprehensives all over the city to become, for a few hours at least, exactly who they wanted to be.

It is no surprise that the most highly valued skills at Crackers were dancing and dressing (I was strictly sartorial), because they are traditionally working-class exploits and expertise, often denigrated and derided by the London haute bourgeoisie with their Hampstead hippy pseudo-intellectualism and shabby attire. It has long been a truism that the middle classes can't dance and the working class can't play tennis. And back then the middle classes didn't really do multiculturalism, we did. Crackers was markedly Afro-Caribbean, but also gay, with a Greek Cypriot DJ playing tunes by Idris Muhammad. And no one cared as long as you felt the funk.

Since then I've spoken to numerous people who shared the same crackling Crackers experience, and realise now that what we were all doing while shuffling and hustling to Lonnie Liston Smith and admiring the coruscating moves and the razor-sharp threads, was staking our place in the heart, the very soul of our city. We were reclaiming the night on a Friday afternoon.

Soho had seriously slipped since its swinging '60s heyday, no famed boutiques, no ranking mod clubs, totally dominated by the grubby mitts of the skin trade. It was underwhelming and overlooked, indeed the whole of the West End was down on its luck by the mid-'70s, the glamour was gone. For thrusting young things, the suburbs were the place to be scene. Yet perhaps, somehow, deep in our collective teen psyche we sensed that as Londoners, whether out of Burnt Oak or Bromley, Ealing or Earlsfield, in order to really fulfil all the promises

London makes to you, and for us to do the best by our city, we had to hold the centre.

It is happening again now, the pendulum is swinging back out to the edge, as the core is rendered plush and bland, too expensive, too touristy. It's great that New Cross and Tottenham are hip, and happening, but unless Soho is thriving, the city is ailing. Back in 1976 the West End was starting to rock again.

Buzzing and blinking into the blinding light of a Friday afternoon, dripping with perspiration and exhilaration after a session of the most thrilling teen traction, I felt like a little princelet, a teen pretender. *Bowling and brazen, cocksure and crowing: I live here; I'm from here.* This time, this town is our town.

The secret of cities is that they are theatrical backdrops, or maybe green screens; each generation projects their own story on to the streets. And swanning down Wardour, heading for a record shop in search of import funk, now a confirmed Crackers kiddy, I was Pete Meadon and Budgie Bird, the Artful Dodger and Nik Cohn rolled into one. In reality of course I was a sixteen-year-old schoolboy with a silly haircut, but in Soho reality is negotiable.

I soon learned that it wasn't just Friday afternoons when they served up the funk, and it wasn't just Crackers (though it was always the pinnacle). There was a whole burgeoning inner-city club scene at places like the Global Village, the Lyceum, Bangs, Sombreros . . . Uptown funk indeed. And it was markedly different to the suburban groove. The music was more intense, the crowd more mixed, more gay, more flamboyant, more savvy, more queues at the toilets, less light ale, less trouble, come to think of it, no trouble. Imagine that in 1976, a club with no trouble.

The people who made the effort and headed up West were a self-selecting group. Only a few of my North London mates got into it, while others preferred to stay entrenched in their own fiefdoms. But you met other like-minded souls who liked soul; kids a lot like yourself from every corner of the city, some becoming friends for life. Others you encountered were nothing like you, though perhaps were templates of who you might like to become. Art students, 'entrepreneurs', models, actors; sexy, scary, intriguing characters. You were stretching out, making contacts, lovers, enemies. London was revealing itself as a web, an interconnected network of the night. And there was no trouble.

There were always fights at suburban clubs, flare-ups and face-offs. Usually they were nothing about nothing and all about pissed-up teen posturing, and therefore dealt with pretty quickly, but occasionally a humdinger would erupt and mayhem would ensue. Some people like mayhem; they're good at it. I personally got good at swerving, dodging my way through the maelstrom. But for those who loved a rumble there was always the Irish clubs.

Many if not most of the lads on the Watling Estate were Irish in origin, and occasionally they would pay a little homage to their roots and go to an Irish Dance Hall. In the 1950s and '60s these had been the fulcrums of that heroically hard working, hard drinking, yet always immaculately washed and pressed community, which did so much to create our town. Girls on one side of the room, boys the other, show-bands in their fancy finery on the revolving stage.

There were a whole network of these big, barn-like dance halls throughout London, nineteen at one time including the National in Kilburn, the Hibernian in Fulham, the Blarney in Tottenham Court Road (now Spearmint Rhino where I mourned), the Gary Owen in Hammersmith (which briefly became the Starlight Roller disco where I fell over repeatedly) the Innisfree in Ealing and mightiest and certainly maddest of them all, our local bear pit the Galtymore, a couple of miles up the Edgware Road in Cricklewood. 'The craic was good in Cricklewood.' It certainly was.

I was far from a regular at the Galty, only ever went a handful of times, as my tolerance for Big Tom and the Mainliners playing 'Green Green Grass of Home' was limited. Although I did have one of the most rollicking nights of my life hollering rebel songs with the Dubliners at the National, one St Patrick's. (Being ginger was definitely a boon that night.)

But there's no doubting the fact that hundreds of the Erin Isle's finest packed into a room with a sprung floor awash with stout can make for a memorable event. Until inevitably a bloke who looks like John Wayne's inebriated brother decides enough is enough. Sometimes the room would erupt into a cartoon bar-room brawl, 'bottles flying, biddies crying'; more commonly it would kick off outside afterwards as lads stripped to the waist would trade riotously windmilling blows up and down the Edgware Road for the entertainment of the crowd. Sadly the Galtymore is gone.

And so has pub rock. At the same time as I was being a soul boy with my Burnt Oak mates, so I was a pub rock habitué with my school chums. Going to see bands was what grammar school boys did. And back before punk redrew the rock'n'roll map, there were a plethora of these muscular old Victorian boozers, clustered north of the Marylebone Road, who would put on a band for ten bob in the big room at the back.

Before gastropubs were invented, rock pubs were the thing. From Fulham to Finchley, there were a score or more of these ornate but grubby gin palaces. Typically there'd be a few old boys supping sedately in the saloon bar, while musical pandemonium erupted as Dr Feelgood or Roogalator ripped it up in the back room, maximum rhythm and booze. Between them they housed a uniquely London scene, which was a vital and often visceral precursor to punk.

Of all the rockin' pubs of the mid-'70s, only the Hope and Anchor on Upper Street and the Dublin Castle in Camden Town are still music venues. Many of the names which follow are no longer even boozers, torn down and reborn as not particularly luxurious luxury flats or far-from-super supermarkets. But in 1975 it was a gloriously grubby circuit of light ale and heavy rhythm and blues, or soul, or country, or 'raspberry ripple rock' as Ian Dury described his band Kilburn and the High Roads, who I saw in the Tally Ho in Kentish Town.

Pub rock wasn't defined by one musical style, but a certain stripped back, back to basics, stylistic purity. The ethos was down to earth, spit and sawdust and stained trousers. Which suited such unreconstructed old drinking dens as the Greyhound, the Brecknock, the Elgin, the

Red Lion, the Red Cow, the Pied Bull, the Bull and Gate, the Pegasus, the George Robey . . . and most memorably for me the Nashville Room in West Kensington, where we watched pub rock morph into punk rock over a matter of frenetic, fantastic, ripped and torn months in 1976.

Part of the appeal of going to see bands in boozers back then was in venturing to parts of the capital you might not otherwise know. This was when I first walked down Islington's Upper Street after dark to see some unknown mob called The Stranglers at the Hope and Anchor, just up from the transvestite shoe shop with a photo of Jimmy Edwards in the window. It was when I first got to know Camden Town, which would later become my home. Walking out of the Tube and into the twilight-gleaming, rubbish-strewn, patchouli- and Guinness-scented *Withnail and I* madness of the market for the first time, looking for a place called Dingwalls.

These were journeys of exploration in every sense; geographical, musical, personal, and they cost almost nothing. Back then nothing cost anything much. Going out in London now is much more swish, much more elegant, efficient and infinitely more expensive. You pay for décor and design, exotic cuisine, craft beers, flat whites, night Tubes and Ubers, service with a smile, suited security and exorbitant exclusivity, red ropes, VIP rooms and VAT on top. You pay through the nose to be part of the groovy 'urban experience', when in living memory it was 50p to experience Eddie and the Hot Rods joyously murdering 'Gloria' in a tiny bare bar room packed to the gunnels with sweat pouring down the walls, beer on the carpets and piss overflowing in the invariably blocked bogs.

One of my favourite stories of nocturnal discovery at a pub gig involved the Clarendon in Hammersmith. Officially the Clarendon Hotel and Ballroom, no traces of this vast Edwardian complex remain, wiped away when Hammersmith station and roundabout was completely redesigned to provide a soothingly bland shopping centre to look at while you sit in the eternal traffic jam. This Brobdingnagian boozer favoured by the local Irish sat between the two bafflingly distant entrances to the Tube station: a warren of rooms, one of which became a noted venue on the post-punk psychobilly scene.

One night while watching the Guana Batz or some such, a lady of my acquaintance was pogoing and canoodling exuberantly with a mohicaned boy she'd just met when they leaned heavily against an old door in a far corner of the venue. It opened, and they fell into a full, ornate, intact, although apparently abandoned, Masonic temple, complete with raised dais and a red velvet throne. Let's just say that they took this unique opportunity to engage in considerably more than a Masonic handshake. And while we're talking temples, can anybody confirm that there was once a network of Masonic meeting houses atop the four grand buildings which make up the circumference of Piccadilly Circus?

You never quite knew what would happen on a night out in that old London. It was a much more random, irrational, irregular city, full of surprises and secrets, unpredictable, undiscovered, unreconstructed, splendidly underdeveloped. It was a breeding ground, a giant petri dish with pot holes. In the pre-internet age, stuff had time to gestate in the grimy, hidden recesses of the city.

One of the many reasons why there has been no truly new indigenous youth movement in the twenty-first century is because nothing has the time and space to grow organically before being exposed to the stultifying glare of iPhones and Instagram. Youth culture is like a fungus, it thrives in dark, dank places, basements and musty backrooms. And back in 1976, a mutant offspring of the high fashion, inner-city funk scene typified by Crackers and the back-to-basics pub rock scene at the Nashville was fermenting and bubbling away, about to blow the night apart. I had to get a new outfit.

It would obviously be an exaggeration to state that everything that has happened in London after dark since 1976 was shaped by safety pins and the Sex Pistols, but I am going to state it anyway. Too many words have been wasted on the origins of punk. Suffice to say it was a fireworks display, a pyrotechnical explosion of creativity and anger and joy, and rebellion and truth and youth and beauty cascading across the sky of two undeniably great, yet decaying and derided cities; New York and London.

Punk rock lit up the urban night for a few short months, enabling us all to see a glimpse of the future, and its reverberations and ramifications are still felt now. Punk was a crashing three-chord restatement of the idea that the metropolis is the perfect arena for gutter-up glory. The city as neon-lit art show.

In 1976, after the longest, hottest, steamiest summer on record, it just got hotter, especially at night. Small gangs of provocatively attired teens, most famously from Bromley, but also contingents from Ealing and Hackney, the Angel, Battersea and the Bush, from council estates and squats, comprehensive schools, art schools, hairdressers, boutiques and building sites, even a small coterie of the coolest kids from Burnt Oak, could be seen moving in peacock packs. They clung to the shadows and to each other for safety, furtive yet flash in a still violently judgemental town. These teen provocateurs, these snotty punks, were on their way to a night out in the future.

The do-it-yourself, have-a-go, start-your-own band, brand, magazine, shop, nightclub, fashion house, record label ethos of punk would lead inexorably to the amazing revitalisation of run-down inner London. And if you follow the logic and the line through to today, ultimately to the corporatised, gentrified, all too homogenised Zone One we know now. Punks were proto-urban entrepreneurs in bondage, led by a pair of maniacally brilliant boutique owners armed with situationist slogans. 'Be reasonable demand the impossible.'

It wasn't just the Pistols of course, an idea as virulent as punk is contagious and soon there were scores of bands, foremost among them The Clash, The Damned, Generation X, Siouxsie and the Banshees, The Slits and my particular favourite lost cause The Subway Sect, all hailing from different parts of town, each with their own ardent followings. Bands of fervent teen partisans, all heading into the W1 wasteland under cover of dark for fun and frolics. Let's go pogo.

If we look at the places punk occurred, it is a veritable masterclass in urban regeneration. By day the King's Road was the locus, especially the clothes shops; Sex, Acme, Johnson's and Boy. Throw in Kensington Market for schmutter and Portobello for records, from Rough Trade and Honest Jon's, and you have West London's most desirable postcodes covered.

The brief career of the Sex Pistols maps out a plan of the way London has changed. They lived in a rancid squat on Denmark Street, leaving graffiti on its walls, which has now been Grade II star listed and is currently the property developers' number one target. Their first gig was just over the Charing Cross Road in St Martins School of Art, which was replaced by Foyles's swish literary superstore and luxury lofts. Later they played Central School of Art, Holborn, now corporate offices, and Westfield College Hampstead, which is flats.

The Pistols played at the Marquee on Wardour Street, which was redeveloped as a Conran restaurant and luxury apartments, and round the corner at the El Paradiso Strip Club on Brewer Street, now a Mexican restaurant, and at Andrew Logan's riverside art studio in Butler's Wharf, which has long been a mecca for fine dining and multimillion pound riverfront apartments. Club Babalu on the Finchley Road was subsumed beneath the O2 Shopping Centre, while the Screen on the Green in Islington – then a flea-pit programmed by Steve Woolley – has remained a cinema but is now part of the upmarket Everyman chain.

They played at the Notre Dame Hall Leicester Square (beneath a bizarre circular French church with a Dan Brownish mystical mural by Jean Cocteau), which is now the Soho Theatre and comedy club. Only the 100 Club on Oxford Street (Motto over the door 'Forget the Doodlebugs and Jitterbug') is still as was, a basement oasis of low down rock'n'roll, saved from closure by corporate sponsorship. Their final London gig was out in Uxbridge, where Freddie came from.

Punk could occur in central London precisely because no one else wanted it. London found its CBGBs on the corner of Neal Street when Andy Czezowski opened the Roxy club in December '76. He took over a truly seedy little gay haunt called Chaguaramas, which could no longer pay the meagre rent, set in a former fruit and veg store, made redundant by the closing of the market.

Going to see bands at the Roxy, wearing a mohair jumper from Acme Attractions (sold to me by Don Letts who was also the DJ at the club), a pair of army surplus strides from Laurence Corner in Camden Town and winklepickers, dead stock from Blackmans off Brick Lane, it felt like walking into the opening scene of a zombie movie. We were literally the only people alighting at 8 p.m. on a Monday or Wednesday at Covent Garden's oxblood Tube station. (Which was closed at weekends because of lack of use.)

The area was completely deserted. A ghost town, stripped out and eerily quiet, the old warehouses emanating a morbid silence, the evacuated streets peopled only by a few locals hurrying home and old-school street drinkers, direct descendants of the denizens of Hogarth's Gin Alley, probably unaware of the market's demise. Plus little groups of us punks, bound to see and be Generation X or The Damned.

Then after a session of crashing tunes and flying spittle, walking through the echoing hull of the Victorian market in bondage gear, speeding past midnight with the ghost of Eliza from Lisson Grove, London felt positively post-apocalyptic. But it felt like ours. We had been bequeathed a former city, to shape and mould just as we were inventing ourselves. London let's you become whoever you want, and we were remaking London in our image. Today the Roxy is the Speedo store and Covent Garden is, well, it is what it is.

The punk conflagration was short lived. I was only ever a teenage ticket, studying the faces; though I did end up splashed over the front cover of the *Melody Maker* after a night watching the Banshees at the Vortex. This was another short-lived punk club, squatting a couple of nights a week in Crackers. I got into a theatrically dramatic argument with a certain drummer from Wembley. Keith Moon, who seemed ancient beyond imagining, was out for a night of old-school hell raising with the punky pretenders, accompanied by a scribe of course. I told this pissed old bore I thought he was a has-been (of course secretly I was a huge Who fan), he told me he would set fire to my jacket. Photos were taken, fleeting fame the following Thursday ensued. The idea that it was easy to get into print was lodged in my brain. Mr Moon died a few months later aged just thirty-two.

My particular favourite night of the three-chord cultural blitzkreig was in the Coliseum, a paint peeling porn cinema in Harlesden. Skanking theatrically to Prince Far I booming from the speakers, before watching my favourites the Subway Sect sing 'Everyone Is a Prostitute', The Slits make their chaotic but coruscating debut, and The Clash in their unbeatably splenetic pomp. Pogoing to songs about the Westway, a wrap of sulphate in my socks, feeling like I'd really arrived in a new Lewis Leather's bikers' jacket and Seditionaries jeans with see-through plastic pockets. I was seventeen and my city was arrayed before me. I was about to learn about hangovers.

Just as I got legally old enough to go to clubs, the Roxy closed down and the punky reggae party petered out. The Clash went off to conquer America, and the Pistols went in for a spot of stage-managed self-immolation, amid a wave of bad drugs and not very good 'new wave' bands. Watching 999 in the Nashville Rooms surrounded by the kind of cartoon mohicans who would charge for photos on the King's Road soon lost its appeal and for a while the city slipped into the muted doldrums again. It was all over before I'd even begun.

The late '70s post-punk malaise was spent slumbering in the slums, a void filled by miserabalist northern bands in long green great coats; Gang of Four, Joy Division, Cabaret Voltaire, all gloomy, monochrome and suicidal Manc tendencies. I hated it. Life simply isn't grim enough down south to do misery with any conviction.

The sounds of this city are reggae and soul, glam, grime, punk, funk and pop, upbeat, up-tempo. From the 2i's in Old Compton Street onwards, the London night has produced a plethora of larger-than-life, brighter-than-a-spotlight pop stars. Tommy Steele and Joe Brown, Cliff Richard and Adam Faith, Mark Bolan and David Bowie, and the Pistols and The Clash were very much in that vein. Early British punk, despite the gobbing and the grungy squats, was utterly glamorous and joyously optimistic, coming from the gutters but looking up at the stars. It was a London thing, and when it burned itself out so the city sulked. But something fungal and fabulous was brewing yet again in a Soho basement.

What became known as new romantic, the outrageous outburst of overdressed, posing and preening youth which sashayed out of London's club-land as the 1970s morphed miraculously into the '80s, has been portrayed as the antithesis of punk. But Boy George and Steve Strange, Spandau Ballet, Marilyn, Sade, Wham, Bananarama, Blue Rondo, Animal Nightlife, Ultravox, Adam Ant and that whole coterie of designers, dancers, directors, mountebanks, mannequins and manqués who emerged from a dodgy wine bar called the Blitz, opposite the Freemasons Hall in Great Queen Street, were essentially punk part two, which was really glam part three.

David Bowie, née Jones, born of Brixton, Bromley boy but invented as Ziggy in Walker's Court in Soho, was the chameleon thread linking all these nocturnal shenanigans. Do it yourself. Create yourself. You better hang on to yourself.

Bowie's death in January 2016 led to an unparalleled outpouring of London love, because we realised he was our shining son, our city made flesh, and Oh what pretty flesh. People of all ages gathering in Brixton to paint flashes on their faces and sing his songs, a celebration of our David's timeless music-hall artifice and shape-shifting genius. Bowie was the one 'old timer' the punks admired and emulated, while the '80s generation, most of whom had been like me, teenage punks pogoing at the back, were unashamed disciples of the shaman Starman. Everybody loved Bowie because he was responsible for all of us.

The first iteration of the neo-glam movement, which would define London in the 1980s, occurred in late 1978 on a Tuesday night in Billy's. This was a grubby subterranean warren with a glitter ball, located beneath a brothel called the Golden Girls Club on the corner of Meard and Dean, owned by a scarily humungous pimp by the name of Vince.

It was explicitly labelled a 'Bowie Night', run by Steve Strange, a delightfully stroppy Welsh shop girl in a forage cap who worked in PX, an experimental boutique serving big shouldered 'space Cossack' tops, which had opened in the still-deserted Covent Garden. And the music played by his mate Rusty from Kilburn was almost exclusively Bowie, Roxy and their acolytes.

All London nights in the 1980s were essentially Bowie nights. Most notably the one when the man himself turned up at the Blitz and Mr Strange and the coolest crowd in town turned into gushing supplicants. I know I was one of them. That famed Covent Garden venue, a fusty wine bar opposite the Freemasons' Hall, adorned with gas masks, tin hats and pictures of Winston Churchill, superseded Billy's when Steve and Vince fell out. The Blitz has become rightly legendary for the lavish gang inside and the large queues outside. Bowie got in but Jagger didn't, not glamorous enough.

Like the 2i's before it, the Blitz was a cauldron of rampaging teenage lust for life, with a critical mass of wannabe suburban oiks like myself. We emerged from every far corner of the city under the safety blanket of darkness. Braving the Number 19 bus in our extravagant dressing-up-box finery and theatrical slap for a Tuesday night of Teutonic electronic music and highly charged flirting and networking.

The Blitz proved that all towns are small towns. The couple of hundred flamboyant teenage regulars who got in every week all knew each other. All young, nearly all working class and skint, it was incestuous and fabulous. Most of them fucked each other and chucked each other, but above all, despite the bitching and the backbiting, helped each other. Climbing up on elaborately padded shoulders. In current parlance it was a community. London at night is communal.

This wine bar was our village hall, gossipy and rife with rumour: 'George says he's starting a band.' 'That little John Galliano said he'd make me a shirt.' 'We've got a room in a squat in Warren Street if you want it.' 'Fancy writing the sleeve notes for our record? Graham's taking the photos.' Crowding into the girls' toilets to spray hair, take drugs and take liberties, posing furiously on the tiny dance floor and bitching, scheming and plotting with every open pore. We were pushing the pendulum, desperately trying to make our city swing again. And it worked.

If the '70s in London had been tough and feral, the 1980s were extravagant and febrile, certainly if you were part of the night shift. And the night began to shift and swing.

Amid all those swinging nocturnes, days were harder to locate, but there is one morning which remains in the memory. That was when fellow LSE student Steve Dagger, Holborn council estate lad, persuasive son of a Fleet Street Father of the Chapel, insisted that I had to come to the Holloway Road of a Saturday a.m. to see his boys play. He even managed to get the Welsh contingent Steve Strange and Chris Sullivan along, neither of whom had ever been glimpsed in daylight. I distinctly remember thinking, 'The Holloway Road on a Saturday morning? They'd better be bleedin' good.'

Dragging a dozen or so of London's most ferociously judgemental and hung-over young scenesters to North London's least attractive, permanently drizzling thoroughfare to see a new band was definitely a gamble. But then Dagger knew that his charges, the four he'd been to Owen's School with and the good-looking one, were indeed good. They had a crap name though, The Gentry, so we changed that in a gloomy old Irish boozer nearby, giving Spandau Ballet their risibly perfect moniker. This was directly after their first-ever public performance in a dismal, malodorous rehearsal studio called Halligan's at 95–101 Holloway Road.

Halligan was one of those Irish blokes with bad teeth and a lovely attitude who had acquired a stretch of Dickensian slum terraces up by Highbury Corner. Just up the road from the scene of Joe Meek's infamous, murderous breakdown above a leather goods shop at 304. Mr Halligan let bands play in his slum for a small fee, while he went off drinking with Arthur Mullard. It was raw, cheap and local to the likes of Madness, The Pogues and the nascent Spandaus, who all rehearsed their racket in his place where all the rooms were painted black. Little did we know that this was, or rather had been the Black House. A very dark story indeed.

A decade before the genial Halligan, a certain Michael de Freitas, known as Michael X, a Trinidadian-born Notting Hill-based pimp and hustler who had been Rachman's rent enforcer turned black power advocate, acquired the place. He wasn't quite so nice, as his other moniker 'the archbishop of violence' might suggest. But this charismatic firebrand was popular with John Lennon and a few other guilt-ridden white hippies, who became his main benefactors in a project to create an exclusively Afrocentric cultural centre/hostel. This was the Black House, a dubbed-up Fagin's lair for Mr X's criminal activities.

The local West Indian youths, still suffering the commonplace racism of the '70s, many excluded from schools or work, were attracted to the Black House as a hang out and occasional sound. Scores of West Indian kids crashing out in the black-painted, filth-strewn rooms, smoking and dancing in the yard. But a hard core of very rude boys indeed gathered round Michael X. Mixing militant black separatism with drug dealing, extortion, robbery and a touch of N7 voodoo.

Amulets were worn, rituals performed. John and Yoko were the only non-black folks let in, and they took part in a bizarre exchange of bodily solids on the roof, when they swapped a bag of their newly shorn hair for a pair of Muhammad Ali's sweat-stained shorts, in a supposed fundraising event, before all appearing on TV on the Simon Dee show together. Strange times.

Michael X was also busy raising money other ways. Including kidnapping a local businessman, putting a spiked chain round his neck and torturing him for £13 he supposedly owed. Not surprisingly the police finally intervened. De Freitas/X fled to Trinidad where he was eventually hanged for murder. The Holloway Road still feels dark. The Black House/Halligan's is now a burger bar.

The night is the vanguard of urban change, it's when new venues and new areas, the Hoxtons and Dalstons, Bermondseys and Brixtons, get discovered and colonised, when the pretty people and the crazy people, the smart, sexy, desirous people gather. The night is contagious, it catches on, and as the '80s unfolded so the habit of clubbing became more and more popular, more and more places to go, more and more fabulously, frantically hedonistic.

The litany of clubs that followed the Blitz is long and blurred, a decade's worth of decadence spent in Hell, St Moritz, Le Kilt, Club for Heroes, Le Beat Route, the Camden Palace, the Electric Ballroom, the Mudd Club, the Dirt Box, Dial 9 for Dolphin, the Limelight, the Africa Centre, the Wag. Oh the Wag, what nights we had, Legends, Taboo, Raw, the Hug Club, the Office, Intensive Care. Squat parties, pay parties, house parties, warehouse parties, blues parties, after parties, launch parties, rent parties and rent-boy parties. I was once invited to a 'gay, rockabilly beachwear party' and spent far too long pondering what to wear.

All those clubs, those swanning, wanton events, were run by people you knew and who largely knew each other. London contained a core coterie of entrepreneurial and piratical kids, wild and industrious, incestuous and inventive, a nocturnal freemasonry, knights of the night. 'Greed is good' has become the crass catchphrase of the '80s, and we were indeed avaricious in the extreme, but never really for money. We were greedy for good times and thrills and sex and clothes and drugs and that uniquely urban commodity, recognition; the ultimate aim to be a face. Ours was an urban avarice, to make the most of our youth in our city playground, and our bashed-up, broken-down city began to respond.

I ran a club or two with my stalwart Welsh pal Chris Sullivan, later of the Wag, who lived for a while in my mum's council house in Burnt Oak. I dabbled at being a DJ, but my speciality was playing the wrong side of the record at the wrong speed. Blame it on the speed. Inner London then had an almost limitless stock of potential venues, from Toyah Willcox's 'Mayhem' warehouse in Battersea to a Battleship on the Thames. Spaces that were cheap or free to hire, almost no rules and no restrictions.

The scuzzier the venue, the better. The Dirtbox was famed for seeking out the most run-down, low-down and dirty spaces for their rockabilly-amid-the-rubble extravaganzas. A dodgy sound system, a big stack of beers to flog from a trestle table, and providing you've got the right people in the room, the street elite, you've got yourself a great night. It was always all about the crowd. At one point I remember leaving my flat with a box of tunes to go to a club run by my buddies Spike and Neville, in a disused chemist on the Euston Road, which didn't start until 4 a.m. and was rammed. Is that the night or the morning?

Those bright nights shone out, siren calling you to go out, full on out and out out, no excuses accepted, no prisoners taken. Be there to the bitter end or be terrified that you were missing out, because you probably were. The end sometimes involved a run to Willesden Lane, where London's only known all-night off-licence would sell you a case of under-the-counter lager. Or else it occurred in a tiny room in Soho, with a bare light bulb, a broken pool table, a transvestite with bad mascara, and a man with a Maltese accent in a camel coat, telling you about his gangster film script. Sometimes of course it ended in bed. All the good stuff goes on at night. And some of the bad stuff too. There was lots of bad stuff out there.

I distinctly recall being both fascinated and terrified as a small boy by overheard mod talk of purple hearts and dexys. 'Uppers and downers, either way blood flows.' I was both attracted and repulsed by the vampire image of the pusher-man lurking in Piccadilly shadows. But of course the cliché of the demonic drug dealer luring his punters couldn't be further from the truth. Dealers are friends of friends in basement flats just off the Harrow or the Holloway Road. Dealers are hard to pin down and always late. Dealers are popular people in a bar at night. Dealers run out. London was playing hard, fuelled by pills and powders, lots of fun was had, lots of fun – trippy, ecstatic, voluble, amiable, passionate, whirling, gurning fun – until it wasn't.

Golden brown ripped through the night in the mid-'80s, inveigling itself into veins, turning good people into tragic, deceitful bores in thrall to muffled, melancholic half-light. (R'n'B took on a sinister new meaning: it was a short hand for rocks and brown, crack and heroin.) Too many friends were mired in the sickly miasma of addiction, locked inside the dragon's den. Most escaped and regained their souls, a couple never did. The night is a dangerous and seductive place.

And soon all London seemed to be seduced by the narcotic, erotic power of nocturnal activity. Bright young things lighting up the firmament, creatives cavorting, supermodels in Soho, actors and pop stars in designer duds, flashlight flash, stretch extravagance, paparazzi in Hoxton. Bloody Hoxton, how did that happen? This early closing, noise abating, drearily conservative and censorious city we'd inherited was certainly swinging again, the wastelands were buzzing. Then it started raving, dancing to a different drug.

Ecstasy started out as an uptown sex aid, a glamorous love drug that fuelled many a mass fumble in a Manhattan loft. But once it was allied with the repetitive beats, the repetitive beats, the repetitive beats of house music, it rocked the house, or rather the sweaty old gym in Bermondsey. Shoom went the night, an onomatopoeic rush of MDMA-driven euphoria and inchoate idiot dancing which transformed grizzly Millwall beer monsters into loved-up hippies in Kickers and dungarees. The second summer of Love in SE1. I went down to Shoom in a Gaultier suit and saw the future. I knew it would end up in a field.

The late '80s rave scene, with all those jolly orbital japes leading the old bill a merry dance round a farmyard somewhere beyond the M25, was probably enormous fun. I wouldn't know. I was now ensconced in an exclusive members' club in Dean Street, my dancing largely done, my distaste for mud and ill-fitting clothes reconfirmed, moaning about the modern generation, showing my age.

In truth, rave was the last great hurrah of British youth culture, the last truly new indigenous, inclusive scene, which shaped the music, clothes, attitudes and lives of its many millions of adherents. And it helped reshape our city, broadening horizons, bringing in Hackney Wick and Wembley. But I've always been an urban elitist, at least at night, a mod at heart; the Scene club in Ham Yard not Glastonbury in Gloucestershire for me.

By the '90s London had started to have it large. The Ministry of Sound was the first sign of what was to come. A vast, swish, corporate, branded, money-making house music machine, in a former bus garage in the Elephant. Founded by a property developer called Palumbo, it's a been-there-bought-the-T-shirt-and-the-CD-and-all-the-merchandise-with-the-logo franchise. Welcome to the era of humungous super-clubs. (Anything described as 'super' is instantly dubious.) With superstar DJs paid vast sums to pump out predictably four-on-the-floor anthems for the huge crowds who now wanted a part of the party. Clubbing as mass entertainment and big bucks business.

London by night is now open for business. Wide awake, busy, bustling, well organised, safe and well-served by transport and, bizarrely, fruit and veg. Who actually buys bananas or cucumbers at 3 a.m. from all those shops on Green Lanes? Compared to the curfew and the drawn curtains of my youth, London is now a genuinely nocturnal city all over the city. The West End is full of tourists, the North is gorging on bourgie restaurants and bars, the East is swamped with Essex 'bridge and tunnel' searching for the hip in Hoxton, while the South is proper hip, scuzzy, impermanent, inspiring: afrobeats in Lewisham anyone, grime in Croydon? London now is saturated and sophisticated after dark. Yet it can still throw up the occasional surprise.

I now only get tempted out to watch jazz, still in thrall to the baffling, beautiful alchemy of improvisation. A jazz night usually involves strolling through Soho to Ronnie's or the Pizza Express, nodding to the regulars, nodding my head sagely at a horn solo or tapping my feet to some poly-rhythms before retiring round the corner to my club for a nightcap.

But recently the air has been crackling with suggestions of a scene, a fuss that has to be seen, a group of brilliant young players, taking this difficult old man's music and remaking it afresh. Yet another UK jazz revival, at least the third in my lifetime, this time blending the beats of afrobeat and drum and bass, dubstep, garage and grime, with some proper out-there instrumentalism. Jazz but not as we know it; jazz not jazz. Played by proper twenty-first century London names like Nubya, Yussef, Shabaka, Zara and Moses, in places like Peckham, New

Cross and Tottenham. It's happening again, and it could only happen here. I had to go witness.

The Total Refreshment Centre is typical, perfect. An unmarked, bare concrete, low-ceilinged, windowless joint behind a car wash in Stoke Newington, the ideal place to see this scene. Paying my sick squid entry to a grinning, wide-eyed girl on the door and getting a rubber stamp on the back of my hand, I felt simultaneously ancient and alive, entering a room filled with young, contemporary London.

The atmosphere was crackling. Energy, energy, laid back but bristling. Dressed down in that very dressed up way; there were a few beards but also afros and crops and locks, beanies and berets, dashikis and guay-aberas, ankles a go-go, loafers no socks. There were girls, lots of girls at a jazz gig, unheard of, and every human hue easy in their skins, with a prevalent mocca tone and a multilingual hum blending Spanish and Italian, Ghanian and Nigerian, Jamaican and Jafaican, all rinsed through current London chatter, amiable and admirable. Cockney not cockney; jazz not jazz.

It was as if all those Benetton adverts had finally come true. The DJ spun vinyl of course, but played too with a computer, mixing and moulding ancient and modern, the tunes inducing nods and shuffles from the groovy, grooving crowd. A truly inspiring, smiling, polyglot, pretty, interracial, gender equal young London at ease with itself, dancing gently to some broken beats. Sipping from two quid tins, comparing work wear, smiling at the old man in the corner.

And then the band came on, sprawling, electronic, acoustic, jazz not jazz, great young players, playing with great skill and easy enthusiasm; kids steeped in the tradition but free to float above it. Truly modern. And the crowd started to dance, and the girl with the curly hair blowing tenor started to soar, and the brilliant drummer snapped staccato rim shots in a grime style that could only come from here, from these streets and these postcodes, and the keyboards boy punched percussive fills and this beautiful hybrid could only come from here, from now, from deep down London.

And the room was moving as one, and I was one of them, lost in the rhythm, totally in the moment, dancing to jazz in an impromptu nightclub in a way I hadn't done since Art Blakey's 'Night in Tunisia' rang out on a night in Camden Town back in '85.

I allowed myself a smile. I felt so proud. God I love London at night.

Jesus's Blood

Every Christmas Eve I play 'Jesus's Blood'. It has become an almost sacred ritual on my radio show that the last record featured before we head home for the festivities is Gavin Bryars's touching, slightly disturbing orchestral accompaniment to a homeless man singing a simple homily to the redeeming power of Christ's corpuscles. Although technically nothing to do with yuletide, it is a timely reminder to us all, especially me, that this great city exacts a cost. It is cacophonous with the voices of the lost and the weary, yet usually we do not hear them above the hubbub.

The story behind Bryars's plaintive, achingly beautiful piece is an interesting one. He was doing field recordings – if you count the piece of grass in front of St John's church opposite Waterloo station as a field – for a documentary about homelessness in London in 1971. One of the recordings, of a man known only as 'the tramp', captured this fellow, his voice frail and ethereal, yet tuneful and strangely compelling, quietly singing this refrain: 'There's one thing I know, for he loves me so, Jesus's Blood never failed me yet.'

We know no more about the singer or the song, but Bryars knew that it would make a powerful piece of music when looped alongside a full orchestra. Indeed it does, soulful and emotional, and my listeners know it heralds that time of year when we are supposed to think of others. But what are we supposed to do the rest of the time?

The homeless, the rootless, the street dwellers and drinkers, the tramps and vagrants of old, are part of the everyday experience of life in a metropolis. But they are also a barometer, a way of discerning how the economy is doing, how parts of the city are faring. Now that London is a truly global metropolis, and those who seek slender shelter on its streets can come from far and wide, it is also a barometer of how the world is doing. And it's a way of ascertaining which particular poison is most popular.

My first real memory of a group of tramps came when I stayed at my cousin Ian's prefab on Fish Island in Bow, back in about 1969. We were no more than nine or ten, and went off on an adventure around Spitalfields, which looked like many bombs had hit it; which of course they had. Today this area is what local artists Gilbert and George call 'the most modern place on Earth'. Back then it was still viciously Victorian, with a sombre, 'end of days' atmosphere.

There was an air of dreadful loss hovering over those cratered and crumbling old streets. Shrouded in a doomy silence, almost bereft of life save for a large huddle of what seemed like ancient creatures, bedraggled and dishevelled, old coats tied with string, skin caked with grime, voices aflame with vivid pink madness.

Sitting around a burning brazier in the middle of the road shouting and cursing, these were 'methies'; imbibers of methylated spirits, openly swigging their bottled addiction. And seeing them, hearing them, smelling them, terrified me. I had nightmares about tramps for years, haunted by the image of those grizzled old geezers on the streets of the far east. In my dreams they would catch me and turn me into one of them. And of course London can do that. Slip, and London can do that.

As time progressed, so I saw successive waves of damaged street souls. In Burnt Oak in the late '70s there was a group of glue sniffers, kids who succumbed so completely to the lure of a tin of Evo-Stik that they lived in their own filth in a 'cave' under the back of the high street behind where Tonibells was, their sticky faces 'black as Newgate's knocker'. Then it was the shambling junkies of St Giles, after that the emaciated King's Cross crack-heads, always agitated, angular, darting, desperate for a pipe. Every city has its collateral damage.

But in the 1980s a different kind of homeless person emerged on the streets, in the underpasses, in the squares and parks and fields and doorways of my town. They were the casualties of neo-liberalism, caught in the not-so-friendly fire of Thatcherism. Many of them young, not yet ravaged but hollowed out by hard times. You stepped over them as they slept.

The Strand in particular was a dormitory by night, every doorway occupied, but every thoroughfare was a wasteland occupied by the lonely and *the lost. And they made vast communal encampments. Lincoln's Inn Fields, one of London's loveliest spots, was Tent City, a veritable shanty town of hundreds of homeless people in permanent occupation. Just over the river in Waterloo, where the Imax is now, was an even more precarious community of human flotsam living in the labyrinthine underpasses of the roundabout. This was Cardboard City, a truly desperate collection huddled together for warmth. Both were demolished in the 1990s, their inhabitants scattered.*

Sometimes, though, one of the characters of the road gains a permanent place in our collective heart. Most areas have their local street ranters or bedraggled eccentrics; Camden Town has scores, from the Stetson wearing 'right-stoned cowboy' to Merlin the magician and the disco granny, but none are a match for Little Jimmy. How we all loved Little Jimmy.

Not technically homeless, Jimmy lived with his old mum Edie in a Dickensian tenement block, but spent all his time prowling the streets of EC1, the veritable King of Clerkenwell. Under four feet tall, of indeterminate age, but very determined views, he hated bad parking, or indeed any kind of parking. Jimmy was a vigilante.

All day, every day, Jimmy patrolled his patch with a notepad and pencil, haranguing car drivers, shouting, waving, directing traffic, guarding yellow lines like a zealot. Everybody knew Little Jimmy and knew not to get on his wrong side. For generations Jimmy ruled EC1.

The police were more than aware of their freelance co-worker and supposedly kept his back from the wrath of enraged motorists. But local legend has it that they once had a big problem with Little Jimmy. The Queen Mother was coming to open a new library on Theobald's Road, and they just knew that Jimmy wouldn't tolerate her limousine parking up on his territory. So to save the Queen Mum from Little Jimmy's ire, they locked him up in a cell for the duration of the royal visit. But to make up for it they apparently fed him in their canteen for years afterwards.

Jimmy, sadly, is gone. The tents, sadly, are back.

Who's the Best Dressed Man in London?

The answer to that question is actually quite easy, except he's not often in London. Charlie Watts, drummer with The Rolling Stones, breeder of Arabian thoroughbreds on his estate down in Devon, and owner of the greatest wardrobe ever created for a jazz fanatic lorry driver's son from Wembley, has long been acknowledged as the consummate stylist.

Look at pictures of his band from every period and it's Charlie who stands out by doing less and doing it just so, never flash, or rather never too flash. Mick is great looking, Keith looks great, but Charlie, who can do Savile Row, can do Ivy League, can do country squire and city slicker, scoop-necked casual and high-buttoned formal, has looked effortlessly immaculate for nearly six decades. I once saw him walking along Frith Street towards Ronnie's where he was playing with his jazz band, and I almost wept at the understated yet pinpoint precision of his attire. Sorry for being soppy, but it was beautiful, a perfect Soho moment.

Bryan Ferry comes close in his soft-shouldered Anderson & Sheppard. Bill Nighy, taking lunch on his own with a book – always in a navy suit – always in Cecconi's. Paul Smith emerging from the RAC Club after his morning swim looks right; David Rosen, who knows London better than any other man, has the best collection of loafers in town; Jeremy King in his slate-grey Bristol 411 is immensely immaculate.

There is indeed a certain group of gentlemen of a certain age and a certain back-story, all self-made men, who keep the traditions alive. But Charlie is unchallenged. He keeps a house in South Ken and stays there a few times a year. I asked him once what he does when he's in town and he said, 'I take a Turkish bath and I visit my tailors.' And he meant tailors plural: 'You have to have two, and you tell them both the other one's better.' I've had loads.

Getting your first whistle made at the local tailors was always a rite of passage, a coming-of-age moment. It was a big day when a man first thrust a tape measure up your teenage particulars and asked you what sort of fabric you wanted. I got my debut suit from Shepherd's Bush, a disastrous attempt to look like Rod Stewart in his bottle green Tommy Nutter on the cover of Never a Dull Moment. Since then I've tried an old Jewish fellow round the back of Altab Ali Park in Whitechapel who did a nice Max Baer back. I visited a part-time soul DJ in a basement in Fitzrovia for that sleek '60s look. I went Soho Sam and I've spent fortunes with such exalted names as Kilgour, French and Stanbury, Nick Tentis, Mark Powell and Timothy Everest.

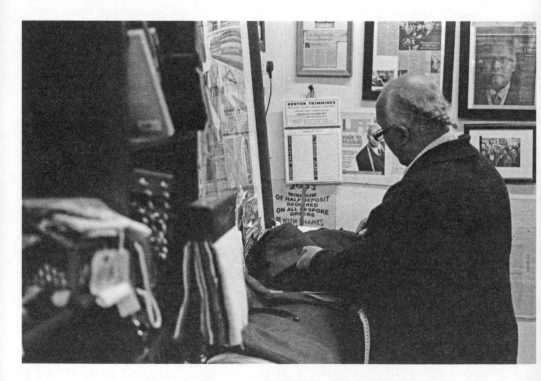

I've been bespoke and I've tried made-to-measure, there was even a time I fell for the ready-to-wear designer trap and gave my money to flighty Italians on Bond Street. I've got a wardrobe full of whistles, some of them thirty years old, but all of which still fit – well, nearly. Yet still I feel the need to go once a year and have a word with my man with a pin in his mouth. Which these days means a trip over the water.

The Savile Row experience is unrivalled, sumptuous. The rich wealth of expertise, the élan of the premises, the exactitude of the process and of course the undoubted excellence of the finished garment, but also unfortunately the exorbitant expense. I still love ambling along the Row; a spot of window watching. It is like twisting the fabric of time, being transported, not so much on trend as beyond trend, ageless, timeless. Just like Eliza wanted to be a 'M(a)yfair Lady' in her Lisson Grove accent, so I love playing the man about Mayfair, but I can no longer justify the price tag.

For a quarter of the cost I can head down the Walworth Road and spend an hour or so with George. We talk frogmouth pockets and English versus American vents, discuss pitched lapels and whether the original modernists would have ever sported turn-ups: he say no, I say yes. Mark Baxter might join us and try and flog me some new band, book or movie project he's involved in. Ed Gray the painter, one of London's finest chroniclers, is also a regular, often popping by just to chew the fat. There's a whole little South London scene based around George's tiny, dishevelled half-a-tailor's shop, in a scruffy money transfer and kebab house parade, just up from the Elephant. And I am honoured that they let me be part of their gang occasionally.

George Dyer is a West-Indian Londoner with an accent just south of the Old Kent Road, a tape measure round his neck and a measured manner, which brings to mind gents of old. He is kind and considered, he knows what he's talking about and also what he's doing, which is making you feel good, because you look good. Most of his clients are in the mod mode: Paul Weller and Martin Freeman can both be seen among the pictures of his punters, which adorn the crowded walls. But he can turn his hand to a conduit cut or a drape back if necessary.

Every high street would once have had a George – they were part of every community – but there aren't very many left, and his little shop now feels like a throwback. It was with great pride that I first took Alfie, then Maude, to the deep South to get some schmutter made. They need to know.

And it was going to see another George one night, also on Frith Street, that I realised just how far and wide a rare craftsman like Mr Dyer now spreads his talents. It was Georgie Fame who was playing Ronnie Scott's, and as usual it was a great show from one of our finest. But rather than watching the band I spent most of the night studying the punters' attire, counting the amount of George Dyer suits sitting in that room. I stopped just short of a dozen, happy that someone is keeping the look alive.

CHAPTER SEVEN

Leaving Home

Aunt Nell, who was married to my mum's brother Jack – a handsome desert rat with a fine moustache, never seen without a tie, rode a moped, worked for the gas board – passed away aged ninety-one about a decade ago. She'd been something of a beauty, a noted dancer at the Hammersmith Palais, friend of Al Bowlly, quite a catch for a chap from White City, always talked a bit posher than us. Nell never really recovered from the loss of her beloved husband, the man she always called 'My Jack', and finally just slipped away in the house in Chiswick they'd lived in together.

On the day of her funeral there weren't that many people present, a sure sign that you've lived a long life, outlived most of your friends; but the remaining family members and a few kindly neighbours gathered at the house afterwards for the obligatory cold sausage rolls and warm words. It was then that somebody told me something remarkable about Aunt Nell, which is that she died in the very room in which she had been born more than nine decades before.

This had been her parents' house, and she and Jack had taken it over, only ever renting, for an entire (long and largely happy) existence in one terraced, two-up two-down – extension on the kitchen, nice little garden – Edwardian semi, in a quiet side street in Chiswick. She never left home. That was her manor. That was her London. That was her life.

There can't be many people, in a city as fluid and dynamic as our contemporary capital, who have stayed put for an entire existence. People move around. They arrive here and flit about, switch postcodes, cross rivers, climb ladders, swap flat shares for flats, flats for houses, flee to the suburbs or make it to the centre. Many come for a few years after college to try and make their name, their fortune, their family, then bugger off again in search of big gardens and small mortgages. Some succumb to the spurious idea that this is no place to bring up kids, who surely need a few more sheep and a little less diversity to prosper, so head off to some dreary white-bread market town and wait for the one bus a week.

But if, like me, you are from here; if this is all you've known and what you're used to in your bones, you have nowhere else to go. We're not just passing through, it isn't a stage of our lives or a phase we're going through, it's a life sentence: we're Londoners, born to the tumult. Though we still have to find our place.

I do know plenty who've left, of course, most of my own family are scattered. My eldest brother Barry has lived in New England for forty years, while Reggie made his life in Hemel Hempstead, part of the diaspora of working-class Londoners who were pushed further and further to the edge-lands. They never so much left their home town as extended it, making large swathes of not-quite-rural Essex, Kent and Hertfordshire into little Londons in exile. That's often where the old accent survives and the old culture thrives. But it's always back into town for the football, the pubs, the shopping, the restaurants, the craic. Their grown-up kids wondering sadly why they no longer live in fashionable Dalston or Brixton, Haggerston or Bermondsey. *What went wrong, Dad?*

Plenty of the elders have cashed in and retired to the coast. Off to Eastbourne or Bournemouth, to spend their last years gazing at the waves, while remembering fresher, friskier days on the Portobello. Too many younger Londoners, appalled at preposterous property prices, unable to make it work here, have also packed up and shipped out to sea. Settling in Brighton, Hastings, Margate; becoming DFLs (down from London) making the most of it, making little enclaves in those coastal outposts come alive with metropolitan brio.

And the first thing they all tell you when you meet them is how easy and quick it is to return, how short the train journey is back to town. I know the look hidden in those nearly convincing eyes, it's what the Portuguese call 'saudade': a longing for your former land. London is in their blood, which is thicker and richer and saltier than any sea water.

*

I left London a couple of times, spent some time in two other great, teeming port cities. I was yo-yoing back and forth to New York in the early 1980s when it was truly the most earth-shattering city on Earth. I was filing reports for *The Face*, DJing in Danceteria, swanning in Area, practising survival skills on the Lower East Side and watching hip hop explode out of the South Bronx. I graduated from a freezing loft on Pitt and Delancey, via Avenue A to Gramercy Park with a key. Then she threw me out and London beckoned.

Later there was an extended sojourn in Barcelona, beginning in 1986, watching that elaborate, elegant but querulous town come joyously back to life after forty years under Franco's suffocating shroud, while living with a fiery Catalan beauty and writing a novel set in Soho. That was the start of a life-long love affair with my Spanish mistress. The lure of Iberia has been a constant pull: elemental and poetic, brutal and romantic, so saturated with light and dark compared to London's relentless sheets of grey. I frequently run off south to indulge her. But I know it is only a dalliance, never doubt I'll be back home.

New York and Barcelona were both exhausting and exhilarating, but even those two great cities veered towards parochialism for me. London always felt more rounded, more outward-looking, more worldly. All that history and all that novelty; a rock of solidity and a springboard of creativity, ensuring you always have to know what's happening here. The unique blend of past and future makes for a compelling present. All towns are small towns compared to mine.

There is actually a certain maiming melancholy, a burden to bear for coming from this city, because deep down you know all the other options pale by comparison. The only way is down, every other urban experience is diminished; everywhere else is less. If a Londoner has left, you know they know they've left something behind; they've lost something.

I'm not saying London is better than everywhere else – and it certainly isn't easier. Of the places I have visited, Paris, Venice, Seville and Prague are probably more beautiful, Rome more ancient, New York and Hong Kong more breathlessly thrusting. LA is more . . . Well, actually LA is more sunny and much more vacuous, what Raymond Chandler brilliantly described as '72 suburbs in search of a city'. Personally I can't stand the place, couldn't find it, but they do make movies, so loads of Londoners rock up there.

Istanbul is just as intriguingly historic and vibrantly contemporary as London; perhaps our closest kin. Mexico City is magnificently mad and incredibly cultured – a truly profound and thrilling metropolis. Berlin is cheap, charismatic and creative, full of techno kids in black but still recovering from its traumas. Tokyo is bafflingly (to me, boringly) modern. I'm told Lisbon and Shanghai are currently happening. But really, come on, compared to here, all these towns are a long way off.

London is doomed to be deemed the centre of the earth. Arne Saknussemm should have just headed to W1. I don't know if this is a permanent position: pendulums swing, zeitgeists shift, contenders rise. Maybe one day an African or Asian megalopolis will emerge, as we become Vienna, a dotage city frozen in former glories, yearning for long-forgotten empires while scoffing cake. But in global terms, London has been paramount, or at least slugging it out for the title with New York throughout my lifetime. And since Manhattan went zero tolerance, minimum creativity, maximum moulah, London has been pretty much the undisputed champ. It's hard to leave the champion of the world.

But its primacy is under threat as never before, besieged from all sides – and from inside. Brexit, which was little England's revenge on its overarching, liberal, polyglot, world-beating capital, threatens to cut us off. Making London isolated, denied the vital blood transfusions immigration brings, while the corporate vultures from Frankfurt and Paris hover over the City.

Property developers threaten to price and bland us out, selling their soulless apartment blocks to absentee owners and their retail units to identikit chains; rendering whole areas ghostlike, but well supplied with scented candles. Does anyone know anyone who lives in Nine Elms? And does anyone know where the next generation of musicians and artists and entrepreneurs and scallywags are going to colonise? Does anyone know where Barkingside is?

Wealth itself is a challenge and London is a far wealthier city now than in my childhood days. Poor cities are dynamic; they change easily, frequently, growing, morphing, striving, improving, but rich ones are frozen by their investment in the status quo, atrophied by affluence. The poor have energy; the rich have inertia.

I chuckled recently when I saw a young man wearing a baseball cap bearing the logo 'Make Peckham Shit Again', but it isn't funny. The young need slums. And I do not mean twenty blokes from Slovenia crammed into a garden shed in Enfield. That is not an opportunity: that is a crime. When you're starting out outside the family home in London, whether you've come from near or far, what you require above all else is somewhere cheap and ideally central enough that you can take advantage of the capital. Remake this city afresh for your generation, instead of watching it from afar.

You don't want luxury apartments, gymnasiums, concierges and endless poxy coffee shops, unless perhaps daddy is rich and you've just arrived to take a post at Goldman Sachs. You want *Withnail and I* with a good supply of Camberwell Carrots.

Finding your niche in this giant jigsaw of a city is never easy. And when you come from here there's another big question: 'Where you from?' When a Londoner asks that of another Londoner, it is loaded, it pins you down, marks you out. It's not the same question as 'Where do you live?' which can be transient, just for now. 'Where you from?' is something you can't easily shake off. The actual form the question traditionally took was, 'Where you out of?' You're actually asking which mould made you, because the different parts of the city are shorthand; branded by the postcode.

A boy from Burnt Oak is immediately a very different proposition from one from Edgware, though they may be separated by just a street or two. Paddington is not the same as Bayswater, which is definitely different to Hyde Park. Peckham is not Dulwich, or at least it wasn't until recently. Islington is Islington, but the Balls Pond Road is a long way from the Angel. Small distances make big differences. Cross Regent Street from Soho to Mayfair and you traverse an unseen border, enter another realm, breathe altogether different air. A Mayfair lady and a Soho girl are worlds apart. Aunt Nell was Chiswick; Uncle Jack was Shepherd's Bush. That was a mixed marriage in West London terms.

Of course, class plays a big part in this. Coming from South London is one thing, but do you mean Southwest, or Southeast? Barnes or Bermondsey? Richmond or Rotherhithe? Literally a class apart. Although the lines have been blurred by gentrification, London is still a stratified, hierarchical city. But it's more than just where you stand on the elaborate British housing ladder.

Different areas have different characters and create different char- acters. We are indelibly shaped by our specific neighbourhood, raised by a village. So for example, if I meet somebody out of, say, Pimlico, I figure I know a bit about them. Chances are they're Chelsea, though they probably don't go any more: too corporate, too Surrey. They're very likely to be smart, into garms, because Pimlico had a big mod cohort, who all hung out in the same youth clubs. The Small Faces even lived there. Despite coming from a council estate, they may well work in the 'creative industries' – photographers, designers, or else in high-end retail. Because the proximity to the Tate and the King's Road on one side and the West End on the other meant opportunities abounded, though there's a fair few cab drivers too. They know London.

A bod from Pimlico will probably have a partner from Pimlico: it's a very cliquey, close-knit place; passports and all that. And chances are they will still be there. You can maybe take Pimlico out of the boy, but it's really hard to take the girl or boy out of Pimlico if they can possibly avoid it. They will certainly never cross the river, which they could see from their window, because despite the SW postcode, Pimlico is ardently north of the Thames. Battersea is another world, which they don't much like.

I liked where I was from. The Watling Estate had been a great place to grow up, I was intensely proud of being a council estate kid – and I couldn't wait to leave. Getting this boy out of Burnt Oak became a mission. The ancestral homelands hovered over me, taunted me, and I knew I wasn't going to stay put on the periphery. I had always intended to aim for the heart, even though at that time inner London was still viewed primarily as a place to flee from. I was searching for home.

I distinctly recall telling Mr Miglio from the Beta Café in Burnt Oak that I fancied living in Clerkenwell. I had discovered EC1 while studying in nearby Holborn, and fallen in love with its winding cobbled streets and steep, storied alleyways, but he looked at me as if I was insane. His family had done everything to escape from what he saw as the slanted slums of Little Italy.

'What do you want to go there for Robert? It's a dump.'

So many times since I've heard that response, whether it is Jewish families in big houses in Mill Hill aghast at their offspring aspiring to Whitechapel, Irish folks cursing Kilburn or my own mum's swift dismissal of Notting Hill: slums, they're all slums.

Back in 1980 I was twenty-one and searching for the keys to any door. The time had come for me to fly the coop and getting a flat was relatively easy. You could rock up at Capital Radio on the Euston Road, where they advertised flat shares on a board in the foyer. Or else you just bought the first edition of the *Standard* (yes you had to buy them then) from a bloke with a foghorn cry outside a station as early as possible on a Thursday morning. You ringed an advert or two with a biro, went to a phone box with a bag full of ten pence pieces and providing you could afford twenty-odd quid a week you could pretty much pick where you wanted to live.

Chances are it would be a shithole, but that's fine – that's all you need and all you really want when you're young. I know one person who lived in Edith Grove in Chelsea for £18 a week, in the '80s: a great address, but only cold water available in the flat. Another in a £22-a-week bedsit in Bayswater got a weekly box of cornflakes put by the door, as their tenancy was officially bed and breakfast. I had never even made my own bed or washed my breakfast bowl, but I was just about to forgo my mum's unceasing love and overcooked vegetables for a place I'd found through a friend, in a crumbling old block on Rosebery Avenue. Fifth floor, no lift, one room with a kitchenette, and a toilet and shared bath up the hall. When suddenly I fell in love and into suburban Wood Green instead.

The girl in question was a half-Nigerian, half-Essex former fashion student from St Martins, who was residing in a run-down but perfectly habitable, and indeed admirably ordered house in Wood Green, N22. I had never knowingly been to that part of North London in my life, certainly had no desire to live there, until I met this extraordinary force of nature in New York on the night Bobby Sands died.

The old line about the rest is history is sort of true, because of course Helen Folasade Adu would go on to became one of the most famous singer/songwriters in British history. Only recently overtaken by Adele (from up the road in Tottenham) as our most successful ever international female artist. But back then Sade was trying to make it in the fashion game and living in a semi-official squat as part of something snappily called the North London Short Life Housing Co-operative. So after a rapid romance I spent the £80 I'd saved as a deposit for a flat in Clerkenwell on a broken 1950s Rockola jukebox (which I somehow later lost) and moved in with her instead.

The NLSLHC, specialised in reclaiming properties owned, but left empty, by local councils (of which there were legion) across a swathe of Northeast London. They were a hangover from the '70s squatting movement, still fired by hippy idealism and soggy roll-ups, but also a steely ability at both breaking and entering and legal technicalities. They were old hands and wise heads.

Sade's buccaneering older brother, Banji, who had his own squat nearby, specialised in the breaking and entering bit. He liked nothing more than shimmying over a pitched roof at dusk with a jemmy between his teeth. He did just that on an old abandoned fire station that had caught his eye. Which was handy, as just a few months after I moved in, we'd been told that we were about to be evicted from the Wood Green house. The council had finally found the money to provide the house with an inside toilet and do it up so that they could legally let it out to families on their waiting list, which meant we had to move on. Fair enough.

The old fire station was on Conway Road, a near-silent, residential backstreet a mile-and-a-half south, just off St Anne's Road in N15. A handsome if neglected three-storey red-brick Edwardian building, with double height space for the fire appliances (the first in London with a petrol-driven engine apparently) on the ground floor and four flats above where the firemen used to sleep. That's where we were going to live.

It had clearly been empty for a very long time when I clambered clumsily in with Banji through the window he'd opened on his recce. The place was covered in cobwebs and the spiders that made them; the only bath was in the kitchen and the only toilet outside on the balcony. There was no electricity and no heating. Perfect.

This area of N15 is one of those in-between bits, a twilight zone, which doesn't really know if it is South Tottenham, Green Lanes or Harringay. Too far from a Tube to be desirable; too solidly residential to be hip. It had, and still has, a slightly forgotten air, with old hand-painted shop fronts and builders' yards with no obvious purpose. We changed the locks, connected the services, sanded the floors, moved our stuff in (that jukebox was a bastard to get up the steep stairs) and informed the council that we would pay rates and bills, strictly following the NLSLHC guidelines.

A couple of pretty good years were spent there, and when I went back recently to take a look, people were still living in the flats we had effectively created. As Sade's ambitions moved from fashion to music, and the place became a crash pad for her band, we had some jolly times. We always got on with the neighbours. Except for one lot of hairy, tattooed, leathery chaps who unilaterally moved into an empty flat in the building and then proceeded to rebuild a series of other people's vehicles in their living room to the sound of heavy metal and panel beating. I think they were the real target when we got noisily raided by a squad of armed police officers one dawn.

That took a little explaining to the people in the houses around us. They were mainly Greek-Cypriot families with bequiffed sons and black-clad grandmothers, but they accepted our profound apologies and protestations of innocence because they liked Sade – everybody liked Sade. The extraordinary tolerance, even kindness of the locals to a bunch of oddly dressed kids squatting in their street was a real lesson in urban manners. This is a city of live and let live and they not only let us live among them, but occasionally gave us food and invited us to funerals.

In retrospect, the Greek-Cypriot community with their fanciful cake shops were nearing the end of their Harringay hegemony, heading north, out to Southgate and beyond. Ironically they were about to be replaced by their eternal enemies, the Turks, with their social clubs and ocakbasis, and their twenty-four-hour greengrocers, which pretty much dominate Green Lanes to this day.

The young West Indian ragamuffins from the nearby Broadwater Farm estate made the area pulse with a reggae-driven rude-boy beat, but you could feel the tension on the neglected and excluded Farm rising before it finally blew. There was also an almost forgotten Irish community who drank morosely in the Salisbury, a wondrously ornate Victorian Gin Palace, which at that stage was down on its elaborate uppers. And neat, smart Indian couples who watched Bollywood films at the flea-pit cinema next to the typewriter shop on Turnpike Lane. Then there was a mass of indeterminate, slightly browbeaten Tottenham supporting locals who mourned the loss of their dog track and their factories. Old London showing its age.

The only real downside of life in the fire station was the outside toilet, on a balcony off the kitchen. (I quite liked the bath being in there, taking a soak while keeping an eye on the pasta sauce is quite soothing.) Whenever the winter thermometer dipped, the water in the bowl froze, and while breaking the ice at parties is one thing (and believe me we had some parties), breaking the ice for your early morning evacuation is another. That was exactly the situation when Sade's first record made it into the charts and she was summoned to appear on *Top of the Pops*. The record company had sent a long shiny car to pick her up, but the toilet had frozen again so she had to take a pee in a bucket. There was a limousine waiting outside the front door, and we literally did not have a pot to piss in.

That situation didn't last long though, and nor did our relationship. Money swept in and Sade moved to a swish new pop-star flat with smoked glass windows overlooking the Victorian clocktower in Highbury. Although I initially went with her, the strains of instant international stardom, including paparazzi parked permanently outside, were pulling us apart, and I found myself back at the fire station sharing with our gay mate Michael Smith. Other adventures ensued, usually involving spotty postmen strewn along the hall, but conditions deteriorated considerably and the aroma of amyl nitrate and unwashed socks hung heavy over the flat. For my health and sanity I had to move on, and besides, this was never really going to be home.

It is something of a myth to suggest it was ever easy to buy a home in London. My parents never managed it, and I'm not sure I would have done if the *New Musical Express* hadn't handily libelled me one Thursday morning. It came after a bout of flailing fisticuffs in the Camden Palace, which resulted in an inaccurate slur in the next edition of that inky pop missive. When Sade's lawyer confirmed that in his august and expensive opinion I had indeed been libelled, she agreed to underwrite my legal fees. Thankfully there were none because the *NME* settled out of court, paying my lawyer's bill and giving me enough for the deposit on a flat, or rather half a flat. But where was it to be? I was looking for my London.

I must have looked for all of twenty minutes. The first place we saw was a two-bedroom 1930s apartment on the fifth floor of a splendidly old-fashioned mansion block called Witley Court on Coram Street, between Russell and Tavistock Squares, just up from the Brunswick Centre in deep WC1. If you had asked me where would be the best place to live in the entire world, I would have said just about there.

I purchased the drum with my mate Graham Ball, a double clever, easy-going Ealing boy who I'd become best mates with at the LSE. Graham now managed bands and ran nightclubs: Blue Rondo à la Turk, Westworld and Wetworld, for those who remember such shenanigans. Fifty-five grand between us, 50 per cent each, plus 600 quid a year service charge for a ninety-nine year lease on a block where we were at least half-a-century younger than the average residents.

That was a lot of money and a lot of figures to cope with, but it was a lot of London. Parquet floors, Crittall windows, grumpy porter in an ill-fitting uniform, lift with chinoiserie panels and cages you had to close yourself, and a smell of overcooked cabbage in the corridors: it was my idea of very heaven. We were now all set to become the Bloomsbury set.

N15 in the 1980s had been an area still drawn in 1950s black and white. When I made it to WC1 – and it really did feel like I'd made it – we stepped straight into the 1930s.

Apart from a famous media sociologist and his infamous ex-villain flatmate, Witley Court was populated almost exclusively by old Jewish ladies, many of whom had fled Nazi persecution in Mittel Europe. Their partners long gone, they would float the carpeted corridors at dead of night in full make-up and frayed dressing gowns like something from *Whatever Happened to Baby Jane*. Some would seek the company of a bald, blazer-wearing, Rolls Royce-driving, late middle-aged lothario who was my next-door neighbour. The place was full of gossip and intrigue, and my new neighbours were full of great stories and gin. My new neighbourhood also had stories to tell and gin to sell.

As I explored the area, I began to understand its parameters and its particulars. I walked the area remorselessly, buzzing to call such a place home, waggle dancing my terrain. To the east was Gray's Inn Road, to the south High Holborn, to the west Tottenham Court Road, to the north the Euston Road. This instantly became my manor, but I never quite knew what to call it.

That depended largely on who I was trying to impress. For literary types it was Bloomsbury, but equally we could lay claim to King's Cross, which sounded much more street, or Holborn, which is what the long-term locals insisted upon. This had been the London Borough of Holborn, the capital's smallest, until it was amalgamated with St Pancras and Hampstead to form Camden in 1968. There are families who have been Holbornites for generation after generation.

This area of WC1 is actually a collection of very different micro-villages. They are connected by an aura of timelessness, which hangs in the muted flat light, and a ragged blanket of charisma covering this still tangibly Georgian/Victorian quarter. Somehow, even today it has survived the ravages of jangly modernity. Despite a clumsy spruce up of the Brunswick, it still isn't generally swish or smart; still feels unreconstructed. And when I walk again those soft, stealthy streets and those inviting but largely unvisited squares I proudly called my own, its rakish charm seeps into me and I fall instantly smitten once again.

This is where the West End looks east, where Dickens walked the night and Foundlings rued the day. It is Virginia Woolf in Gordon Square and sheep in Coram's Fields (where adults must be accompanied by children at all times). Cab drivers in their Russell Square shelter and businessmen rutting in the nearby bushes, Gay's the Word. The Brunswick's brutal geometry hard-by Handel's harmonious symmetry. Dodgy geezers from the Peabodies, drinking alongside eager undergrads from the colleges.

Stroll these streets as I did so often and you will encounter Horatio Nelson's undertakers and Uncle Harry's bookmakers, Lutherans, Quakers, the Society of Friends and the Friend at Hand. The Duke, the Lamb and the Fryer's Delight. The Ethical Society and the Swedenborgians, Reds in Red Lion Square, Nazis in Argyle Square, Gandhi in Tavistock Square. The Children's Hospital, the Italian Hospital, the Horse hospital, the Queen's Larder, the old Dairy, the Mazzini and Garibaldi Club, John Nash's plaque and Paul Nash's plaque. Condor Cycles, Conway Hall, Congress House, with Epstein's master- piece in the courtyard. Senate House, which Hitler had earmarked for his headquarters, Dickens House, Pushkin House, Sir John Soane's House, the Egyptian rooms, my flat. I lived near mummies.

The two grandest edifices, the neoclassical British Museum and the stripped modernism of Senate House, with its notorious room 101, were cut-throughs to Witley Court from the West End. I would make a point of popping in to see a totem pole or a sarcophagus on my way home, before pointedly walking through Charles Holden's grand art deco entrance hall, star of so many episodes of *Poirot*, and a public right of way even at night. It felt special just being there.

Throughout the area was a large, often forgotten, community of Londoners of all kinds. The elegant mansion blocks in Bloomsbury proper, up towards Tottenham Court Road, were generally posher. Bob Marley lived in one of them, but some were council-owned and really run down, the bookish bohemians mixing with nervous looking asylum seekers.

North, over towards the Cross, but still south of the Euston Road, were the wildlands of St Pancras. This was made up of a series of sprawling, gloomy, dark red-brick council estates in various stages of decay and pubs, loads and loads of pubs. The most broken of the blocks were squats full of Scots, rampaging Caledonian punk rockers who made their chosen boozer, the Skinners Arms, the rowdiest I'd known since the Bald Faced Stag in full flight.

Other blocks, like the labyrinthine Cromer Estate behind the Town Hall, were still peopled with occasionally grumpy old-time locals.

Chelsea boys, drinking in the Boot and reminiscing about Kenneth Williams' dad's barbers. In amongst them, an emerging population of brightly coloured Bengali families were playing street cricket and opening sari stores. The three groups seemingly co-existed by failing to notice that the others existed at all.

The Brunswick Centre, at the end of our street, now hailed as a masterpiece replete with a Waitrose, was then a desolate wasteland of empty shop units and overlooked, under-appreciated concrete; a wind-swept brutalist vision with a bizarre metallic-clad disco-pub where toothless junkies bought and sold. But just a little south and east was the glorious Georgian enclave of the Rugby Estate and its elegant main drag, Lamb's Conduit Street. Here was a still vibrant hold-out tribe of sagacious old London families who had lived in these streets for generations.

Gregarious, generous, but guarded, these were proper old Holbornites: I always felt like an interloper in their presence. Some were of Italian descent, members of the mysterious Mazzini and Garibaldi Club on Red Lion Street, where I would peer through the letterbox at the pristine 1950s interior. They took part in the procession at St Peter's, had terrible tales of family members interred during the war and excellent packed lunches. I was taught to drive by the Scuola Guida, the Italian driving school on Clerkenwell Road, which could account for a lot. Others were Irish; almost all were Catholic.

They worked the flower stalls and fruit stalls, did scene shifting in the West End or mined the last seams of Fleet Street gold. Some ducked, others dived. They bought Stone Island and Smedley from a shop run by a pair of local characters on Lamb's Conduit Street and import soul records from City Sounds, where Pete Tong once worked, on Proctor Street. They all knew A. France & Son, who had organised Lord Nelson's send off, would one day bury them.

Steve was one such local boy. Born and bred in the Peabody buildings on Herbrand Street, schooled at St Joseph's in Macklin Street, where the subterranean playground is unique in all London, he followed the Arsenal, delivered copies of the *Standard* from a stripy van and drank every Sunday in my local, the Marquis of Cornwallis. Until he didn't. We were never close friends, but a pint or two while talking about George Graham's dour defensive strategies or Peter Storey's criminal escapades was a pleasant weekend diversion, and I missed Steve when he didn't show up for a few weeks.

When finally he reappeared, I asked casually where he'd been. He looked as sheepish as the ewes grazing round the corner in Coram's fields. I thought he was going to tell me he'd done a bit of time for some minor transgression, but instead he said, 'I met a girl and we've moved out of London.' I realised he was feeling rather ashamed of such apostasy so enquired where he was now living in as non-condemnatory a manner as I could manage. His reply stays with me to this day, as he shamefully muttered, 'Putney.'

If anywhere feels like that elusive beast, 'real' London, Bloomsbury is it. Drenched in Dickensian apparitions and bookish aspirations, this neighbourhood goes about its business, lives its life, amid a barrage of tourists and visitors and the highest urban concentration of students on earth. A constant chaotic hum of bewilderment and wonder rings around its streets and squares, yet somehow it remains sane, gentle, grown-up and shabbily gracious, its denizens deeply ingrained.

I spent the best part of a decade in WC1 and almost every day there would be some sort of minor memorable incident. One occurred almost thirty years to the day as I write, on the night of 15–16 October 1987 to be precise. That was the night of the hurricane that never was, or rather the hurricane which was, but the weather report insisted wasn't going to be. I didn't even notice. You get rather good at sleeping through noise if you live in a flat overlooking Woburn Place, with no double glazing, so I snored right through Michael Fish's manifest nightmare.

Next morning I awoke with my then paramour, the Spanish lady I'd met in Barcelona, who was visiting London. We walked out and into Russell Square in search of breakfast to see a scene of almost post-apocalyptic devastation. Silent, still, the calm after the storm, but with debris strewn everywhere and trees lying prostrate on the ground. It looked like there had been a hurricane.

One particularly proud old ash at the southern end of the square was looking especially tragic, sprawled across the railings, uprooted and contorted, and as we got closer we could see an elderly gentleman standing by it, tears running down his cheeks. We asked gently if he was OK. He explained that he lived nearby and for nearly thirty years had come, most every day, to read on a bench in the shade of this particular tree. He called it his 'friend' and was mourning the loss of so close a Bloomsbury companion.

Another morning event which sticks in my mind occurred at the other, at that stage less literary, end of the neighbourhood. It was a couple of years after the hurricane, and a different girlfriend and I were standing on the Euston Road in King's Cross, waiting for a bus north to go and see some friends in Stoke Newington. It was definitely a Sunday morning because I've always thought that what happened next was possibly a sign of God's generosity on the Sabbath.

The bus stop was directly in front of a huge building site, next to the then derelict St Pancras Hotel, which had been there for most of my adult life. This would eventually become the British Library, a piece of architecture as splendid inside as it is wretched outside. But at this stage it was just a giant hole next to a Gothic ruin. All was quiet as the two of us waited for the Number 73 bus on a fine, blue but blustery Sunday morning.

The only other people within sight were a pair of African ladies in full flowing headgear, dressed in their finery, presumably to go to church. Perhaps it was their prayers that were answered, because suddenly there was cash money floating in the air. Five, ten and twenty pound notes blowing in the breeze, emanating from a gap in the tarpaulin-clad fence around the Library site. In a strangely silent dream-like state, the four of us were grabbing handfuls of notes for a minute or two, manna from heaven. Then the bus duly arrived and we dutifully jumped on board, dazed, delighted, a couple of hundred quid better off, but with free money still floating away down the street.

I've thought many times about what really happened that WC1 morning. Unless it actually was an act of God, chances are the money was the ill-gotten gains of a local pimp/pusher, of which there were plenty. At this time King's Cross was the place most rank with sex and drugs in the entire land (and some rather good rock'n'roll at the Water Rats), both openly on sale in the middle of the street in the middle of the day. Gangs of grisly blokes lined up outside the post office opposite to proffer crack, smack or anything else. I was once offered a blow job by a sorry-looking lady pushing a poor child in a pram at 11 o'clock in the morning, about a hundred yards from that bus stop.

So I can only assume that one of the big dealers was holding a large stash on a Saturday night when he felt the need to hide his bag of cash behind that fence in rather a hurry, perhaps with plod on his tail. Drug dealers don't do early mornings, so he hadn't yet come back to reclaim it, when the wind whipped up and notes, like so much sweet street music, were sent floating through the air. We had a very good lunch.

Bloomsbury back then was redolent with secrets, and thick with the dusty motes of sedition and spying. It was a hotbed. There were meeting halls and community centres and book fairs and congresses and conferences, with that mix of superannuated students, perpetual revolutionaries, old comrades and young hot heads. However, the grand institutions of the British state were never far away.

Conway Hall in Holborn, home of the Ethical Society, was the epicentre of agitation, with the great leap forward prophesised in its main hall most nights. But I used to chuckle when the militant vegetarian types in the meetings bought chips from the Fryer's Delight next door, as it cooked them in beef dripping.

Our local bookshop, just round the corner from the flat on Marchmont Street, was Gay's the Word, which as the name implies was pretty specialist, but very much part of the community. They were the oldest LGBT bookshop in town; a rather serious, veritably venerable institution, where marginalised groups of all kinds met in the back room round a piano, including those who supported the miners in their struggle and became immortalised in the film *Pride*.

They were pitched against the might of the state when the shop was raided at the height of Margaret Thatcher's anti-gay Clause 28 hysteria. Doors were smashed in, its directors charged with conspiracy, and tomes by such seditious souls as Tennessee Williams, Gore Vidal and Armistead Maupin were impounded as evidence. 'I've always wanted to be seized,' said Mr Maupin when he recalled the events of 1984 on my radio show. The place became a real cause célèbre and locals were still rightly proud of the stand the shop took and the support they received. It's hard to be anything but tolerant when you live in WC1.

Next door to Gay's the Word is the Marchmont Centre, a community hall where local grannies congregated for crosswords and macramé and mother-and-baby sessions took place. But this being Bloomsbury, it was also where the Stalinist Society and the Anarchist Federation both met, thankfully on different days.

I actually went to a couple of anarchist meetings there out of curiosity and was amazed to meet a remarkable old girl known as the Makhnovist Granny. This sweetly ancient Eastern European lady, whose real name I later discovered was Leah Feldman, spoke faltering English and fluent Russian and Yiddish. In an incredible life, full of adventure and tempest, she had fought for the black flag, against both the reds and the whites, alongside the legendary anarchist guerillero Nestor Makhno in the Ukraine during the Russian civil war. She had been at Kropotkin's funeral, smuggled arms into Republican Spain and now sat with her handbag on her lap on chilly Wednesday nights in WC1 plotting the downfall of the state. It was very Bloomsbury.

I would not be surprised to learn that there were spooks in those meetings. Keeping an eye on people, drinking strong tea and preaching strong politics was a longstanding tradition in those parts. Lenin had been regularly spied upon when he lived up the road in Percy Circus and was known to sup in the Water Rats, long before Oasis made their London debut there.

There's also a story of a British agent hiding for hours in a cramped cupboard in the upstairs room at the sadly vanished Crown and

Woolpack pub on St John Street. He had to eavesdrop on a meeting of Vladimir Ilyich and his commie comrades, only to find that the entire meeting was conducted in Russian, a language he did not speak a word of. So it was no real shock when I was told about the Soviet spy drop and the camera concealed in the brick round the back of Coram's Fields.

Always known as the Foundlings to the locals, this had been the foremost home for abandoned babies in Victorian London, with so many terrible and beautiful tales of its own. Now the Foundling Museum, you can see the swing-gate contraption where the swaddling-wrapped newly born could be placed by despairing mothers and swung inside never to be seen again. But the story I was told centred on deliveries of a different kind in a tiny alleyway at the back of the fields, where the tennis courts are today.

This is a little used cut-through known only by locals – and, it seems, Russian agents and their British counterparts. A rubbish bin by a tree was apparently a dead letter drop for Soviet spies to leave their seditious missives en route to Moscow. But because Oleg Gordievsky, the KGB chief, had been turned and was working for MI6, they knew what was going on and had placed a secret camera in a fake brick in the wall opposite to monitor exactly who was dropping what. As I regularly used that cut-through to head up to a mate's house in Islington, I can only assume the secret service have me on film and on file as a fellow traveller.

Another local secret spy story only came to light many years later. We were talking on my radio show about much-loved London signs. The illuminated Lucozade masterpiece, which heralded your arrival back from Heathrow on the elevated A40 near Brentford, was a perennial favourite. Many also fondly remembered the strangely compelling Veneer of the Week, which used to appear on a large shed by the eastern fringes of the North Circular. It advertised the wares of Shadbolt's veneer suppliers with an ever-changing paean to the delights of Crown Cut American Walnut or Straight Cut Burr Vavona. Then someone mentioned the Fancy Cheese People.

This was a prominent, flamboyantly 1950s-style sign emblazoned in yellow on the side of a squat, scruffy, permanently closed building. Just to the east of Bloomsbury at 27 Farringdon Road, as it flows down towards the Thames with the Fleet river raging beneath it and the Holborn Viaduct above. It actually read 'Crowson & Sons Ltd: The Fancy Cheese People' and enlightened a rather gloomy stretch of road to the north of Smithfield.

We all raved about its fantastic font and wondered what had become of the Fancy Cheese family. Then a caller, who in classic radio fashion wished to remain anonymous, told us that 27 Farringdon Road was the exact address he had to send his forms to when he applied for a graduate job with MI5. Others concurred and locals told of lights mysteriously on in the apparently abandoned building and strange comings and goings from the back entrance. One caller even claimed to have seen Fancy Cheese vans loitering outside with antenna on top. Not long after our conversation, the entire building was demolished and the beautiful sign vanished. I hope it wasn't because we had blown their cover.

I was incredibly lucky to live so centrally at a time when the West End and Soho was very much the focus of the city, when it was still ours. The walk from Bloomsbury into town became my almost daily perambulation, and I became acutely attuned to the tiny changes in atmosphere from street to street. I adopted the Londoner's tactic of weaving, always swerving the main, straight streets; partly to avoid the hordes (tourists throughout the world stick to the obvious and travel in straight lines in packs), but also because the back ways are always more compelling.

Kingsway, High Holborn, Aldwych, New Oxford Street, Charing Cross Road, Euston Road: these wide, noisome thoroughfares lined with grand, bland Edwardian architecture, are ponderous and serious. They are also unmarked boundaries: cross them and you enter a markedly different zone on either side. Unless you specifically need something from one of their shops, it's natural to deviate away from them into the succour of the backstreets. They don't feel right. Has anybody ever strolled New Oxford Street for pleasure?

This is because those wide, cheerless boulevards are interlopers; impositions upon London's natural flow in the name of metropolitan improvements. They were driven mercilessly through ancient settlements in a frenzy of turn-of-the-century rationalisation and sanitisation, a slum clearance/social cleansing fervour, which robbed us of some of our most vivid and visceral enclaves long before the Luftwaffe.

I took to walking the old ways, trying to envisage this earlier, more intricate and intense London. Crooked and convoluted, cramped and polluted, but full of the urban intensity, intimacy and authenticity we now value so highly. How much would those slums be worth now?

Perhaps the greatest loss was one I first sensed as a student at the LSE. A temple to twentieth-century rationalism, its largely nondescript buildings were clearly plonked upon a much more ancient plot, contested by twisting, cobbled roads and the occasional Dickensian remnant among the bland lecture halls and offices. At the northern end of the area, beyond Lincoln's Inn Fields, is an intriguingly obscure alley. The Ship public house dates back to the sixteenth century and a tiny dog-leg called New Turnstile is the only surviving sign that this was once a Tudor drovers' route to the fields. It was also the entrance to the Clare Market, perhaps our greatest lost redoubt.

This was a shambles, overflowing with flesh and fish, cow houses and tripe dressers, butchers and costers, including a kosher section in the small Jewish ghetto. Clare Market was one of the last surviving medieval enclaves, too far west for the Great Fire, which by the end of Victoria's reign had become a teeming, shaming slum of murky dead ends and toppling Tudor houses full of the hustling inner-London poor. Smelly, noisy, lively in so many ways, it was a positive provocation to the rational, imperial mind. So it was wiped clean away, with the bloated stodge of Edwardian Kingsway, one of London's coldest, most clinical highways, driven right through it. What vandalism.

Clare Market survived only in a couple of street names and an LSE student magazine. But as I walked the streets just to the west of my

Bloomsbury home, heading habitually for sweet Soho, so my urban antennae became attuned to another notorious slum: a desperate rookery, which despite being all but erased by generations of planners and developers, had somehow seeped back into the streets of 1980s London. The theory of psychogeography, as postulated by the likes of Peter Ackroyd and Iain Sinclair, was made suppurating flesh every time I entered the dark innards of St Giles.

Today, a much shrunken St Giles is rigidly circumscribed by New Oxford Street, Charing Cross Road and Shaftsbury Avenue; a tiny in-between triangle of land usually avoided en route to elsewhere. But all of those were new roads, specifically created for slum clearance schemes, firewalls erected to contain the spread of poverty.

Before those wide, dull roads existed, St Giles would have been larger, less confined and defined, a ragged blot bleeding into Bloomsbury, Seven Dials and Soho. Think of Centre Point, Seifert's soaring '60s masterpiece, as the dark heart of this pivotal crossroads, with the spire of the church of St Giles as its soul. I spent many hours searching for its spirit.

The story of St Giles is all suffering. A seeping bog, a leper hospital, a plague pit, a gallows, a sunken well into which the poor and luckless fell; this was where the hopeful became the hopeless. The bubonic plague began here and countless short lives ended here, bound hand and foot, and bound for Tyburn's fatal, final blessing.

The rookery of St Giles was the favela of the doomed and the damned. But as with so many slums, it was so many homes. The urban story told time and again, of arrival and disappointment, country bumpkin, Irish and African, the noted blackbirds of St Giles, rubbing more than shoulders together, creating a mongrel creed, dying but also living and breathing and breeding here in this teeming town incarnate. When St Giles had sufficiently shamed the burgeoning bourgeois city and was finally razed in the 1850s, many of its inhabitants were pushed further west, finding themselves in the claggy shanties of Notting Dale, where they were joined by a certain Freddie Elms a few years later.

Today St Giles is a pit yet again: Crossrail has cut deep until it bleeds. All but obliterated by the works, Renzo Piano has imposed a tacky kindergarten-coloured block upon it, the surviving remnants of its always stunted High Street have been maimed and obscured, its circus smashed apart, the last labyrinthine twists of its tale torn down, erased. No mercy given, no respect shown. They do not want you to know this place ever existed, as if the stain of generations has to be scrubbed away. But still. But still, cross from singing Soho over to the other side and the darkness descends, the miasma wraps itself around you. You can still feel St Giles.

My first noted night in the rookery involved dancing naked in Seifert's splendid, now removed, fountains, which stood in front of Centre Point. It was the finale of my brother Reggie's stag do at the Astoria, over the Charing Cross Road, where Crosse & Blackwell's pickle factory had once stood. The basement contained a soul club called Busby's, where the night before his wedding, a big group of Big Oak – the older lads from Burnt Oak – and little me, drank to Reggie Elms's future. By midnight, tiny teenage Robert Elms was drunk enough to fully disrobe and leap into Centre Point's murky shallow waters. I never quite lived that down. But nor did it put me off.

Arriving at Tottenham Court Road Underground station, admiring Paolozzi's mural, up into the subway, past the retching bogs and out into St Giles's thrilling, fetid air was how so many glorious nights in my London began. I knew nothing then of history, hadn't even heard of the rookery, but was already attracted to such fecund badness. Those public toilets in the tunnel were spectacularly dodgy and seedy in a way we no longer accept. Renal of smell and venal of intent, like prison khazis with added loitering. They were apt. As you walked past a sickly stranger, he might have asked you if you have 'a works' he could use. They often did.

Once dubbed 'the Holy Land' because so many of St Giles's inhabitants were devout Irish Catholics, the handsome St Patrick's Soho Square was built specifically for their salvation. Throughout the 1980s, directly opposite the church on the eastern junction of Tottenham

Court and Charing Cross, from the station entrance to Denmark Street, was where supplicants of the opiate faith came to pray; their habits long, their stigmata on display.

Where once plague sufferers had pleaded for alms and lepers had painfully decomposed a millennia before, so bits fell off the scarred bodies of the junk-sickened. Where once had been Hogarth's Gin Lane was now smack alley.

Living in adjacent Bloomsbury, I passed here all the time, at all hours. I would see them saddest in the mid-morning, arriving, waiting, shaking; scabrous, skinny methadone actors playing the part of Hogarth's wretches in this tragic tableau. With all London to choose, what made them gather there? They probably hadn't read Ackroyd, yet they were ineluctably drawn to this precise place of ancient want as if by a magnet pulling them through time to this spot, where misery is so deep in the soil.

I would stand and watch, repelled and fascinated; could see when a dealer had arrived. Suddenly these damaged and weary souls, normally so shuffling and lifeless, would become agitated, animated, scurrying off into the rookery to score and to fill their aching veins. Hey hey we're the junkies. This was their manor.

Yet tourists would walk blithely by: bookish types would head to the other end of Charing Cross Road to more wholesome dealers; guitar nerds would turn into Tin Pan Alley to play the solo from 'Smoke on the Water'. I would walk into the churchyard of St Giles itself, to muse on its many mysteries dating back to the eleventh century; the tortured Catholic martyrs and the swinging cut-purses. I would peer into the peerless interior, maybe stop in the Angel next door for 'One for the road', as so many condemned men had done en route to Tyburn.

Amid the scant remains of St Giles, there is a lovely little garden. The Phoenix: born of a bombsite, kept verdant by volunteers, where office workers can canoodle over lunch; a sign of hope springing from despair. There is also a little row of humble council houses built in the 1980s where luxury flats would surely now stand, a tiny London community, in an oasis, in a swamp. I love it here, but then

I loved the swamp and even spent the occasional afternoon with the alligators.

Denmark Street's place in Britain's music-biz history is unique. This was our tiny Tin Pan Alley, the dishevelled home of avaricious music publishers for generations. Elton John writing 'Your Song' in an upstairs room, David Bowie virtually camping out there to get noticed, hit after hit, hype after hype. Instrument shops on ground level, publisher's offices and small record companies above, rehearsal rooms, nightclubs and tattoo parlours round the back in Denmark Place; the last of the enclosed seventeenth-century warrens to survive.

La Giaconda, the café where so many fabulous pop plots were hatched, was perfect to sit and watch. But a couple of doors away was the TPA, or Tin Pan Alley Club, one of those dodgy, closed doors, afternoon drinkers, which used to abound in London when the licensing laws insisted pubs must shut after lunch and after ten thirty.

I was first taken to the TPA by one of the many music biz bottom feeders who hustled their way round W1, back when money was flowing; Rizzo in a satin tour jacket. I certainly never became a regular: that would have been deeply deleterious to the prospects. But once it was established that I was down by law – kosher so to speak – the occasional knock on the door, followed by a couple of hours ensconced in a scene from a cheap British version of *Goodfellas*, was an entertainment and an education. Though there was always an edge, the unsettling sense that it could all go a bit Joe Pesci.

St Giles Greek was the name of the criminal slang spoken by the low-down denizens of the rookery in the eighteenth century. More than two hundred years later, the geezers who frequented the TPA spoke a vivid argot all their own. These were men who had been around the block, on the wing, over the pavement, through the slips, under the counter, behind the jump.

I would literally struggle to understand a word as a collection of scalpers, bilkers, blaggers and drummers, jigglers, dippers, but definitely no fiddlers, conversed in their convoluted combination of rhyming slang, back slang, prison speak, Romani, and just wantonly bizarre obfuscation. 'I just punted a pair of snide briefs to a bice of luke rich-ards for a carpet,' said a happy chap who'd been working tickets over the road at the Astoria. Took me an age to decode that one.

I have no idea how many of these funny, dodgy, label-laden, Corona quaffing, occasionally scary, always lairy men were bonafide bad people, but they were good company until the charlie kicked in. Most, I suspect, just worked the angles; some of them worked the hot dogs.

Over the road from the TPA at number 18 Denmark Place, which links St Giles High Street and Denmark Street, the very heart of the rookery, was a shabby old three-storey building, with green metal double doors that were usually locked. But it regularly opened up late at night when the hot dog boys had done their rounds. These were the men who pushed those metal trollies round London selling sausages and burgers you really wouldn't want to eat, on illegal pitches at tourist sites and outside clubs around town. They stored the trolleys and the tins of whatever they were selling in this building. A shabby storehouse rumoured to be owned by the same people who owned the TPA. No one really talked about number 18 much.

The Astoria and the Tottenham Court Road toilets and the Centre Point fountains and the TPA and the Giaconda and the junkies and 18 Denmark Place have all gone now: too much has gone now. St Giles's scars sacrificed for the Lizzie Line, torn down for a bland new station entrance, which sits precisely where I danced naked at a stag do. A clumsy glass pyramid, where once music and money were made, deals were shaken on and swiftly forgotten, where smackheads scored and shot, where gobby villains drank bottled beer in designer gear and generations of piss poor Londoners before them eked out a life and too many were sentenced to death by hanging. Death hangs heavy here.

We're told Crossrail is necessary to keep London moving, though turning Reading into a western suburb of the city and pouring millions more people into the centre of town every day will have consequences. It has already taken away another little slice of what we thought of as our own, turning an intimate if occasionally intimidating enclave into a tacky no-mans land of wheelie suitcases and bemused out-of-towners. Demolishing one of the remaining slithers of the old, storied West End and replacing it with a shiny reception centre, with glass pyramids and high definition touchscreen 'entertainment portals', feels like a slight to the past, a disservice to history.

This is yet another attempt to eradicate the often terrible but always powerful story of St Giles. But will it work this time, or will the dark past work its way up through the concrete and glass, like the fingers of the living dead, rising from a shallow grave? For 18 Denmark Place and whatever replaces it will always be haunted by what occurred there on one night in August 1980.

Dreadful events happen here. Plagues happen here, fires and floods happen here. Where the Dominion Theatre is now was once the site of the Horseshoe brewery, a memory which was kept alive as recently as the 1980s, when there was a pub called the Horseshoe, where DJ Paul Murphy opened the first of his famed jazz dance clubs. I saw Jay Hoggard play there once. But on that exact site on 17 October 1814, a vast vat of beer exploded, leading to a positive tsunami of porter flowing down into the rookery: 9,000 barrels of foaming dark hooch, a wave fifteen feet high, rushing into overcrowded basements, which led to eight deaths by drowning, some of them children. If the gin didn't get you, the beer would. Only in St Giles.

I would occasionally find myself drowning in beer in a late-night blues in one of the rooms above Denmark Place in the late '80s. It was a club organised by Phil Dirtbox, a legendary nocturnal host, the latest in a long line of impromptu shebeens, which colonised any available space in W1. Somewhere in the back of my undoubtedly addled brain, I knew then that we were dancing very close to death. For I had heard tell of John Thompson. Have you heard of John 'The Gypsy' Thompson?

Before Harold Shipman GP took his dubious title, John Thompson was the most prolific mass murderer in British history, topped only by Doctor Death in the number of people he topped. He is still arguably the murderer who killed most victims on a single occasion, and it happened in living memory. Yet almost nobody has ever heard of Mr Thompson, a notorious man with no notoriety. Because his terrible crime occurred in St Giles and dreadful things happen in St Giles. What do you expect if you go there?

It was that building, 18 Denmark Place, where the hot dog stalls were kept, a ramshackle structure that dated back to the old rookery itself. In 1980 it contained two unregulated, illegal clubs on its upper floors. On the top was the Spanish Rooms, or El Hueco, 'the hole', and below it Rodos, or the Colombian club, both accessed by hollering up for a key, which would be thrown down. As their names suggest, they were used by the large community of Spanish and South Americans who worked by night, often as waiters in the West End. But it was also frequented by the myriad Londoners who didn't want to go to bed, and maybe fancied sampling some of South America's most famous export. It was a port of call for people of the night.

That Friday night into Saturday morning, John Thompson, a local low-life, would-be gangster, got in a row over the price of a gin and tonic, got thrown out but wouldn't let it rest. He took a minicab from one of the local kiosks, drove to a petrol station in Camden Town, bought a can of fuel, returned to the Spanish rooms, poured it through the letter box and lit a match. Within a few unimaginably diabolical moments, thirty-seven people were dead, as flames raged and raced and ravaged through those rooms. Some survived by clambering over the rookery rooftops, using guitars from the shop next door to smash open windows and locked fire escapes; thirty-seven did not. Many of those who died were never even formally identified, left just burned bones.

For years I spoke about this fire, told people the story, or at least the version of it I knew, as there was so little information. I would always think of those incinerated souls every time I passed by their unmarked resting place. No plaque, no sign, no nothing. It was as if, like St Giles itself, there was a desire to entirely wipe it away, pretend such a terrible thing never happened just a few years ago in our shiny new city. But it did.

I heard from a man whose brother-in-law had died in the conflagration, a young lad from Ladbroke Grove who had gone into town with a mate on a Friday night looking for the craic and ended up in the Hole. His spar got away by climbing over roofs, but he never made it. The family member I spoke to was so saddened, and still angered and bemused by the fact that this whole terrible event – the biggest mass murder on a single occasion in British history – had been forgotten: those lives as well as those deaths had been forgotten.

Truth is, even at the time, this terrible crime went almost unreported. Probably because many of those who died were people of the darkness: foreigners, undesirables, illegals, what one paper called 'pimps, lesbian prostitutes, screeching homosexual queens, hash dealers and drooping addicts'. There were also architects and nurses and boys from the Grove having a night out. I, too, was out that night, over the road in a club in safe Soho, preening and prancing in my pretty New Romantic gear. There but for the grace. The night is a dangerous place.

But they haven't quite been forgotten. A journalist called Simon Usborne did some painstaking research and gathered what scant information exists, getting together relatives, and eventually organising a memorial service. It took place in the church of St Giles, of course, where the martyrs and the lepers are remembered, too, and maybe those who died that night were somewhere between the two. There is talk of a memorial plaque on the new Crossrail development to honour those lost souls, but whether the future really wants to acknowledge such a tormented past remains to be seen.

And now another little bit of St Giles and its history has died too, sacrificed to development, to Crossrail and clean lines and clean sheets and balance sheets. But can you ever really get rid of a stain? St Giles, patron saint of cripples, last redoubt of the hopeless remains.

Thompson died handcuffed to a hospital bed on the anniversary of the fire in 2008. He'd been nabbed nine days after the blaze, drinking in a bar 100 yards away, as stupid as he was cruel.

The Brigadistas

'They went because their open eyes could see no other way.'

Every time I read that inscription down by the river I choke up a little. Even typing it out just then made me feel simultaneously sad and intensely proud, because I know what it means. I know even more what it meant to the men and women, many of them Londoners, young and strong, who heard the call and with open eyes and clear minds headed off to sunny, dusty, deadly Spain to fight for what they knew was right, many never to return. I met them, I knew them; I adored and admired them. Now they are all dead, not one left to tell their tale. So we must.

Those fine, true words, originally written by C. Day Lewis, adorn a humble but handsome bronze sculpture on a plinth on the South Bank, honouring the 2,100 men and women who left these shores in 1936 to fight for freedom and against fascism, with the International Brigades in the Spanish Civil War. It's in Jubilee Gardens, a patch of green right by the ever-revolving frippery of the London Eye.

I have nothing against the big wheel, but it is indicative of the way in which the riverside has been Disneyfied. The South Bank, now the premier tourist passeggiato, used to be staunchly working class; factories, breweries, power stations and council estates. It's why the Festival Hall – 'The People's Palace' – was placed there on the proletarian side of the river. It's why it's still apt, if a little incongruous, that the old commies and the ragged lefties and the arch anti-fascists meet there, at that memorial every first Saturday in July, to clench their fists and sing their rousing songs. And I am always among them.

I became entranced by Spain as but a boy. My first ever trip abroad as a sixteen-year-old took me to those merciless skies, blue, bleached bone-white towns, parched and stripped, austere yet ripe, hard, rich, a place of blood and duende. The spell Spain cast over me has never wavered; it is my other

place. I have lived in Barcelona and Madrid, and have a home now in Cadiz. I still feel fire in the scalding air, still understand why those young people went all those years ago. I hope I would fight for Spain, but I don't know if I am brave enough.

My first brush with the proud, brave Brigadistas was back in the 1990s when a fair few were still here among us. Three of them came on my radio show, to talk about their annual remembrance ceremony at that statue by the river. There was David Lomon, a former rag-and-bone man from Hackney, a Jewish lad who had first fought fascists at Cable Street and was nineteen years old when he volunteered to head to Spain and pick up a gun. Lou Kenton, a Stepney boy whose family had fled pogroms in the Ukraine, another veteran of Cable Street, who rode his motorbike to Albacete, where he swapped it for an ambulance and worked as a medic on the front line, later he served in the merchant navy on the arctic convoys. The third was Sam Lesser, another son of Hackney, born an orthodox Jew, but converted to communism during his early anti-fascist struggles. He was among the first thirty British volunteers, and found himself defending Madrid in one of the bitterest battles of the war. Later he became a journalist for the Morning Star.

I was in awe of these London men, old now, humble, wise, but still staunch. I loved hearing their tales of Brunete and Jarama, the political debates, the howling shells, how they lost so many comrades but never lost their passion or their conviction: they knew they were right. These were men who had fought alongside Durutti and Dolores Ibárruri, who had lived the history I only read about. I asked them many questions, and at one point I said, 'Do you know if you killed anybody?'

I think it was David Lomon, small and hard of hearing, who spoke, looking at me as if it were a very naive question. To this day his answer sends shivers down my spine.

'Did I kill anybody? Of course I did, many, they were fascists and I hope they stayed dead.'

From that moment on I knew I had to know more of these remarkable people. I discovered the International Brigades Memorial Trust, the IBMT, who look after the memory of the 15th Brigade, the British unit, and who organise their annual memorial ceremony. At my first July event there were probably seven or eight veterans present, including a couple of the incredible women who had made that fateful journey. Jack Jones, the trades unions leader was there, so was fierce Paddy Cochrane in his wheelchair and his beret. And when the time came to sing, they clenched their fists and roared 'The Internationale'. They said they wanted Tories to hear it over the river in Westminster.

The proudest moment came in 2009 when all surviving International Brigade members were awarded Spanish passports by the now-democratic government, keeping a pledge made almost seventy years before. In a ceremony at the Spanish embassy, Sam Lesser, then ninety-four years old, made a speech in which he said in fluent Spanish, 'We've taken a while but now we've come home. But there are those of us who did not come home, who sleep under the sun, the soil and the olive trees of Spain.'

In fact, over 500 British volunteers gave their lives for the Republic, and time took the rest. I was honoured to be asked to make a speech down by the river one July and spoke of my undying admiration, and of how although we lost, we finally won a free and democratic Spain. At the end of my speech, Sam Lesser, then one of only three men standing, came up to ask me a question.

'Robert Elms, are you the son of Albert Elms?'

Yes, I replied, amazed, as my dad had died fifty years before, and I had never met anybody outside the immediate family who knew him. Sam looked me up and down.

'Albert Elms, the building site trades unionist. He was a good comrade.'

CHAPTER EIGHT

Finding Home

We met in the middle. Actually, we met years before in a nightclub, when she walked downstairs looking preternaturally elegant. She married a very good friend, I was best man, they had a kid. They grew apart; we stayed close, we fell in love and got married in the registry office on the Marylebone Road, where pop stars frequently wed. I didn't have a best man. The registry office is currently closed for refurbishment, but twenty-four years later, our marriage is still up and running. We still live in the middle, which is an excellent place to be.

When we got together, my wife, Christina, and her daughter Alice, were in a flat in Belsize Park, when I was thirty-six and still sharing with Graham Ball in Bloomsbury. It was finally time to grow up and set up home somewhere with my new family, but where? She loved the proximity of Hampstead, the Heath and all that; I thought anywhere north of the Euston Road was the suburbia I had escaped from. So we split the difference and settled on Camden Town. It was generally not considered a very good idea at that stage, which is precisely why it was a very good idea indeed.

We'd both made a bit out of the flats we sold: the property market was in one of its periodic slumps, mortgages were easy to come by, and so were houses in areas still considered a bit dodgy by most. We hadn't yet got to the point in London where places like Hackney and Brixton were deemed fair game for 'nice' people, and although Camden Town wasn't quite Murder Central, the reputation of the area was pretty scuzzy: there was a major drugs market, the streets were pretty lively and plenty said we were crazy to move there.

Of course I knew Camden Town from Dingwalls and the Music Machine, Rock On Records and Red or Dead. But I didn't know the

elegantly wide, tree-lined terrace of early Victorian, flat-fronted, half-stuccoed houses, interspersed with bomb-damaged fill-in council flats, that was about to become our home. Running parallel to the railway line into Euston at the southern (Mornington Crescent) end of Camden Town, it is close to the craziness yet a distinct place apart.

In the few brief minutes we spent deciding to buy the house, I was rendered overwrought by wrought iron railings, London stock brick, high ceilings, floor-to-ceiling sash windows and panelled shutters. A proper, listed, London terraced house, albeit one which had been pretty bashed about. This was a considerable distance from a council house in Burnt Oak. I was about to own and live in a part of our collective story. I was about to commit the sin of pride.

But a short while before we actually took possession of this run-down, chopped up, mucked about but still strikingly handsome house, which we lived in as a building site for many months, all the portents of doom and danger were realised. Our about-to-be next-door neighbour was mugged and stabbed by a teenager within 200 metres of his front door and came within millimetres of dying. Because his wife was the Director of Public Prosecutions, it was a big national news story, and my wife was understandably jittery about our new home, especially as she was now pregnant.

As we lugged the boxes of records and books up the short flight of steps, police helicopters were hovering overhead, and I remember saying uneasily that if we didn't like it we could go somewhere else. I had moved here for love but had no idea just how much I would love this place which would become our family home, our manor, our London.

Thankfully John next door survived, and is still John next door. But the fact that his wife Dame Barbara was the head of the British legal system provided us with a few moments. Two members of Oasis, this new band from Manchester everybody was talking about, shared a flat in the house directly on the other side of us, while Noel lived opposite. So we were a physical buffer between wild Britpop parties and the head of the British legal establishment.

There was also permanent police surveillance on our house as Barbara had locked up numerous felons and they feared revenge. Watching the old bill watching us made us feel simultaneously uneasy and secure, and made some of my old scally mates very nervous indeed about visiting our drum. At least we weren't likely to get burgled.

We hired a hippy gardener who toured the area in milk floats painted in Rastafarian colours to plant up our tiny garden. A few weeks later I was standing talking to Dame DPP over the fence when I noticed some mysterious looking fungi poking out of our pots. I remember hoping that the big law chief next door wasn't au fait with the sight of psilocybin. At that stage I had no idea of the link between our street and one of the great psychedelic moments in British cultural history – 'my thumbs have gone weird'. Once ensconced, though, I would learn a lot about the past of our future home.

Like so much of London, our street has been something of a roller-coaster road. It is part of a distinct enclave of similar roads built in the mid-1840s, in the honeymoon period of Victoria's reign, and has gone up and down and up and down ever since. The product of a speculative builder, these houses and the even grander ones on Mornington Crescent itself, were made for the emerging middle classes, or what one old local called 'the carriage trade'.

With its proximity to the Regent's Park and the West End, this should have been an affluent area – and perhaps for a while it was. But the smoke and noise from the nearby railways was always a problem, steam trains smothering the houses in layers of soot and cinders, blackening the stucco, stinging the eyes. The arrival of the Underground in 1907, plus a large influx of Irish immigrants dropped off at Euston, drove the area further downhill. And when the massive, Egyptionate, Carreras Black Cat cigarette factory replaced the communal gardens in front of Mornington Crescent in the 1920s, any remaining respectable types evacuated.

One sign of the decline is the fact that the mews at the end of our road where those carriage horses had been kept became a paint factory. That was knocked down in the 1970s and is now council-run sheltered housing where one of the residents plays melodious but melancholy polkas and tangos on their gramophone.

Very like the Notting Hill Freddie first rocked up in, Camden Town went from well-to-do, to down-at-heel in a rapid decline. Poor immigrant families superseded the middle classes, who fled to the outer suburbs, and these generous family homes got subdivided into multiple occupancy dwellings for the transient poor. Albert Street had fallen so low that some of these once gracious homes, quite possibly ours, had been 'flop houses'. These were rooms of last resort, where itinerant navvies could rent a spot on a rope strung from wall to wall and flop out for a few hours, before heading back to the building site or the boozer. This was when Camden Town first developed a reputation as home to the fighting Irish.

The house next door to ours, where the Oasis people lived and the famed Mick the Fish still resides in the basement, is one of the last surviving 'rooms to rent' establishments in the street. It is owned by a Greek-Cypriot family, who were part of another major wave of migration in the early 1950s.

The Greek Orthodox cathedral, where Archbishop Makarios once preached to crowds of thousands, is just around the corner on Camden Street. The very last little old lady in black sadly passed away recently, but there are still a couple of local tavernas selling tired tarama.

The loveliest reminder of our neighbourhood's Cypriot past is George the coffee man. This wonderful, ancient yet ageless fellow in a dun-coloured coat on Delancey Street, still sorts, roasts and grinds his beans daily, amid a tiny shop full of hessian sacks and anachronistic machinery, as he has done since the '70s. The almost narcotic aroma of his coffee shrouds us all in a sumptuous fog that heralds home.

By the late 1960s, a new type of person washed up in NW1, although if you've seen *Withnail and I*, you'll know washing up wasn't high on their list of priorities. Perhaps it was the proximity of the Roundhouse with its hippy happenings. Camden Lock also happens to be up the road, with its plethora of split-knee loon-pant purveyors, head shops and musical pit stops, so a kind of hippy, actory, arty, literary type sought out cheap digs here. Among them the man who was I.

Interviewing writer and director Bruce Robinson years later, I mentioned off air that I lived in Camden Town. He asked where, exactly? I told him, and he smiled. It turns out he'd lived a dozen or so doors to the north with Vivian MacKerrell: the real life Withnail. The whole splendid film had been based on their adventures in the street. This was where his thumbs went weird, lighter fuel was drunk and the Camberwell Carrot was smoked. He'd even been the man who got the trees planted. One stoned night, Bruce wrote a letter to Camden Council complaining that only the posh people in Primrose Hill had trees, and they responded by planting the planes, which are still there today. We have a lot to thank Mr Robinson for.

The ghost of Withnail still moved among us, and there was a palpable aroma of shabby chic and second-hand furniture hovering over the street when we first moved in.

Beryl Bainbridge lived down the road with a stuffed buffalo; A.N. Wilson wore a liturgical beret; Jazzy B had a host of motors parked up; Dylan Thomas even has his plaque fifty yards away on Delancey Street, where he'd lived in a caravan in the garden. There were drunken old philosophers and a few surviving superannuated music biz types with too-tight trousers, long frizzy hair and a general air of arty ennui. Oh, and Madness: you always saw members of Madness.

A handful of the houses were – and still are – owned by the council. You can tell because the doors are all painted black. There are also a couple of council hostels nearby, and two houses up towards Parkway are knocked together to make a home for lost girls. It's a halfway house, a shelter for teenage females who've been kicked out of their family home, sometimes because they are with child. You see them sitting together in the street talking, while their whey-faced boyfriends wait nervously on the corner for a kiss.

Another house in the street is a kind of unofficial reception centre for South Americans. Originally it was for refugees fleeing Pinochet's Chile, but now it is full of all kinds of cheery Latin types, carrying guitars, holding great parties, making great neighbours. They give me another opportunity to practise my Spanish.

There's a compelling book called *The London County Council Bomb Damage Maps 1939–1945*, which chronicles exactly where the Luftwaffe landed a direct hit, but it isn't hard to work out. There are half-a-dozen blocks of flats at the southern end of the street in the low-rise, four-storey, red-brick, post-war social housing style, which correspond exactly to the map. And it isn't too controversial to say that the Germans did us a favour.

The combination of big private houses and council flats in the same street has ensured that, as gentrification has slowly changed the nature of the place, we still have a genuinely mixed community here. Noisy families with kids on bikes, boys on mopeds, girls on hormones; working-class families, many of them old-school Camden Town, some of them exotic new arrivals, interspersed with the arty archetypes. That combination is one of the things that makes London so special.

So is seeing the man in brown.

In among the regimented, stylistically Georgian uniformity of the terrace, there is one odd, high-Victorian, gothic-style house – all dark bricks, pointy roof and arched windows – and a row of similarly styled artists' studios leading off it. For years I saw a slight, bald, elderly man, always in a brown tweed suit, walking towards the studios every morning – every morning without fail, sometimes clutching a carrier bag. We would nod as he went by, but I had no idea who he was.

It was literally a decade or so before the penny dropped, and I realised that he is the chronicler of the Crescent, maestro Frank Auerbach no less. One of our greatest living painters, Frank came here as part of the Kindertransport of Jewish children fleeing the Nazis in the '30s. He has obsessively painted the streets where he found sanctuary time and time and time again: a lifetime of chiaroscuro love songs to his salvation in Camden Town.

I love seeing Frank going to work every day from my front window, or nodding to him in the street as he walks, now slowly, by. A glimpse of Frank is one of my favourite things. I have never said more than two words to the man, but he is – to my eyes – more welcome and more wondrous a sight than any flock of birds or pretty pastoral scene. He is Albert Street. He is London.

As I referred to in Chapter Two, when my dad first settled in Burnt Oak with his family, it is said he applied the pub test to see if the Watling Estate was a decent place to live, and it only just passed. He would have had no such problem in Camden Town. There were six boozers within a two-minute stroll of our front door when we first moved in, and double that within five.

Let's see how many names I can remember: the Victoria, the Crown and Goose, the Spread Eagle, the Sheephaven, the Pig and Whistle, the Edinboro Castle, the Windsor Castle (blimey that was rough), the Dublin Castle, the Mornington Arms, the Good Mixer, the Mother Black Cap, the Cobden, the Camden Head, the Camden Stores, the Beatrice, the one next to Camden Palace with the green tiles. There was also the heavy metal pub called the Purple Turtle, but I never went in there. There may have been more – certainly there were loads more if you ventured over towards the market. Eight on that list have since vanished.

The heyday of the famed Camden Town drinkers had been back in the 1950s and '60s when the massive Irish population used the locals as social centres and second homes. Some of those rollicking old Irish pubs were still roaring, albeit faintly, when I first took my place at the bar. The local newspaper stall still stocked all the Irish regional titles: the *Waterford News & Star* and the *Roscommon Herald*. There was a shop on Arlington Road, in the front room of a terraced house next to the Catholic church, which sold Irish records and musical instruments. This was still Irishtown.

You could hear those bodhráns and penny whistles played in the Stag's Head, an authentic Athlone pub over towards Chalk Farm where the craic and the céilí were damn good. A rebel song, a pint of Guinness and a Pogue or two makes for a mighty time, and the diddle-I tunes were reeled off deep into the locked-in night. Oh what headaches were had.

The Stag's Head and the music shop and the papers are gone, all gone. Only the Irish Centre remains, still going in a big old house up by Camden Square, still feeding the elders, still teaching the young to dance, still holding literary events, still holding on. Keeping alive the memories of the ghosts of penguins past.

Penguin Island is the local name for the pedestrian intersection of five roads, which come together in front of Camden Town Tube station, where the subterranean gents' toilets are. Back in the day, that pedestrian plot would be filled of a Sunday morning with scores of eager Irish fellows, fresh out of mass in Our Lady of Hal round the corner on Arlington Road, all dressed in their regulation Sunday best – black suits and white shirts. Massing together like so many monochrome Antarctic birds, these men from Tip and Tyrone, Meath, Mayo and Monaghan were waiting for the 12 o'clock bell to sound. When it did, they would migrate en masse to the pubs, which stood on all four corners before them, waddling rapidly to the bar like a colony of penguins with a ferocious thirst. Love those men. Love those proud Irish men.

They called it 'Camden Town where the rough lie down.' You would still see the old boys back then, in the street behind the bingo hall, the lonely fellows living in the bare cells of Arlington House, the largest Victorian spike in the country. This gaunt and daunting hostel has been done up, tourists stay there now, but it cannot escape its melancholy. This was where so many big strong fellows saw themselves shrink and wither over the lonely years. Veined of face and weary of limb they sat on corners cradling a bottle, or if they were flush, sat for hours imbibing the shabby warmth of the Good Mixer next door. Supping poison, quietly telling tales and singing songs of the old country as their lives drained into Camden Town.

Then the Mixer became the home to a different type of singer. Blur and Pulp, Oasis and Amy, standing with the old boys by the bar, adding a veneer of authenticity to slumming rockers, postmodern irony mingling with men of iron. Those Irish chaps had come here in the '50s to build this city – many built lives, their kids doing well and dispersing, buying houses, moving on, but some never got beyond the muddy trench and the magnetic bar stool. Camden Town was awash in unshed tears.

On Parkway, which is now almost exclusively chain restaurants and estate agents, the scuzziest of the boozers was the Windsor Castle. This was a proper rough house where the drinking men and women slumped on stained seats, the smell of urine overpowering, the chaos of lives unravelling. It kept no known hours, nor obeyed any licensing laws, and was a great place to go when deeply drunk and in need of an incomprehensible conversation with an inebriate stranger. But technically none of the Irish lads should have been in the Windsor Castle: the Dublin Castle, a hundred yards up the road, was their nominated redoubt.

The Castles of Camden were a wonderful piece of social history enshrined in nomenclature. The Windsor Castle for the English, the Dublin Castle for the Irish, the Edinboro Castle for the Scots and two, the Pembroke Castle and the Caernarvon Castle, for the Welsh. These places were established in the mid-nineteenth century when navvies or navigators from all four corners of the kingdom were cutting the canals and later the railways that lacerate this area.

So to keep apart these rambunctious and thirsty fellows, and stop them brawling and fighting against each other on a Friday night, each nationality had its own castle and keep. Just up from the Pembroke Castle is a pub called the Engineer, which showed that class as well as nationality was a factor. This was the pub for the bosses and the superior sort, no soiled work clothing in there. It's still posh today.

But the Windsor Castle has gone. No doubt it needed a little love, but at some point they ejected the last of the pissheads and reopened as a bland bar called NW1. A century of stories jettisoned in favour of a postcode. That lasted a couple of years before closing down and morphing into a faux French chain restaurant. Commerce trumping history, money over memories.

The ultimate irony for the Irish pubs of Camden Town was when the Beatrice on Camden High Road, another decidedly old-school drinking house which still gave succour and supping space to the last of the local Irish, closed its doors to be replaced by an O'Neill's. It was now one of a chain of faux Irish pubs complete with fake Gaelic road signs, twee Celtic nick nacks and not an actual Irishman in sight.

But my real sadness comes from the fact 'our' pub has gone. The Victoria was a classic London local, buried deep in the backstreets near our gaff, overlooking the railway line. A lovely old curved mahogany bar, a garden at the back and the sweetest view to the Post Office Tower from the benches out the front on a sunny day. Run by an engaging if enjoyably unpredictable landlady, Scottish Alison, the morose Bulgarian barman who could locate any football match in the known world on the satellite TV and his flamboyantly gay and impossibly good-looking co-worker who attracted admirers from miles away.

My step-daughter Alice worked behind the jump for a while and so did many of the local teens. There were rocking lock-ins of a Friday night and chilled afternoons reading the papers and gossiping with the staff. It was the perfect pub.

Somehow the Victoria managed to mingle all the usually disparate elements of our local community. The bookish sorts and the hardened drinkers, the punky poseurs, the Polish builders, the skinny kids from the fashion magazines; Kate Moss and her mob had parties there, alongside the postmen from the local sorting office. When a crack den opened in an empty council flat over the road, a delegation from the Victoria made sure it closed again pretty quickly.

As a family we had our big moments there, birthdays and celebrations, and when my mum died just up the road at UCH her wake was held in the Victoria. The remaining members of the old Elms clan gathered at that venerable bar; uncles from the Bush and the Grove; people I hadn't seen for ages and assumed lost in Acton; ageing aunties brought up from the coast. I held my brother Reggie's hand in that pub and wept quietly. Then it closed.

There's a moment in every ever-changing London micro-community when it is in balance. When the newcomers and the old timers, the estate dwellers and the house owners, the hipsters, the office workers, the builders and the brokers, the eastern Europeans, the Africans and the lesbians can all stand side by side at the bar.

I ventured out to Homerton a while back and wandered into a vast old Victorian gin palace, which had clearly been taken over by pierced and bearded types. This was the absolute front line of Hackney gentrification, and I feared for the worst. But over in one corner were the Jamaican lads playing dominoes, there was a group of local mothers chattering over white wine; a couple of wide boys were playing pool and the beardy people were on their laptops. There were signs up for both the yoga classes and the darts league. I ordered a pint and sat down and marvelled at the scene. I wanted to hug that pub, because it was in balance. It was the new London and the old London rubbing along. It was a paragon, and I wanted it to stay like this forever. I also wanted the Victoria back.

It closed. Many of those Camden Town pubs closed because not enough of the local community used them, and critically because they were worth so much more as real estate than as drinking houses. Our area has changed. Much slower than most, much less than some, but it crept off when we weren't looking. The people buying those houses now are not really the types to wander into a public house for a pint. They live their lives privately, have their children educated privately: they are international, internal; you rarely see them, living behind their immaculately kept facades or in their burly cars, their provisions delivered, their proclivities unknown.

The newcomers are decent people, I'm sure. They're successful people, certainly: smart gay couples with small neat dogs, French families with small neat children, Americans, people in finance, people in the Cotswolds for the weekend, Tuscany for the summer. Not a stuffed buffalo between them. Camden Town is still admirably scruffy, but it is public squalor masking private wealth.

Everyone who owns a house in my street now is a millionaire more than once, and anyone who buys one has that kind of cash to spend, and then plenty more to do it up to their exacting standards. But what does that mean? What has this incredible Klondike of bricks and mortar actually meant? Well, it has theoretically enriched a generation of Londoners beyond anything we could have imagined.

If you were lucky enough, or savvy enough, to have bought a house or a flat in inner London at any point from the 1970s to the early twenty-first century, you have been catapulted across the economic classes. But if you didn't, or couldn't, you got left on the other side of the ravine, with all the bridges burned. And if you sell up and leave for a period, you ain't never coming back. Families split, communities fractured, generations divided.

And while we were all secretly consulting Zoopla, revelling in every hundred grand on the price tag, boasting at dinner parties, as if the preposterous property inflation were some great skill we had acquired, no one thought to ask where our kids would live. It's a question I can't begin to answer.

Like most, I am still baffled by what has happened, still don't really know how we got here and who buys all these places. Who has three million pounds for a former flop house in Camden Town, or a million-and-a-half for a railway cottage in Kilburn, or half-a-million for a one-bedroom flat in Brixton where no cat could ever be swung? Don't even ask how much a house in Notting Hill will set you back. I guess it is self-perpetuating: you sell, you buy; a money-go-round. Don't know where it will end.

I do know that selling shiny new apartments in bland new towers to foreign investors who have no intention of living there or even renting them out is a scandal of our age. I called up about a flat in a new development in King's Cross once, when we were having one of our periodical 'maybe we should move' moments. The girl in the estate agents asked me why I was interested in the property. I said I wanted to live there; she answered 'Oh, that's unusual.'

I also spoke to a property developer about the apartments going up around Battersea Power Station. That building is an absolute icon of our city, a shared symbol of our smoky past, yet those apartments had been promoted primarily to the Malaysian market as investments. When I questioned why they were so spectacularly expensive that no ordinary Londoner would ever live there, the marketing man said, sniffily, 'You cannot expect ordinary people to live in prime central London.'

I'm sorry, but when did Battersea, fucking Battersea (no offence Battersea) SW bloody 11 become Mayfair? And where are ordinary Londoners supposed to live? Reading?

I think we're all angry. And all this theoretical money we're sitting on and living in only gets realised if we move out. I don't want to move out. But where will my kids, Alfie and Maude, both of them born in this house, raised in this street, schooled in these ways, deep in this community, where will they live? They don't want to move out either. I spoke to a young Londoner the other day who said they had been priced out to the far east of the city. They were living in Canvey

Island. Is that where my proud Camden Town kids will be forced to settle?

I remember a conversation with my youngsters when we were talking about their heritage. To call them mixed is an understatement: they are a magnificent agglomeration of English and Irish, Jewish, Romany and now Chinese, just to include the bits we know about. It was my littlest one Maude who said to me 'What does that make us dad?' I replied, 'It makes you Londoners.' And they would rather like to stay that way.

Raising children here has been a treat and a test. We spent many hours among the swings and roustabouts of the Regent's Park when they were little, lucky indeed for such verdant largesse on our doorstep. We took them to the zoo, and when we didn't want to pay, just stood on the mound in the park and peeked over the fence. We visited the great museums on rainy days, dragged them reluctantly to galleries (all kids are philistines, but they love art now), went to the pictures on Parkway and to the theatre at the Tricycle in Kilburn every Saturday morning.

But then we also had Camden Lock just up the road, where the waft of skunk and the whispered song of the dealers is a constant backdrop to every stroll. We once walked past a junkie shooting up in his groin in a phone box and had to explain that. A lecture on the politics of the far right was delivered when a skinhead was hurling racist abuse at some Somali kids.

They learned to scan the horizon, but Alfie got mugged a couple of times when he was in his early teens. He was lucky, he lost only a phone, a pair of football boots and some innocence, but he gained a tranche of priceless street wisdom along the way. Others of course are not so fortunate. On the day I write this, two boys were stabbed to death just up the road in Kentish Town, one of them the second member of his family to die by the blade.

Learning to navigate through the booby-trapped maze of urban life is no bad thing. Nor is growing up in a place where one of your neighbours is an extravagant transvestite, who appears in cabaret at the gay pub round the corner (the Black Cap, now tragically gone) and another is Alan Bennett. It is a boon when your fellow schoolmates speak a fabulous forty-eight languages between them, and a Godsend when your peers celebrate every known religious festival and their kitchen tables are laden with the goodies of the world. Some lived in Hampstead mansions, others in tower blocks with broken lifts.

It is very Camden Town to go to school with the progeny of politicians and plumbers, musicians and physicians, caretakers and risk-takers, painters, and painters and decorators. My son played football on the windswept, artificial pitches at Market Road, where the always-shivering air turned blue with curses, but also elegant cricket at dreamy Lord's. My daughter did sweaty kickboxing under the railway arches and sang in a choir at the Royal Albert Hall. They both forged ID to get into Koko.

One of the most memorable days in their early education came when we took them one Saturday to a children's theatre production involving flouncy thespians and flaccid puppets. It was in a temporary site over by those football pitches in Islington in a former industrial warehouse. There were other pop-up events going on in the complex, including, we discovered later, the London fetish convention. So when a fire alarm went off halfway through the show, two groups were evacuated into the same courtyard: here were families with small children, and here, too, were S&M types in leather chaps, spiky dog collars and rubber basques, all mingling together. Some started recognising each other from the school playground or the workplace, and struck up conversations, the kids blithely ran around, clearly unconcerned by Prince Alberts and peep-hole bras. I was just disappointed when the all-clear sounded and we had to go back to the bloody puppets. Nobody complained.

I also made sure my mob got to know their local history. I'm sure they got bored rotten when I dragged them round to Royal College Street to stand in front of the Poet's House, while I recited the astonishing tale of Verlaine and Rimbaud. I actually went all the way to

Harar in Ethiopia to see a Rimbaud house before I even knew there was one round the corner in Camden Town.

This was where the two star-crossed, absinthe-soaked French lovers, in exile for their homosexual sins, rented rooms and came to blows after a slap across the face with a wet fish bought in Pratt Street Market. Later, Verlaine shot his young punk-poet lover and they split forever. But not before the wild Gallic boy genius wrote 'A Season In Hell', perhaps the most powerful invocation of the compelling horrors of life in nineteenth-century Smoke Town. Maude is studying Rimbaud as I write.

A few yards away from where the poets lived and loved and fought over fish is the old St Pancras workhouse. A grim but always sobering reminder of our own London roots via Freddie and Eliza Elms, born in the strictures of Victorian penury. Over on Bayham Street, in a house now blown away, lived the young Charlie Dickens, a boy boot-black, destined to become the greatest ever chronicler of this city we co-habit. He walked these streets. My kids share this thick Camden Town air, this very space, with the boy who wanted more and the man who gave us more than any other. This is Dickenstown.

Up at the Roundhouse, I pointed out where Pink Floyd held their first psychedelic happenings, and where their van ran over a giant six-foot jelly made for the occasion. I told them, too, of the catacombs beneath our feet, which stretch all the way to Euston. I was taken down there once, into a beautiful herringbone underworld of Victorian ingenuity and engineering where subterranean horses once lived; a fabulous lost city beneath the city.

I also pointed out the Rehearsal Rehearsals studio where the mighty Clash first honed their sound and cultivated their look. Splattering Jack the Dripper swirls on their combat fatigues; living, so the mythology goes, on the flour and water they used to fly-post the area, with posters announcing their clamorous, glamorous arrival. Paul Simenon fell off the roof of the Roundhouse sneaking in to see Patti Smith, who then briefly became his paramour. We all saw Patti Smith at the Roundhouse, remembering that she is even more obsessed with Rimbaud than I am and she, too, made the short pilgrimage to the Poet's House.

Rock'n'roll is part of the pavement; you step over it, bump into it. One evening, walking back from the shops, I got run over by it. Lee Thompson from Madness backed his car over my feet trying to park outside the Dublin Castle, then invited us to a secret gig to commemorate their first ever appearance at the pub in 1979. We were still skanking hours later during a lock-in at the Goose. Oh what a night. Oftentimes we would see Mitch Winehouse's bee-hived daughter walking to the pub. She would smile at us and say hello. Her first ever radio appearance had been on my show. Then one day, she would smile at us and say hello no more: a dark day in the Town.

As my kids grew, so they took all this in, took it for granted, knew they lived in a place where people from all around the world travelled to. When they told others that they came from Camden Town you could see the sparkle in their eyes. Yet like everyone who lives here they were driven mad by it too. The tawdry stalls, the tatty tat, the incessant insanity as you walk out of the station, the crowds, the crap buskers, the bloody jugglers, the standing gawping stragglers in dreadful dreadlocks, the bemused families, the school parties, the out-of-towners and hander-outers, the chuggers and the chancers. *Please get out of my way; I am trying to get home: I LIVE HERE; I'M FROM HERE.*

My kids have lived all their lives in this vagabond barrio, used it as a springboard, a starting point for their own nascent Londons. But they don't often go out at night here; it's too touristy, too pricey, too mainstream. Camden Town was a big part of the punk story in the 1970s – it was funky and jazzy in the '80s and the epicentre of Britpop in the '90s, but today? Well, tourists still like it.

You can still see examples of every teen trouser tribe, from skins to goths, steampunks to mods; they all take part in the brilliant parade, the living museum of British street style, a mobile Madame Tussauds with mohicans. There are still clubs and bars and bands, but the buzz isn't here, the cultural axis has shifted: first east, to Shoreditch, Hoxton; then south, to Brixton, Peckham. The grime and the afrobeats, and the jazz not jazz; the movers and shakers have moved on, leaving rocking Camden Town as a chimera. That just leaves Soho. And you can never really leave Soho.

There comes a point in the London journey when you claim Soho as your own. The name comes from an ancient hunting cry, and it has remained the place to go on the hunt. I recall walking what cab drivers call the 'dirty dozen', the twisting route of twelve turns from Regent Street to the Charing Cross Road, with Alf when he was maybe twelve or thirteen years old, and he was taking it all in. Eyes darting, ears primed, imbibing and absorbing, and as we strolled down Wardour Street he said to me, 'I really like it here, Dad. It feels special.'

I smiled with pride and gave a little speech about how it *is* special, how these few streets making up the un-square mile represent the soul of our city, our collective creative urge, our hedonism and our humanism, our shared sense of urban exaltation.

All that is good and all that is splendidly bad in our cumulative London experience has a place here among these multistoried buildings and alleyways crammed with anecdotes: William Blake incubating visions; De Quincy eating opium; Dylan Thomas drinking whiskey; John Snow not drinking the choleric water; Karl Marx starting communism; John Logie Baird starting television. The revolution undoubtedly will be televised, probably on pay-per-view; and the post-production will take place on Poland Street.

Soho set the beat. Scores of angsty, angular kids in skinny jeans started the whole teen caper in the basement of an Old Compton Street coffee bar. This is where the British pop scene first percolated up amid the espresso machines, and Adam Faith, artful dodger extraordinaire from East Acton and my favourite-ever fictional character, was invented.

It all happened here: naked ladies in the Windmill; Free French in the Minster; zoot suits in Archer Street; Tubby Hayes in trouble; Ziggy Stardust in Trident Studios. Every turn has a tale to tell, and as you grow into these streets so you absorb their pattern and their patina.

I then told Alfie the dodgy mnemonic I'd been taught by a London cab driver to remember the order of the grid: 'Good For Dirty Women' – Greek, Frith, Dean, Wardour. I don't think he had a clue what I was talking about. I hope not anyway.

Turning from Wardour into Old Compton, best experienced as twilight first touches the sky, I still feel that pulsing frisson of all possibilities. The look of wonder on a young man's face, perhaps a kid down to town for the first time – maybe he's gay, maybe not, who knows, who cares? Nobody does and that is the wonder of this place.

The big secret Soho keeps for you is that you can become and be whoever you so desire. This London is a non-judgemental jungle, this ancient parish a petri dish of all personas. You can come to Soho to find yourself or lose yourself, you can invent and reinvent, dress up, play up, get pissed, piss people off then piss off again. You can get on down, move on up, hone your back story, devise your destiny. No questions asked; no excuses necessary. Soho invites you to the party, fancy dress optional. Or at least, it did.

My first Soho excursions were back in the oh-so-seedy '70s. Then it was all Budgie jacket wide boys in spunk shops, biker jacket know-it-alls in record shops and runners with round tins of film stock. The market was still shouting its wares, and the girls were certainly flaunting theirs. The Dilly was the rent-boy meat-rack, skinny lads leaning against the railings, pouting seductively, their dancing bags by their side.

Carnaby Street was mods and skinheads kicking off, Wardour Street was rockers in the Ship before recording in heavy metal alley, Greek Street was 'retired' actresses fallen on hard times. Meard Street was brothels, Walker's Court was clippers, Dean Street was funky knitting and twelve-inchers. This was a scrappy, scruffy, but neon-bright tenderloin with 'models' available up every stairway, 'dancers' in every cabaret and chancers in every boozer: sex, sex, sex; sell, sell, sell.

There were peep shows and tableaus, dirty book shops, arty book shops, nosh bars, a couple of posh bars, mini-cab kiosks selling a bit of gear and tailors selling gear of a different kind. You could find the Italian deli, the French church, the Algerian coffee shop, the Chinese herbalist, the Swiss restaurant, the Thai massage and the Greek barber. French and Greek were also advertised in every phone box.

There was the Durex shop in Wardour Street, the Vintage Magazine Shop on Brewer Street, and Borovick's for the needle merchants on Berwick Street. And then there were the clubs: strip clubs, drinking clubs, nightclubs, gentleman's clubs, hostess clubs, gambling clubs, gay clubs, tranny clubs, after-hours clubs, 'Scandinavian' cinema clubs, 50p membership to get round the licensing law clubs. But absolutely no swanky members' clubs whatsoever.

There were rumours of blokes with clubs or maybe baseball bats or coshes under the counter, a sense of villainy unseen. But providing you didn't push it, you wouldn't know. Up in the Maltese social club on Frith Street there were still men alive who could claim to know what really happened to boxer Freddie Mills, found dead in his motor in the alleyway behind the Astoria. Or tell you they had seen Reggie and Ronnie with George Raft down in Chinatown before the Chinese came, or even Jack Spot and Albert Dimes blade to blade outside the Bar Italia. There is still an unopened magnum of champagne behind the bar at Ronnie's, given by Dimes to Ronnie Scott himself, from when the 'old place' on Gerrard Street first opened in 1959, supposedly to be drunk when the club first turns a profit.

Soho is smothered in the folklore of glam gangsterism, but it's all a front. Once you've fallen in love, accepted its mucky advances, given in to its giddy embrace, Soho feels like the safest place on earth; thrilling, heady, scary but safe, warm, cosseting, even on the darkest night. Straight away it felt like home. It was ours.

Technically Soho in the late '70s was still the domain of the last lot, the black-and-white, gin-and-tonic generation, as captured by Dan Farson. There was George Melly and Francis Bacon, Peter O'Toole and Jeffrey Bernard, Muriel Belcher and Molly Parkin, John Deakin and Lucian Freud, falling out of Norman's and up the dirty stairs into the bilious green hell of the Colony, then out again into the gutter. Geniuses and giants of art and acting and swearing, foul of mouth, brilliant of mind and open of heart. If they felt for a moment that you were a Soho sort, you would be invited into their grubby, glamorous world and called every foul name imaginable. They had a bitter but genuine generosity.

As a Soho stripling I was propositioned by George Melly and Molly Parkin on the same night: 'Do you swing, darling?' said Molly. I was given an astonishing ad hoc acting lesson by Peter O'Toole, playing Jeffrey Bernard, and a few writing lessons by Jeffrey himself. Bernard, by this stage, bereft of one of his legs and almost all his charm, would insult me on a regular basis, but took a genuine interest in my work. He gave me occasional tips and frequent quips. One morning, drunk rotten already at 11 a.m., I chided him gently on his sozzled condition at such an early hour and he said, 'Elms you cunt, you must understand I now lead a nocturnal existence entirely by day.' Pissed and passed out by 5 p.m., it was occasionally my job to help push him back home in a wheelchair to his council flat in a tower block on Berwick Street. Jeffrey Bernard was unwell. But Soho was doing just fine.

Night after night we'd go 'down, down past the Talk of the Town'. Meet first in the Spice of Life, or the Ship, or the Blue Posts, then off to Le Beat Route or the Kilt or St Moritz or the Wag or any one of the scores and scores of nocturnal haunts, many of which came and went by the week. But Soho was much more than just a disco playground. It was our shared ground, our common land in this vast, disparate city. It was where we came together in more ways than one.

Very few tourists entered the redoubt; there wasn't much for them. Soho back then was still secretive, furtive, hidden away, revealing its pleasures and treasures only to those who knew which alleyway to go up, which door to knock on, which stairs to descend, which name to drop. Lots of Londoners too were too scared or too straight to go to Soho, put off by the queers and the villains and the poseurs and the funny foreign-sounding stuff. Choosing to hang out there was like a badge of cosmopolitan pride, a statement of urban intent. So Soho contained a self-selecting, self-promoting, self-satisfied clique of gad-abouts and misfits, and I fitted in perfectly.

By the time the '80s had really kicked in, it was a new generation creating the Soho stories. John Pearse and Mark Powell were the new tailors in town, dapper men who knew exactly which side you dressed. (Mark, who lives in Wardour Street, once told me that he hadn't set foot outside Soho for over three months.) Chris Sullivan opened the Wag; my mate from the baths Ollie O'Donnell, Le Beat Route. Boy George had a clothes shop in Foubert's Place; Black Market records and Sounds of the Universe were the cool places to procure tunes. Alistair Little opened his restaurant, Fred opened Fred's, Pam Hogg and Phil Dirtbox and Bernie Katz and Philip Sallon and a legion of my fellow nightclub compatriots opened doors and began to put their stamp on the streets – or rather the dens – below and above them. Then they opened Groucho's.

It was the first and it is still the best, but there is no doubt it was also the symbol of the changing face and faces of Soho. A club, which despite the origins of its name, you might actually want to join, Groucho's premiered in May 1985. It was the very centre of the decade and a pivotal point indeed. Formed by members of the media fraternity; publishers and writers, filmmakers and troublemakers, fed up with stuffy old male-dominated members' clubs with their dress codes and arcane rules. The aim was to create a place where the bright young things and the right old things could combine business with pleasure, which is always the best combination. I was there the day it opened and most days for the rest of the 1980s.

The Groucho Club, housed in what had been Gennaro's long-closed Italian restaurant, was a portent of the newly emerging Soho: slicker, hipper, sharper – more exclusive, more expensive, but just as joyously dodgy. For a decade or two it was riotously, almost industrially good fun. All of the excess and exuberance of the age was played out here, and a list of the players is pretty exhausting.

Stephen Fry and Noel Fielding, Julie Burchill and Zadie Smith, Keith Allen and Lily Allen, Tracey Emin and Damien Hirst, John Lloyd and Emma Freud, Terry Pratchett and Melvyn Bragg, Alex James and Robbie Williams, Rachel Weiss and Richard Bacon . . . YBAs and Britpoppers, movie and media moguls, models, editors, luvvies, druggies and still enough Soho flotsam to feel suitably bohemian. Long lunches becoming endless nights, becoming bleary mornings in the snooker room were legion and legendary, and tales of good times and appalling behaviour rightly celebrated.

My own small but noted contribution to Groucho's lore came on Thursday 26 February 1987. I can be sure of the precise date, because that was when we awoke to the announcement that two of London's great old football clubs, Queens Park Rangers and Fulham FC, were about to merge and become a Frankenstein's monster of a team called Fulham Park Rangers.

This was essentially a land grab by a property company anxious to get their hands on Craven Cottage, Fulham's lovely riverside real estate. (QPR's White City ground, where this bastard hybrid would play, was still a long way from gentrification.) This foul and unnatural coupling was presented as a fait accompli: the team my father loved and I love in turn was about to vanish. I received an urgent early morning phone call from my fast Fulham friend, Spike Denton, saying we must meet at the club to do something about it.

We settled in the sofa in front of the old bar at just after 11 a.m. and effectively sat there for something like sixteen hours straight, plotting. It wasn't just our stamina which impressed – epic sessions in Dean Street were not exactly unusual – it was the resulting bar bill. For years this record of our imbibing was pinned up on the wall of the manager Liam Carson's office as an exemplar. Between us we consumed seventy-eight bottles of Becks, a bottle of champagne and a club sandwich. We argue to this day about which one of us had the sandwich.

But what is unarguable is that it worked. The merger was called off and our individual teams lived on to disappoint us to this day. Quite how we survived the ordeal I'm not sure. We had pledged that Fulham Park Rangers would happen 'over our dead bodies' and seventy-nine bottles later it very nearly came to pass. Two days later, still hungover beyond imagining, we both sat together on the pitch at Loftus Road during a game as part of a demonstration, with no beer whatsoever.

The hedonism of the 1980s and '90s in Soho was something to behold, and it was sometimes tough just holding on. But there was also a palpable, sometimes visceral sense of collective creativity, an exhausting but exhilarating vortex of projects. Magazines, movies and art, clubs, music and fashion, drinking and snorting and talking and blagging and bragging and just doing what city folk do when you let them loose in the playground. It was corny old cool Britannia being born, but Soho was so far from cool as to be scalding, no place for the glacial, but it certainly felt like our place. It felt like this was our neighbourhood, like we owned those streets. But of course we didn't: Paul Raymond did.

The success of the Groucho Club in attracting the good, the bad and the pretty had a knock-on effect. Other clubs opened, most notably Soho House in an old knocking shop on Old Compton Street. Always known in Groucho's as 'the other place', it was destined to become a twenty-first century international empire, cashing in on the realisation that plenty of people want to feel like they're in with the in crowd and are prepared to pay handsomely for the privilege of joining the party.

But it wasn't just the rash of private members' clubs springing up, it was the restaurants and the bars and the boutiques, the swanky offices and the hip hotels replacing the peep shows and the clip joints, the subterranean nightclubs and the grumpy, second-hand record shops. It was Soho getting cleaned up. Sex was going out of fashion – or rather on to the internet – and seedy was being replaced by greedy as rents rose and rose. Soho had always been about desire, but now it became desirable.

The gay colonisation and standardisation of Old Compton Street was another factor. Of course this had always been a queer quarter, a nobody-gives-a-fuck-who-you-fuck quarter, but suddenly it was codified; lines were drawn, flags flown, neat men with facial hair spending their cosy, rosy pounds to make old Soho into a facsimile of New York's West Village.

Soho isn't a village; it's an Alamo, a fortress under siege from the forces of conformity and all the better for it. But we began to let the defences down, invite in visitors, lure the tourists, the curious and the spurious, began to see Soho morph into Covent Garden.

To my mind there had always been an implicit pact. Once the fruit and veg went and the frou-frou tourist tat arrived, Covent Garden was for them, but that was OK, because Soho was for us. Covent Garden was big-name brands and commercialisation, people gawping and looking lost, sitting outside eating overpriced food and buying candles; Soho was not. Soho was a place for those in the know, where outsiders were on the inside, where the inverts were in charge and Londoners ruled. It was ours. But of course it wasn't: it was Paul Raymond's.

The real issue is real estate. Paul Raymond made his many fortunes from smut and invested it in land to the point where he owned nearly half of the properties in the Soho salient. Then when it tipped over from seedy red-light district to central boutique location, his heirs set about maximising their portfolio or whatever it is business-type people do.

So the place changes even more. The hardware stores and the hard-on shops get replaced by something altogether swisher, and the chains attach themselves to every available lease. The ragged fruit and veg market gets trimmed and tamed, and the ancient market in fresh flesh vanishes.

Open, inviting glass frontages take the place of secretive doorways and gaudy neon. International brands stake their place and suburban souls visit their 'clubs'. Provincial coach parties dropped off at musicals on Shaftesbury Avenue turn the corner to mingle with the nice gay men, while tourists and manipulable millennials stand neatly in line outside the latest, no-booking restaurant raved about on TripAdvisor. Suddenly, Soho, shorn of its always cosmetic bad reputation and its messy excesses, is for everybody. But is it still Soho?

We can't really blame the Raymonds and the other property people for this. They've just ridden the wave. We can't blame anybody but ourselves, because this contemporary tenderloin is a reflection of us. London gets the Soho it deserves. If this is really our soul, then it is we who have changed.

All London now is more open, easy going and cosmopolitan, a liberal redoubt, so there is less need for a designated bohemian enclave as an antidote to little England's oppressive rigidity. This is a more bourgeois, materialistic, conformist, corporate city, so we patronise the poxy coffee shops and the identikit eateries with their franchise menus, we buy into that lifestyle magazine boutique buzz. This is a more ordered, top-down, safe and predictable town, so we don't want rancid dumps full of dangerous artists, buccaneering one-night entrepreneurs or rip-off clip joints with swaggering gangsters, don't really fancy barrow boys or working girls with our fine dining and our prime retail. We want Soho to be nice, like us.

There are more tourists and visitors then ever and they want to visit the mythologically edgy red-light district they've read about in reviews. But to accommodate them, the edge has been blunted, the sleaze has been all but eradicated, and even the myth is receding. It's a red-light district with no red lights, and the disturbing absence of the smell of semen and Parazone, which once leaked from every neon bright alleyway. Sex has become a digital transaction, so you wank over a keyboard, buy your dildo online and arrange an assignation through an escort agency or Tinder or Grindr rather than visit a W1 sex shop or a dodgy nightclub to meet someone for potential how's-your-father.

Soho today, with its al fresco dining and busy pavement cafés, its designer bars with muted lights and wafting music, its Michelin-starred restaurants and elegant minimalist boutiques, chocolatiers, patisseries and galleries, discreet hotels and flash sommeliers, has become positively Parisian. Truth be told, I've never much liked Paris.

It is easy to get a little maudlin about our wounded soul. Easy to understand why there is such a vociferous 'Save Soho' campaign and a collective yearning for lost guilt. It is easy to echo the words of my

mum on her UCH deathbed and lament: 'This is no longer my Soho.'
And for the most part, it isn't.

My Soho, like my London, like all our Londons, is slip-sliding away.
But then I go there and something remarkable happens. Using that
trick which only London can pull off, it transforms itself. If I am in
the right mood, and the neighbourhood is in the right mood, suddenly
Soho hasn't changed at all. More than anywhere else in this city, these
streets, replete with so many apparitions, crawling with so many collective memories, can still become the place you long for it to be. It can
still be as it was and as it is simultaneously; it can still be your Soho,
providing you squint a little and want a lot.

It usually happens on a Friday. A couple of times a month, early
afternoon before the bridge and tunnel pour in for a night out, but
when there's a fair chance that a few of the bods will be about.

I have a route that takes in the remaining record shops, especially
the 'secret' one upstairs on D'Arblay Street, where there will invariably
be an old music head or two chewing the fat with JC. The Blue Posts
on Berwick Street, the French and Norman's are bound to proffer a
disreputable acquaintance or three, maybe a Sullivan or a Suggs with
his mum. I might have a mooch for garms with Mark Powell or the
Peckham Rye boys, see if any of the South London mob are up.

Then check the Bar Italia and take a coffee, maybe a cake with
Christos, watch the waves, take the pulse, before finally going into
Groucho's to sit at the bar and see who occurs. Usually I'm back home
before the offices have even turned out. But occasionally – thankfully
only very occasionally – the old Soho voodoo kicks in, and I get
kidnapped by the streets.

Then the clocks have stopped, all bets are off; all options are available. The night starts to shine and the mischief starts to occur. Soho
is in its pomp when you are, it responds to your desires, repays your
investment. Soho is so precious because, like gin, it is London distilled
and concentrated, intoxicating, addictive, it is essence of us.

It may become jazz, in which case Ian Shaw will probably be involved,
and you had better call your insurers. It could be art, an opening or a

happening, where Philip Sallon will probably arrive wearing a wedding dress and a policeman's helmet, as he did when I first saw him in Soho when I was sixteen. For some it's theatre, but more likely for me it's film, perhaps a showing in one of those little preview theatres with warm red wine and nuts followed by deep drunken debate with an actor with a faux cockney accent, a director or a critic called Solomons.

It may just be that you find yourself in very good, very bad company; terrific, terrible, terrifying company who lead you astray, perhaps even to Peckham. Get your coat. Or else you barely move at all and the parade comes to you; a conveyor belt of fellow travellers, faces old and new, but most likely old, like me. Like my Soho. Like my London.

Old like me. I know I am now chasing shadows, know this wondrous warren is not the shameful, disgraceful, lustrous, lustful place it once was, but then nor am I, though just occasionally we have a go together. And when we do it feels like coming home.

This is my home town. My home, my town.

Postscript

London plays the long game.

Just before I embarked upon this book, my wife bought me a birthday present. It is a history of the city of my obsession, called *Old and New London* by one Walter Thornbury. Written in 1872 and published in six large, handsome, but dauntingly dense and voluminous volumes. I opened the first of thousands of pages of closely packed Victorian type and almost stopped in my tracks. It begins:

'Writing the history of a vast city like London is like writing a history of the ocean – the area is so vast, its inhabitants are so multifarious, the treasures that lie in its depths so countless. What aspect of the great chameleon city shall one select? . . . Perpetually renewing and to all intents inexhaustible . . . Old London is passing away even as we dip our pen in the ink.'

That's pretty much what I was going to say. Except for the bit about the ink. Those words, written when Freddie Elms was first becoming a Londoner, struck such a chord because they are just as true, just as apt, as I sit at my keyboard nearly a century-and-a-half later trying to finish my one slim tome.

I don't want to get all biblical on you but it certainly reminded me of (and I paraphrase), 'What has been will be again, what has been done will be done again, there is nothing new under the sun.' Nor under sullen skies, which haven't seen a glimpse of sunshine for weeks. This great grey city is still unfathomable, the ocean is still in perpetual motion and old London is still passing away as we write.

Already aware of the enormity and inherent impossibility of trying to capture an endless swirling sea, which ebbs and flows through the ages, and changes shape and shade with every tide, I became even more concerned about the task I had undertaken when I discovered that Mr Thornbury ended his life in a lunatic asylum, penniless and mad.

Those half-a-dozen, musty Victorian volumes of his are just part of my library of hundreds of books on the same subject. They're all around me in the room where I write, inspiring me, chiding me, taunting me. There are hundreds more to collect, and there will no doubt be count-less more to come. This city is a subject of limitless fascination, a place of infinite words. If Paris is a town of painters and New York is a cinematic city, then London is literary. We cannot stop writing about it, reading about it, talking about it, precisely because it is impossible to pin down. No one can have the last word on London.

For, as the *News of the World* used to boast, 'All human life is here.' This is a churning sea of souls. It is a living entity, an organism that simultaneously was and is and will be; it is the sum of all its pasts and all its parts, which means all of us. We make London as London makes us. Each generation reinvents not just themselves as Londoners, but London as themselves.

And the place we have collectively constructed is currently pretty good. For the most part, it works. In most ways it is a striking success. You can moan all you like, and we all like a moan, but in so many ways this city is better than ever before. If you live here and fancy swapping places, millions of souls from every corner of the globe will do so in a moment. This is a good moment for London. But of course pendulums swing. We must never rest.

That London is once again a great global magnet is a sign of our intrinsic attractiveness. Great cities, the crowning glories of civilisation, are a coming together, an agglomeration of human desires. The very fact that so many humans of every hue and every cry, every turn and talent, have wished and worked and scraped and schemed, some risking their lives to make their lives here is perhaps the greatest compliment you can pay an old boy like London. They still fancy us.

This modern urban success story has undergone what doctors call an 'autoresuscitation', a Lazarus-like leap from the sickbed of 1940s ruination and 1970s stagnation. After years of decline, depopulation and disinvestment, it has been revived by a kiss of life, the cumulative breath of more and more and more of us. And I like that, because I like people. Oh come all ye faithless.

Of course that influx has brought pressures. The eerily, joyously empty swathes of my youth have been filled in, replaced by built-up blocks and teeming hordes in all directions. There are no more debris to play run-outs on, precious few empty warehouses to hold raves in, no unwanted council houses or disused fire stations to squat in. They were all remnants of a city in decline.

Everything is more crowded now, from art galleries to train carriages. There is no rush hour in London anymore; there is just one long continual rush and crush. But I take a certain pleasure in the fact that eleven miles an hour was the average speed of a horse-drawn Hackney carriage in Victorian times, and a little less than eleven miles an hour is the average speed of a typical car journey in town today. You can't hurry love.

The London little Freddie walked to was a momentous, teeming metropolis. The town my mum and dad courted in was crowded, noisy, polluted and congested, just as it is now, just as it should be. A cab driver stuck in a morass of road works and construction jams once said exasperatedly to me, 'London is great, but it will be better when it's finished.' But of course the opposite is true, London will be finished when it's finished.

In Chinese culture, which I have come to know a little, cranes are considered auspicious, lucky birds to see flying on the horizon, a sign of prosperity. Well, in London, seeing cranes of a different kind on the skyline is a very good sign indeed. This city must be a perpetual work in progress.

But we have to do the right work if we are to progress. After the First World War we built homes for heroes. Places like the Watling Estate and White City, which housed me and mine, gave us a chance. After the Second World War my dad and so many strong men and women like him built the Royal Festival Hall, the Post Office Tower, the Brunswick Centre, Trellick Tower . . . Now we use our energies and resources to construct ghost towers for speculators. But London plays a long game. All those hundreds of towers going up, boasting luxury flats, will one day come crashing down. If the history of Notting Hill or Camden Town is anything to go by, they will be slums in a few years' time.

The blitzed-out, worn-out town my mum and dad met and married in was born again through their sterling endeavours. People like my parents born proudly of these streets and people like their neighbours arriving on boats in beautiful suits to live in slums, to work and play and do and be done by, bequeathed new lives, new Londoners. They have refreshed and replenished and for the most part infinitely enhanced this place. What heroes. What an inheritance.

And the London my kids have been bequeathed is even better in so many ways. London in my time has become a much more open, hopeful, dynamic city, less reserved, less judgemental, more tolerant, more accepting. Always cosmopolitan, it has evolved into something beyond, something new and perhaps unique, the greatest city in the world, because all the world is here and what's more, it's welcome here. They are us, we are them; we are London.

For the most part, we get along pretty well, rubbing much more than just shoulders together. This is the western world's capital of miscegenation. Those beautiful, resourceful mongrels of mine are typical twenty-first century Londoners. And their generation, kind and positive, decent and diligent, give me – give us all – great hope.

But of course change is a double-edged sword, every gain a loss. You can be simultaneously better in many ways, yet worse in others. There is more to do in London today but perhaps less fun to be had. This cool, easy-going town is tougher to live in, harder working, harsher on its poor, much more expensive and exclusive, shamefully banishing its own far away. We are much less rigidly class conscious and deferential than before, yet much more painfully divided between haves and have-nots. This genuinely gentler, less aggressive, more tolerant town tolerates its young being stabbed to death in doorways.

This cool, gluten-free, artisan-produced city of ours can also be cruelly avaricious, materialistic and monetised. This city of individualistic, creative entrepreneurs with interesting facial hair has also become crushingly corporate. Uber Google. Our now beautifully designed, well-lit, tasteful town does bling and brash like never before. Money has left its ugly mark. London today does have no-go zones. Why would you go to Knightsbridge, Kensington or the King's Road? But then there are now so many great reasons to head to Lewisham, Walthamstow or Clapton. A shape-shifter indeed.

This fractured multiplicity of cities is baffling, challenging, but I am up for the challenge, loving the new while lamenting the old, missing the familiar and the familial but happy to pass the baton. Run, kids, run. I am eager to see what my city becomes as the next generation reinvent it in their image. The long game goes on.

London can contain so many contradictions, because there are so many Londons. But my one is fading; I can feel it fading. I can no longer smell it by the river. I cannot leap from its open platform or dive into its seedy dens to learn from its denizens. I rarely hear its voice any more; its accent is kept alive only in gambling ads and gangster films; its mores and its modes look more and more like an old black-and-white Ealing comedy.

As I look around so many of my landmarks have vanished, it is getting harder to navigate by eye. Instead if I shut my mince pies and try to remember, I can see them all. And so I end with these, the lost monuments of the city that made us. These were places of good times and bad, old times, which once were new; the haunts of our forebears and the playgrounds of our youth, our London. Do you remember, can you recall?

The Hammersmith Palais
Ward's Irish House
Bloom's Restaurant
The Beta Café
Madame Jojos
The Astoria
The Wag Club
Laurence Corner

Compendium
Warren Street Car Dealers
Collet's Bookshop
Fleet Street
Fleet Street Printers
Fathers of the Chapel
Norland Gardens
Orange Hill School
The Mazzini and Garibaldi Club
White City Stadium
Walthamstow Dog Track
The Watling Boys' Club
The Galtymore
Denmark Place
The Colony Club
The Fridge
Jack Straw's Castle
The Toffee Apple Man
The Monkey Nut Man
The GLC
County Hall
Woolworths
Arsenal Stadium
The General Smuts
R.G. Elms & Sons
Groove Records
Bagley's Yard
Ray's Jazz Kings X
The Albanian Shop
Tonibells
The Scala Cinema
Pimlico School
Club Row Market
Truman's Brewery

Centre Point Fountains
Cheapo Cheapo
Contempo
Dobells
Dionysius Kebab House
The Routemaster
Robot
The Ivy Shop
Crolla
PX
Finchley Lido
Soho Market
Mill Hill Baths
Kingsbury Baths
Demob
Dub Vendor
Modern Classics
The Heygate Estate
Clippies
Nippies
Aldwych Station
The Victoria
Frestonia
Rumours
The Rainbow
The Marquee
The Academy Cinema
Daddy Kool
The Boleyn Ground
The Shelf
The Clock End
The Mother Black Cap
Smoking Carriages
The Hole in the Wall

The Odeon Marble Arch
The Africa Centre
Jimmy's
Pollo
The New Piccadilly
The Bald Faced Stag
Cold Blow Lane
Mappin & Webb
Veneer of the Week
Gamages
Battersea Funfair
Battersea Power Station
Broad Street Station
Whitechapel Bell Foundry
ABC Bakery
Sports Pages
Flip
The Lucozade Sign
The Fancy Cheese People
Rosetti's
Rock On Records
Swan & Edgar
Johnson & Johnson
Kensington Market
Cooks' Pie and Mash
Covent Garden Market
The Docks
Dockers
Porters
Blustons
The Embassy Club
The TPA
Grenfell Tower
Albert and Eileen Elms

List of Photographs

Page 4 – Albert and Eileen Elms, St James' Church, Norland, 1946

Page 18–19 – The Westway

Page 24 – Shepherd's Bush Market

Page 33 – Robert & Ian, the Watling Estate

Page 52–53 – Latimer Road Station

Page 59 – Top deck from the top deck

Page 88 – The author aged 6

Page 147 – The Ferreira Delicatessen, Camden Town

Page 177 – Giro the Nazi Dog

Page 181 – Greet House, the true centre of London

Page 183 – The plaque for the centre of London

Page 186 – A wedding with Aunt Dot and Ian

Page 190–1 – Ska records, including Rita and Bennie

Page 222 – George the Tailor, Walworth Road

Page 229 – Peckham girls

Page 253 – St Giles' Circus from the bus

Page 257 – International Brigades Memorial Trust Monument, Jubilee Gardens

Page 261 – Robert & Christina, Marylebone Registry Office, 1995

Page 263 – Mornington Crescent Station

Page 265 – The Camden Coffee Man

Acknowledgements

Thank you to:

Jamie Byng for being brilliant.

Hannah Knowles for editing with care, flair and wine.

My beautiful wife Christina for gracing my city and my life, she has improved both by her presence.